THE R[▮] FAR EAST

850

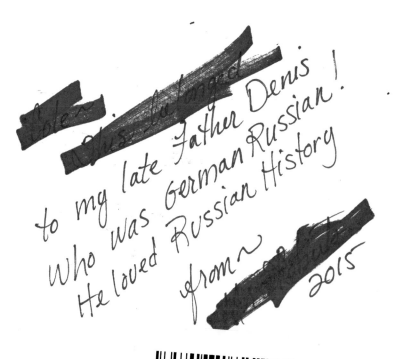

[▮▮▮ ▮▮▮ ▮▮▮]

to my late Father Denis !
who was German Russian
He loved Russian History

from~ [▮▮▮] 2015

D1293532

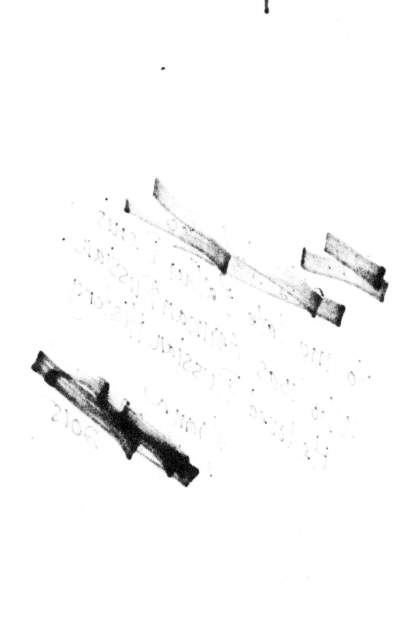

THE RUSSIAN FAR EAST

Erik Azulay
Allegra Harris Azulay

HIPPOCRENE BOOKS
New York

For information, address:
HIPPOCRENE BOOKS, INC.
171 Madison Avenue
New York, NY 10016

Azulay, Erik
      The Russian Far East / Erik Azulay, Allegra Harris Azulay.
             p.   cm.
      Includes index.
      ISBN 0-7818-0325-X
      1. The Russian Far East (Russia)--Guidebooks.   I. Azulay, Allegra
Harris. II. Title.
DK771.D3A98   1995   95-11919
915.7'70486--dc20   CIP

Printed in the United States of America.

This book is dedicated to our parents, who opened our eyes to the world and who knew we would like traveling even before we did.

Table of Contents

City Maps

ACKNOWLEDGMENTS

A lot of research goes into a book like this, and we couldn't have done it without the help of our friends and colleagues, many of whom shared with us their experiences of living and working in the Russian Far East, and commiserated with us over bottles of vodka and *zakuski* as we compared Aeroflot horror stories. Our special thanks go out to:

Kristin Rogers, for her invaluable work on Sakhalin, sharing with us her years of Yuzhno experience and taking time out of her busy last days on the island to write up her knowledge. Without Kristin's work the section on Sakhalin would be a mere shadow of its present self.

Vice Mayor **Rimma Valentinovna Kim** and the City Administration of Chita, for their hospitality and kind assistance; **Volodya** and **Anna Popravko**, for their excellent work on our maps; **Andrew Wilson**, for his insights into Nakhodka and Provideniya; **Lena Kostenko**, for long investigative walks in freezing weather, and for eating raw pony liver with a smile; **Will Saunders**, for obtaining hard-to-find maps and river information on Yakutsk, and for his perceptive comments on Aeroflot; **Semyon Vladimirovich Manturov,** for providing insight into Buryat customs and traditions; **Lydia Moskwin**, for her help with Khabarovsk and her boisterous enthusiasm; **Katie Sauter,** for vital Kamchatka input at a crucial moment, **Leonid Bannikov,** for exciting trips and sharing his years of wilderness experience to enrich our appreciation of the variety of nature in the Far East; **Jeff Wheeler** of The Register, for his collaboration on finding phone directories; **Marina Sharshavina**, for taking days off her vacation to make calls; **Dan Gotham**, for information on Magadan and a vicious jump shot; **Cheri McConnell,** for her assistance on Arsenyev; **Lauren Hockstetter,** for information on the northern regions; **Dan Spatz, Ben Hanson Jeff McQuaid** and **Andrei Gorodilov** for choice nuggets of info gleaned from their own travels; **Rich** and **Marcia Balmadier,** for many enjoyable late-night talk sessions and moral support; **Scott Yates** and **Carol Richman**, for invaluable assistance with printing; and **Jeff Azulay,** for perusing the libraries of Ecuador and Texas for needed historical research.

Photo Credits

The authors are grateful to the following for permission to reproduce photos in the book: Dan Spatz for Khabarovsk tower in winter on p. 94; Valery Nemerov for reproductions from his book *Chita: Istoriya, Pamyatnie Mesta, Sudba,* on pages 138, 143, 144; Mrs. Eduard Martsenko for Kamchatka photos on pages 238, 244, 259, 262; and author photo by Rick Azulay. All other photos are by the authors. The cover photo is of the monument in the main square of Vladivostok.

Note: All information in the book is current at time of printing. However, due to the rapid pace of change in the Russian Far East, stores or restaurants may have raised their prices, improved their service, changed their hours, or gone out of business. The authors appreciate your comments and would be grateful for notice of any changes.

Introduction to the Far East

Siberia and the Far East: to the Western reader these names conjure up visions of hard labor camps, vast tracts of snow and forest, large industrial cities, and of a simple, hardened people scraping out a living under harsh conditions. To the Russians, however, Siberia and the Far East represent the frontier, a mixture of familiar Europe and exotic Asia. Just as the Americans spread to the west coast, claiming a "manifest destiny", so too did the Russians expand eastwards in the 17th century until reaching the Pacific Ocean. It was here in the East that Russia got her natural resources, sent her exiles and obtained a "window on the East".

The first to come were military expeditions of Cossacks and other Tsarist troops, looking to expand the Russian Empire during the reign of Ivan the Terrible. They were followed by the fur trappers and traders, seeking new markets and cheap goods. Next came the exiles, some of whom had served their time and were looking for a fresh start, some with no choice at all. These were followed in turn by the peasants looking to make a life for themselves as free men, away from serfdom in the west. Over the years towns developed and grew to cities, and the Far Eastern fur exports became a substantial part of the Russian Empire's economy.

The early Soviet years were a period of purges and restructuring. Stalin sent waves of prisoners and "enemies of the people" to exile in the Far Eastern work camps and through their labor mines, railroads, harbors, even entire cities sprang up, seemingly overnight. Through their efforts, the Far East became one vast industrial and military zone, providing needed raw materials and labor, "the muscle" in the Soviet economy.

Many regions, such as Kamchatka, Magadan, Khabarovsk and others are perhaps most typical of what westerners imagine the area to be like: beautiful scenery, a harsh climate, and a people with a more independent, dynamic outlook than their counterparts in the west. However, few know of the regions of Chita, Buryatiya, and the Republic of Sakha (Yakutia), which are probably the least-known in all of Russia. This is a shame, because each region is graced with a unique culture, history and ethnic makeup, as well as natural beauty.

From the Buryats with their strong ties to Mongolia and Tibet, to the Republic of Sakha with its rich gold and diamond resources locked in permafrost, to Sakhalin, once owned by Japan and now looking to Japan and the West for economic cooperation, this area has much to offer the traveler looking to explore one of the least traveled areas on earth, the Russian Far East.

Definitions

The following Russian words are used in the text and are useful to know from the beginning:

babushka	granny
banya	sauna
dacha	garden plot
kassa	cashier or box office
peregovorni punkt	long-distance telephone calling office
ploschad	square
stolovaya	cafeteria
ulitsa	street
vokzal	station

Krai and *Oblast* translate variously as "territory" or "region," and most closely correspond in regional authority to a state within the Russian Federation. *Krais* and *Oblasts* are headed by a governor. Republics are headed by a president.

Zakaznik: originally land set aside for hunting, these preserves are still favorite recreation areas. They are often created to help preserve a single species of plant or animal or a unique landform. Entrance is usually free.

National Parks have three missions of equal importance: conservation, education and recreation. Permits and modest entrance fees are required.

Zapovedniks (Nature Reserves) are areas given the highest form of protection. Their primary mission is conservation, with scientific research and education as secondary functions. Although recreation is generally discouraged in these highly sensitive areas, some individual *zapovedniks* have recently begun welcoming ecotourists in limited numbers.

RUSSIAN FAR EAST

RUSSIAN FEDERATION

☆ Moscow

1 Republic of Buryatiya
2 Chitinskaya Oblast
3 Republic of Sakha (Yakutia)
4 Amurskaya Oblast
5 Khabarovski Krai

6 Jewish Autonomous Oblast
7 Primorski Krai
8 Sakhalinskaya Oblast
9 Kamchatskaya Oblast
10 Magadanskaya Oblast

CHAPTER 1

BEFORE YOU GO

Russian Hardships

Russia is an interesting country, an exciting country, a dynamic country, but not a particularly comfortable country to travel in. This is especially true of the Russian Far East. The tourism infrastructure, recently developed in the cities of Western European Russia such as Moscow and St. Petersburg, is only just starting to appear in the larger cities in the Far East.

Travelers can expect varying sanitation levels in hotels and restaurants, frequent delays in timetables due to weather or lack of fuel, and a service industry that is more focused on industry than service. Most hotels are still state-run, or if "privatized" are staffed by the same people as before. For many it is just a matter of not knowing what a real service industry entails. Flexibility and a good (stoic) sense of humor are essential.

Despite the difficulties, travelers who are willing to explore off-the-beaten-track and who make the effort to get to know the people and the history of the Far East will be rewarded with a wonderful traveling experience.

Weather

Although it is hard to generalize about such a huge area weather-wise, the Russian Far East can be split into three main groups; the coastal regions, including the island of Sakhalin; the far northern regions of Yakutia, Northern Kamchatka, Chukotka and Magadan; and the internal regions, including Chita and Buryatiya. In general, the best time to visit the Russian Far East is from August to the end of September. The temperature is mild, the foliage is in full splendor and the markets have more fruits and vegetables than other times of the year. The salmon run in late July so caviar and smoked salmon are plentiful. If you are interested in a photo safari, this is the best time to take pictures, especially of bears when they are not hungry and mean.

However, if you have your heart set on a typical Russian snow-covered wonderland, the best time to visit the coastal and internal regions is from November to January. In the northern regions the snow falls earlier and stays longer. People have been able to ski in Kamchatka as late as May and it stays cold in Chukotka for the majority of the year. Be forewarned though, the average winter temperature is from -15 to -20 C in the south and can dip below -50 C in the north.

Early spring should, if possible, be avoided, especially in the coastal regions. This time is characterized by sudden storms, frequent rainfalls and fog. The saying goes in Vladivostok that it only rains twice in June: once for 13 days and once for 14. Road travel is made more difficult than usual by the large amounts of mud generated by melting snow and rain.

What to Bring

Medical precautions

Any prescription medicine, however basic, should be brought along with you; don't expect to be able to refill a prescription in Russia. Aspirin and antacid tablets are also a good idea. Women should bring all the feminine hygiene products they need, for although western tampons are starting to appear in stores, there is no guarantee they can be found when needed. This also goes for contraceptives. People with contact lenses should bring enough saline solution, disinfectant, etc. In short, if you really need it, bring it with you.

Food

As the Far East opens up to imports, more snack foods such as candy bars are available in stores and kiosks, but if you have any particular tastes, like cream in your coffee or artificial sweetener in your tea, you'd better bring your own supply of packets.

Food tends to be heavy on meat and oil. For vegetarians this makes eating out a complicated experience. If the waitress is in a good mood, you can probably order just the *garnir*, which is usually potatoes or rice and a couple of pieces of cucumber or a few canned peas. However, it is a good idea to bring a supply of vitamins, and possibly peanut butter or some other simple-to-carry source of protein.

Clothing

Be prepared; winters in the Far East are **cold**. Winter temperatures vary from area to area, but travelers can expect an average temperature of -10 to -20C, with temperatures dropping to -40 or -50 in the northern regions. The wind chill factor will drop those temperatures even more. If you plan to be outside a lot, especially in the north, a winter parka with a hood is essential. Thermal underwear, gloves and warm socks are also a must and a fur hat is recommended. You will also need to buy some insulated, waterproof boots; Sorels are excellent. Business travelers who do not plan to be outside a lot can get by with rubber-soled dress shoes and thick socks.

In spring, waterproof shoes, raincoats and umbrellas are essential. These will also carry you through much of the summer in the coastal regions, which tend to be cool and cloudy, with frequent rainfalls. Dry cleaning (*khimchistka*) services are hard to find and the chemicals used might harm your more delicate clothes. Bring strong, hardy clothes that can withstand heavy detergents and industrial washing machines.

Other Items

Travelers should not expect to find toiletries such as toothpaste or shampoo in hotels, especially in the more northern regions. Toilet paper is more readily available than before, but it is still wise to have your own supply when you are outside your hotel.

Most apartment blocks have no lights in their entranceways, and negotiating the stairs in the dark can be tricky. Some hotels also conserve energy by not lighting the hallways, which makes it difficult to find your keyhole. A pocket flashlight is a useful item to carry at all times.

The following are items which should be included in the kit of any intrepid traveler to the Russian Far East: pocket knife with bottle/can opener, electric transformer for small appliances (to 220v), batteries, film, flashlight, sunglasses, chapstick and postcards of your home city as souvenir gifts. An immersion heater with the proper plug and voltage can be obtained in Russia. A water filter is also a good idea, as there are often "scares" about the drinking water. Last but not least, those who plan to be traveling in the spring and summer should bring lots of tick and mosquito repellent.

In general, try to strike a balance between weight and preparedness. The business traveler staying in the more expensive hotels geared to western tourism will probably not have a problem obtaining basic amenities. However, for the average tourist and adventure traveler the best advice is still to "be prepared."

Gifts

It is always a good idea to bring several small gifts with you when traveling to Russia. Small gifts to helpful *dezhurnayas*, to friends you meet during your travels, or, if you are invited to a person's home, to the host, go a long way toward creating good will and making friends. Although a pack of Marlboro's or a pair of jeans no longer hold the allure they did 5 years ago, a picture book of your home town or the latest cassette of a popular music group will still be appreciated.

Arriving in Russia

Visa

Anyone wishing to visit Russia is required to have a visa, which is issued at Russian consulates around the world. To get a visa, you must have a completed application, a copy of your passport, 3 signed photographs and a letter of invitation from a Russian organization or individual. For a business visa, the invitation must be issued by a legally registered Russian organization; for a private or tourist visa, by a private individual or tourist organization. Lately, "invitation services" have popped up, offering invitations for a price. Visas cost different amounts depending on the type of visa needed and how quickly it has to be issued. Your visa is your most important document besides your passport, and should be kept with you in a secure place at all times. Hotels are required to check your visa when registering you and will not let you stay if you cannot show them a valid visa.

Currently, there is debate between the Russian consulates abroad and the local administrations in Russia as to whether it is necessary to list on your visa every city you will visit. Some hotels will not allow you to register if you are not "authorized" to be in their city. This is a very thorny issue. If you know which cities you plan to visit, it is a good idea to list them on your visa application and make sure they are listed on your visa, just in case.

Customs

When entering Russia, you must fill out a customs declaration, reporting how much money and other valuables you are bringing in. This declaration should be kept with you for the duration of your visit. You no longer have to list every exchange of money on your declaration, but losing your declaration could subject you to fines and other unpleasantness upon departure. When leaving the country you will fill out a second declaration, listing all your same valuables and current money, as well as whatever valuable things you bought in Russia that you want to bring out. The various border points differ in their strictness, but in general, besides the usual items (drugs, weapons, pornography), the following are considered illegal to take out of Russia: antique samovars and icons (what is an antique is up to the customs person), paintings without a stamp from the Ministry of Culture, gold and silver items made before 1968, military medals, and certain books, stamps and coins depending on the mood of the customs official. Rubles are also illegal to export, so spend them before you pass through customs.

Registration

All visitors must register with the local police within 72 hours of arriving in Russia, and any time they go to a new city. This will be done automatically if you are staying in hotels or private apartments rented through an official agency. If you are staying elsewhere, such as a friend's apartment, you have to go to the local police or OVIR station and fill out forms detailing where you are staying, for how long, and so on. They will put a stamp in your visa, stating your length of stay. This should be done with a Russian contact or friend, to make the process as painless as possible. Failure to register could make for a very unpleasant time when you try to leave the country.

Hotels

Hotel services in Russia vary greatly, and often in the moderate-to-expensive range the cost has little to do with the quality of the hotel. Most hotels rely on the city hot water system, which means that hot water may be shut off for months during the summer while pipes are repaired and "winterized." A few of the more expensive hotels have their own hot water systems, but these are rare.

Since prices change so quickly in Russia, we have not listed specific prices, but have graded hotels on the following scale (based on a single room):

Very expensive - over $100
Expensive - $76 - $100
Moderate - $41 - $75
Inexpensive - $25 - $40
Cheap - under $25

Although to some business travelers $76-$100 per night is not thought of as expensive, considering the level of service in many hotels, it is expensive for what you get.

Most hotel rooms come with a TV and refrigerator as standard equipment. In some budget hotels you can get rooms without these amenities.

Russian hotels usually require an application (*zayavka*) before they will let you stay. This application is a letter of guarantee from a local organization, promising that it will cover all costs if you skip out without paying. For the independent traveler this can be a complication, but there are hotels which will accept you without a *zayavka*. Usually it is the newer, more expensive hotels which might not be such sticklers. Foreigners always have to pay the special (higher) foreigner rate, unless they have a humanitarian aid or student visa. At the less expensive hotels, a reservation fee might be added to your first night's charge (whether you made a reservation or not), sometimes up to 50% of the room charge. Keep in mind that tax (currently 23%) is added to your bill.

In state-run and some newly-privatized hotels, each floor is served (guarded) by a *dezhurnaya*. She is the keeper-of-the-keys, tea-maker and housekeeper. Every time you leave the hotel you are supposed to drop off your key with the *dezhurnaya* in exchange for your hotel card. Unfortunately, *dezhurnayas* have a frustrating habit of disappearing when you need to pick up your key. The best advice is to quickly make friends with the *dezhurnayas*, as they can make or break your stay.

Travel in the Far East

Travel on Aeroflot is usually an uncomfortable experience with crowded, smelly planes, indifferent service and scary flights during bad weather, but it is the only practical method for covering the large distances between cities in the Russian Far East, and in more than one region will be your only choice.

If your schedule allows it, train travel is cheaper, more interesting and much more pleasant. The conductors will supply you with blankets and linen on an overnight trip and will sell you hot tea, too. Tickets should be purchased as far in advance as possible, as seats sell out quickly.

Bus travel is available for shorter distances, but is generally unpleasant due to the bad conditions of the roads throughout the region. On the other hand, bus prices make it one of the cheapest methods of travel from city to city.

For those who wish to travel by car, be forewarned: roads in Russia quickly deteriorate once out of the main cities and there are few signs along the way to direct you to your destination. Gas stations are few and far between.

Air Travel

Aeroflot structure

Contrary to popular belief, Aeroflot is not a single monolithic monster...it is several different monsters all using the same name. In essence, the post-Soviet air system is a bit like the post-Soviet bus system: every airport was given a bunch of planes and told to organize some flights. The control is very local and for this reason it is very difficult to get return tickets for anywhere—the bookkeeping involved in reciprocal ticketing is too complicated. Tickets for foreigners (excluding students who are able to pay the Russian rate) are a little different—return tickets can sometimes be paid for, but return seat assignment (if any) is usually done at the destination.

Tickets

The following applies only to "normal" operating conditions. During fuel shortages, political crises or epidemics the rules change unpredictably.

Tickets first go on sale 15 days before the flight. Under normal conditions, tickets are "freely" available up to about 8-10 days before departure, when things start to fill up fast. It can be very difficult to get air tickets on short notice.

However, there are traditionally a number of organizations in every city that have permanent reservations (the Mayor, people's deputies, military institutes and factories, etc.). This means that on every flight out of the given city, a certain number of seats are held for these people whether they ask for them or not. If, however, they don't call and confirm/order these tickets, the spaces are sold on the day of the flight or possibly the day before, and usually only at the airport. Same-day tickets are sold only at the airports, all others are sold at the city Aeroflot office. What this all means is, even if they tell you there are no tickets, if you go to the airport the day of the flight and wait around for a while, you have a good chance of getting a ticket at the last minute.

Tickets for transit flights (to get on at a stopover) are almost never available except the day of, usually at the very last moment, since tickets for seats emptied by departing passengers are sold only after the plane has landed. Do not despair, there are probably seats available.

Luggage

If you are traveling on a package tour where transportation is provided, then weight and style are not a primary concern, however, it is always a good idea to pack light. Don't count on luggage with wheels, now so popular, to lighten your burden, as you will be confronted with stairs, broken sidewalks, narrow doorways, tall doorjambs, etc. Be prepared to carry your bags. Luggage should be lightweight, but strong enough to endure the rigors of Russian travel.

Overly fashionable or expensive luggage should be avoided, as it advertises the fact that you are a foreigner. Suitcases and hockey bags are less conspicuous than nice travel-packs, duffels, backpacks, etc. Russians tend to wrap their bags in paper and string; this discourages people from tampering with them, keeps the bags dry and clean, and makes them look like everybody else's. Although it doesn't happen as often as you might think, bags have been delayed, or have arrived with slashes in them and things removed. Make sure all bags are securely locked and leave nothing interesting open to view.

If your bags do not arrive with you, immediately find the supervisor (*kommandir smeny*—shift supervisor or the *nachalnik bagazhnovo otdeleniya*—head of baggage department, etc.); learn their names and phone numbers; tell them that you are a foreigner and your bags did not come in on your flight and fill out the papers they give you. Ask questions and get your face known, then contact them by phone and visit at least twice daily until your bags appear. Keep in mind; you must repeatedly say that you are sure the fault lies not with the honest people you are talking to, but with the incompetents at the airport from which you departed.

Weight Limitations

On international Aeroflot flights, you are allowed two bags at 23 kilos for free, a bit more weight if you pay, and a carry-on.

On domestic Aeroflot flights, you are allowed 20 kilos of checked baggage, another 20 kilos overweight (charged at 1% of ticket price for each kilo), and 5-10 kilos of carry-on. These are the official rules posted in all airports, and thus subject to change or interpretation at the whim of the lady behind the counter. Usually, Aeroflot will allow you to bring more overweight baggage if you pay for it, but flights that have been subject to delays or rescheduling may limit you to 20 kilos checked, max. Ilyushin 62's are low on baggage capacity, and more likely to involve low weight limits.

Airport Routine/Demeanor ("what to do")

Aeroflot suggests that you get to the airport 2 hours before departure. In any case, you <u>must</u> be there <u>no less than</u> one hour before, or your place may be sold to someone else and you won't be allowed on the flight.

Once you arrive at the airport, take a few minutes to get to know your new home. Some airports put departures and arrivals on a big departure/arrival board (Magadan, Khabarovsk); most just announce it over the public address system.

Most airports have an Intourist Hall. They are known by various names like International Sector (*Mezhdunarodnii Zal* or *MezhSector*), Delegations Room, VIP Lounge, etc., but are really Intourist Halls. Intourist was the mega-company charged with the care, feeding, looting and leading of "foreign guests" around the Soviet Union; it has now disintegrated into a dozen or so organizations all warring for control. Intourist always had lots of pull, and the special halls for foreigners are usually outfitted with soft couches, heat, bathrooms with toilets, and an expensive bar selling beer, vodka, stale cookies and so on. In most cases they are nicer to wait in than the rest of the airport. Intourist ladies have the ability to make or wreck your week, and can be persuaded to like Westerners in most cases. Remember the following:

- You almost always have to go outside to get to the Intourist Hall.
- Some Intourist Halls are now charging to check you in.
- Most Intourist Halls like to have foreigners all to themselves. They frequently do not take kindly to friends and well-wishers unless they are either recognizably foreign or else play the role of *soprovozhdayushi*—the native guide who translates, carries luggage, passes tickets etc. from you to them.

Registration begins for domestic flights about 60-90 minutes before scheduled departure. At this point, give the counter person your passport and ticket. She will examine these documents, write you on the passenger manifest, and tell you to weigh your bags on the scale next to the counter. Do not weigh your carry-on unless somebody yells at you to do so. You are then given the stubs of the tags they put on your luggage, your ticket and documents, and you can go.

If your bags are overweight, you must leave your ticket, passport and bags at the counter, take the overweight slip to the cashier that accepts payment for overweight baggage, pay your extra weight, then come back and trade the stamped overweight slip for your ticket, passport and claim stubs. Boarding usually takes place about 20-50 minutes before the plane leaves. Foreigners are either put on first or last. Remember, the best things to take with you on Aeroflot flights are a sense of humor and patience.

Leaving the Airport

If you don't have previous arrangements for being picked up at the airport, you should allow lots of time to locate the bus/taxi/dog sled that will take you to town. When in doubt, ask. Airports are frequently far from the center of town, and a long ride on the wrong bus could really ruin your day. Generally, there will be a crowd of people at a bus stop, so just point to the bus sign and ask "*v gorod?*" (to the city?) A taxi to or from the airport will be your most expensive choice.

City Transport

Taxis

If you are only going a short way, it's more than likely that a regular taxi won't take you unless you pay dollars. (They hold out for long trips to the airport and other places). If so, stick your hand out, pointing to the ground, and a regular person will stop to pick you up. Establish where you're going and the price before getting in. **Use common sense: if you don't like the looks of the people, just wave them on and wait for the next car.**

Public transportation

Most cities have buses (*avtobus*), trolleys (*troleibus*) and/or trams (*tramvai*).

Tickets are purchased at a kiosk near the stop, usually in packs of 10, with some cities offering monthly passes. On some routes you can buy tickets from the driver. Don't be surprised to see that these flimsy papers still say "15 kopecks" on them. Either they have millions of these tickets stockpiled in some warehouse, or it is too expensive to change the die. In any case, ticket prices vary from city to city, but are universally low.

Standard procedure is to punch your ticket once you get on the bus/tram/trolley. There are punchers placed near the doors and windows. If you are standing near a puncher and someone taps you on the shoulder, they probably want you to punch their ticket and hand it back. People are quite meticulous about punching their tickets. As it says above many bus doors, "A good conscience is the best controller." However, as verification of your conscience, controllers sometimes do come around to check. There are stiff fines for failure to punch your ticket.

The speed with which mass quantities of people stream in and out of the doors of buses/trams/trolleys is simply amazing. This is because people prepare to exit well in advance of arriving at their stop, especially at peak hours when cars are packed. If you are standing near or in the pathway to a door and someone speaks to you, they are probably asking *"vykhoditye?"* (are you getting out?). If you're not, let them squeeze by. If you are, simply nod, but be sure you can get to the door yourself! *Babushkas* (the Russian breed of grannies) and burly men are good at shouldering their way through crowds, so follow in their wake if you get the chance.

Miscellaneous

Telephones

In this country of standardization, the telephone system has more variety than you can imagine. Pay phones in most cities are currently free, but they may adapt the phones to accept tokens, which you will probably be able to obtain at kiosks. Pay phones can only make local calls. In general, local calls are relatively straightforward, although sometimes you can be certain you dialed one number, only to find you have landed at a completely different one. A hint—if your call doesn't go through properly, dial again s-l-o-w-l-y. Surprisingly enough, this often helps.

For out-of-town calls the procedure can be more complicated. Many houses and offices and some hotels have direct-dial phone lines: dial 8, wait for new tone, then dial city code and number. Or you might have to dial your own phone number after the phone number you are calling, so the call gets charged to your phone. If you are in a hotel you will probably have to order a call through the operator (dial 07), wait by the phone while the operator checks that you really are registered at that hotel under that name in that room, and pay the *dezhurnaya* after your call comes through. Or you might have to pay in advance, either at the hotel desk or at the phone station, stating how many minutes you want to speak and paying for that amount. If your call doesn't go through, you'll get your money back. If you use only some of the time, you may or may not get the balance back. But beware, you cannot go overtime, you will simply be cut off.

For international calls the procedure is similar to out-of-town calls, except you dial a different number for the operator. Very few homes have direct-dial international lines, and only a few businesses can afford that luxury. Rates for international calls, which used to be cheap, have skyrocketed in the past couple of years. $5-7 per minute is not unusual. Some hotels offer satellite phone connections—instant, clear and exorbitantly expensive (as much as $25 for 3 minute minimum). The best rule of thumb for international calls, whether from home, office or hotel, is to ask what the procedure is and find out the cost per minute in advance. Also, there is no such thing as a collect call or a credit card call in Russia, so if you plan to call home, prepare to pay cash.

A full list of telephone city codes is listed in the Practical Information at the end of the book.

Shopping

Shopping is one of the most exhausting, yet rewarding experiences you can have in Russia. Goods appear and disappear without notice and unless you have a good network of contacts, finding what you need is a continual process of "trawling" through stores. Lines are nowhere near the size they were during communism, but they can still be pretty long. State-run stores (and some private ones as well) are staffed by bored, unfriendly workers who find that customers are constantly distracting them from what they would rather be doing. Despite all this, or because of it, there are great buys and finding something nice like pretty china or a fur hat for a good price is very rewarding.

Shopping in a state-run store can be confusing and entails a three-step process. First, attract the salesperson's attention and find out the price of the item you are interested in. If you already know what you want and the price, you can go straight to step two.

Second, go to the central cashier, tell (or show) her how much your item costs and give her the money. She will then punch it out on the register and give you a small white receipt with the money amount printed on it.

Finally, go back to the counter and give the receipt to the salesperson, who will give you your purchase.

Some state-run stores have given up this process and have counters that take the money directly. However, other stores still demand the old system, so be prepared. A last word of advice: most stores close for lunch from 1-2 or 2-3, so try to avoid shopping during these hours.

Hours

All shops have their hours posted on a sign outside. In the secular Soviet system, the week begins with Monday, so if there are 7 bars on the sign and the last two are a different color (probably red), then the store is closed on Saturday and Sunday. Furthermore, hours are posted according to a 24-hour clock, with lunch hour usually highlighted or in parentheses, so 8-19 (13-14) means that the store is open from 8:00 am to 7:00 pm, with a lunch break from 1:00 to 2:00 pm.

Markets

Some of the best shopping in the former Soviet Union used to be found in the state marketplaces. Farmers were allowed to have a small personal/family plot and sell a percentage of their produce at markets for a profit. As a result, the produce found at markets was always a lot more expensive but fresher, cleaner and better looking than anything you could find in the state-run stores.

With the fall of communism and the relaxation of laws which used to restrict Russians from buying and selling goods in the open, non-state-run "markets" have spontaneously sprung up everywhere you look. However, the permanent, "organized" markets are still good places to find produce, imported clothes (mostly Chinese) and various knick-knacks that are hard to find or are unavailable elsewhere. Try to bargain in Russian, otherwise be prepared to pay up to several times more than the normal asking price.

Market scene, Petropavlovsk-Kamchatski

Lines

Everyone has heard of the lines in Russia: lines for bread, lines for soap, lines for ice cream. Well, the Russians have been standing in line so long, that there is a particular way to do it. For one thing, lines tend to form to the right. The proper way to be next in line at a counter is to be right next to the person in "front"' of you. This of course makes for lines which run right along the counter until they bump into the lines from another window, and are forced to slant back. Which makes for the question: How do you know who is last? Lines tend to be amorphous rather than linear, which makes it difficult to sort out who's who, yet everyone knows where they stand in the line, or who is holding their place. So if you want to join a line, ask "*Kto poslyedni?*" for "Who's last?", then fall in behind the person who acknowledges. Veterans of World War II usually do not have to wait in line, one of the many privileges they enjoy as an honored member of society. The Russians have developed line-standing into an art, which takes time and practice to perfect. If you will be buying your traveling tickets in Russia, or have to visit some official organization (like OVIR or Aeroflot), you will have plenty of opportunities to develop your own style of line-standing.

Banyas

One of the great Russian traditions is the *banya* or sauna. *Banyas* not only provide a fun way to experience Russian culture and traditions, they are also an excellent way to get squeaky clean in the winter (or summer) when there is no hot water.

There are various ways to experience a *banya*: there are public *banyas*, which anyone can go to; privatized *banyas*, which can be rented out to small groups; and private *banyas* which you can enjoy if you are lucky enough to have a friend who lives in the country.

Public *banyas* are strictly segregated, with either separate rooms and pools for each sex, or perhaps separate hour or days. Public *banyas* are usually small, although in Almaty in Kazakhstan there is a huge public *banya* with marble porticoes and scenic pools. Privatized *banyas* for small groups can usually fit anywhere from 5-10 people, and your group can decide to go naked, or wrap yourselves in sheets. Private *banyas* belonging to a family are rare, except in smaller villages where they might be the best way of getting clean in a place with no running water.

The whole *banya* procedure is quite a ritual in Russia. Basically, you sit naked in the sauna until the sweat starts running (and remember, it is hotter at the top so beginners should take a seat on the lower level), then run out and jump into the cold water pool or, if the water looks a suspicious color, take a cold shower. The first couple of cycles are just to warm up. Now it is time to *paritsa*, from the root *par*, meaning "to steam." Here is where you get out the wet branches (*venninki*) and start hitting yourself (or a neighbor) to bring the blood to the surface. Throughout the process, people will be throwing water on the stove to get more steam and a higher temperature. Russians occasionally wear felt or knit hats to protect their ears from burning and sometimes use portable boards to sit on to prevent burning elsewhere. If you are out in the country you might substitute a roll in the snow for a pool. Another idea while you *paritsa* is to rub honey all over, to stimulate circulation and leave you with silky skin. Others recommend smearing a mixture of coffee grounds and *smetana* (sour cream) over your body for nice, smooth skin. You will find that everyone has their own traditions and strong ideas about how to take a *banya*.

In between courses in the *banya* you can sip tea, or in some public *banyas*, receive a massage. Afterwards, wrapped in a sheet, you retire to an adjoining room for more tea, beer, or, for the hard-core, cognac or vodka. Be very careful about drinking, as your body will be dehydrated and much more susceptible to alcohol.

No matter how it is done or in what season, *banyas* are great fun and a great way to experience Russian culture.

S lyogkim parom!

Customs and Etiquette

Russia is a country steeped in tradition, and it is best for travelers to know about the customs of the country they are visiting to better enjoy the culture. The following tips will help you get along on your trip.

Men and Women

Many customs revolve around the relations between men and women. Despite the fact that Russians claim to have an egalitarian society, men still insist on carrying a lady's heavy bag, opening doors for her, and some men are still prone to hand-kissing. Ladies who turn down the services of bag-carrying, door-holding, etc. are not seen as free-willed and independent, but rather as rude and abrasive. March 8 is International Women's Day, and it is customary for men to give gifts of flowers or chocolates to all their female colleagues and acquaintances.

Terms of address

Since the fall of communism there has been confusion over how to address other people. It used to be easy to simply call everyone "comrade." Nowadays, "comrade" is out, but nothing has replaced it. *Gospadin* and *gospazha* (Mr. and Miss) are considered too old-fashioned for everyday conversation, although they are occasionally used when addressing foreigners (*meester* and *mees* are also used). The formal form of address in Russian is to call someone by their first name and patronymic. Therefore, when you are introduced to someone, you have a lot of names to keep track of. If you meet Alexander Sergeevich Ivanov, whom you would like to call "Mr. Ivanov" if there were a word for "Mr.", you can call him Alexander Sergeevich. Once you know him better you might call him Alexander. But probably only his close friends and his mother call him Sasha.

Another difference is the way in which waitresses, shop clerks and other women strangers are addressed. The proper way to get their attention is to call out "*dyevushka!*", which means "girl." This is not nearly as rude as it sounds in English. Women of 50 can still be called *dyevushka,* because the alternative is worse. *Zhenschina* ("woman") tends to sound rude, so the next stage is *babushka*, or granny! If you're not comfortable with *dyevushka,* you can always fall back on *izvinitye pazhalsta*, which means "excuse me, please."

Dress

Russians tend to dress quite formally for business and parties. Ladies most often wear skirts and dresses, even in the coldest weather. Shorts are usually worn only for sports, although "dress" shorts for ladies are becoming accepted. Ladies carry their bags in their hands (not over their shoulders), and you can easily spot the foreigners by their daypacks.

Hats

It is considered vital to keep your head covered in winter. If you try to walk around without a hat, even if you don't consider it cold, your friends will have a fit, and possibly even strangers will yell at you for endangering your health. Ladies can get away with a woolen scarf, children sometimes wear knit hats for skiing, but the most common form of hat is fur. For men there is a standard style, with flaps which come down to cover your ears (but it is considered "macho" to never put your flaps down). For ladies there are numerous shapes and styles to choose from: the *beret* or rounded style; the *kubanka*, modeled on the Kuban Cossack's style; the *chalma* or turban style, and more. In Buryatiya and Yakutia there are also traditional styles. Furs range from the humble bunny, to the sleek mink, to the fluffy Arctic fox.

Business dealings

Russians have spent decades doing most of their business through *blat* or personal connections. Personal relationships mean more than signed contracts. For this reason, Russians are often surprised at Westerners who want to come in, lay out the plan, and sign the papers. Business is most often conducted over a couple of cups of tea, or, more likely, a few shots of vodka and perhaps a trip to the *banya*.

Shaking hands

Men shake hands upon greeting and also upon departure. Women rarely if ever shake hands, and American business women who insist on shaking hands are often thought of as quite forward.

The following are some other customs to be aware of:

Always take off your shoes at the door when you visit someone's home. They will offer you slippers (*tapochki*) to keep your feet warm.

If you bring flowers for your hostess, make sure you have an odd number (4 flowers are what you bring to the cemetery).

At dinners and other gatherings, toasts are frequent and long-winded. You will probably be expected to join in with a flowery toast of your own.

When you enter a restaurant, theater, or some office buildings, you will see a *garderobe* or coat-check. It is not only considered a convenience to leave your coat there, it is also required. It is considered quite rude to walk into the theater with your coat on, although ladies can sometimes leave on their hats.

On a last note, a few Russian proverbs are good to remember: "Work is not a wolf, it won't run away into the forest," and "War may be war, but we'll have lunch on schedule!"

Food

In the past, Russian cuisine was considered to rank among the world's finest. Unfortunately, under communism it was allowed to lapse into mediocrity. Soviet rule, with its zeal for standardization and conformity, excelled in suppressing creativity, and "Russification" was applied not only to the peoples of the Soviet Union, but their diets as well. Collective farms and a bad distribution system where up to 50% of a harvest could spoil before reaching the stores further limited the variety and quality of food available. Individual families were able to supplement their diets with a variety of foods grown on their summer plots but restaurants, relying on the government infrastructure, tended to offer a bland and repetitive selection based mostly on beef, potatoes and cabbage. The dining experience was damaged further by the indifferent service offered by the restaurant staff to its clientele. Fortunately, private restaurants and cafes have emerged in the last few years to offer an attractive alternative to state establishments. Today, although eating out in Russia is still viewed as a roll-of-the-dice adventure rather than a relaxing dining experience, there are restaurants to be found that have delicious food, served by attentive staff in a pleasant atmosphere.

The best way to taste Russian food and to experience Russian hospitality is to be invited to someone's home. As is often the case around the world, home-cooked food is tastier and more plentiful than restaurant fare. Russians take their responsibility as hosts seriously, and you will be plied with food and drink until you burst, followed by tea, cakes and candies.

Russian meals are served in several courses, starting with appetizers (*zakuski* or *pyervoe*), followed by the main meal (*vtoroe or goryachoe*) and ending with dessert (*sladkoe*). Soups are usually served only at lunch.

Dinner is usually accompanied by a bottle of vodka (or two) drunk in toasts spaced about 5 minutes apart to friendship, the hostess, mothers, women, world peace, and lots of other things. Be forewarned: Russian custom dictates that once a bottle is opened it must be finished and toasts are drunk "*do dnya*," meaning to the bottom. If you don't want to drink, be firm from the very beginning, otherwise you might be on the tenth shot saying: "THIS is the last one, I mean it!"

Food will vary from region to region but typical Russian dishes include *pelmeni*, a Siberian dish of a type of meat ravioli in broth, and *blini,* a thin pancake eaten plain or wrapped around mushrooms, caviar or various other fillings. *Piroshki* are baked or fried stuffed rolls that can be bought from street vendors and are filled with cabbage, egg, potatoes or rice. *Borsch*, a beet and cabbage soup, is actually a Ukrainian dish but can be found everywhere. *Smetana* (sour cream) is added to most soups and salads. Local cuisine in the Russian Far East includes *paporotniki* (fiddle head ferns) and *uha* (boiled fish soup). In the coastal regions, all sorts of seafood are available such as *grebeshki* (scallops) and *kalmar* (squid). *Ikra* (caviar) is plentiful when in season and can be bought in liter size jars at local markets. *Krasnaya ryba* (smoked salmon) can be found at markets and seafood stores year round. *Morozhenoe* (ice cream) is usually soft-serve and plentiful. *Kvas* is a bitter, slightly alcoholic drink made from fermented bread with various herbs added for extra taste. It can be quite tasty or nasty depending on how it's made. *Balzam* is a local alcoholic drink made from different herbs and spices which one adds to vodka or tea. Vodka is everywhere, but unless you are a serious drinker, be careful if your hosts pull out the *samagon* (homemade vodka or moonshine). *Pivo* (beer) is sold "fresh" at stands throughout cities in the Far East and can be bought by the gallon or the glass. When the light above the stand is lit, that means there's fresh beer to be had, or just look for a line of men holding 3-liter jars.

Stolovayas

A *stolovaya* (sto-LO-vaya) is a cafeteria, the kind where you pick up a tray, pick out your food from the choices on the counter, and pay the cashier at the end. The advantage of *stolovayas* is that they are usually dirt cheap. *Stolovayas* can be found in universities, or sometimes in certain office buildings. They are usually intended for the students or staff of that building, but often don't mind if people walk in off the street, or they might have separate hours for the general public. The disadvantage of *stolovayas* is that they are usually run with all the concern of the post office, and the cleanliness of the sanitation department during a strike.

Stolovayas have their own etiquette. The first thing you do when you walk into a *stolovaya* is pick up a tray and wipe it off with the (unappealing) rag which lies nearby. Pick out your aluminum utensils (check them for cleanliness). Then get in line. After you have gotten your food, head for the cashier. It is advisable to pick up the receipt she throws at you, as it is very useful for wiping off your utensils (don't expect napkins at a *stolovaya*). Head for a table. You may well have to join a table with strangers if it is crowded. When you get to the table, unload your tray and return it to the pile where you first got it. When you are finished, pile your dishes and bring them to the window or table where dirty dishes are already piled high.

We mention *stolovayas* here for the adventurous, for those who want to see how the "other half" lives, and for the budget conscious. Despite their flaws, *stolovayas* usually offer filling, if plain, food. If the meat doesn't appeal to you, you can get a double helping of the potatoes or rice. Just point to the potatoes and say "*Mnye dvoynuyu portsiyu.*"

Priyatnovo apetita! (Bon appetit!)

HISTORY

Russia is a vast land with a long history. Thick books have been written about the history of Russia, but we have attempted here to give a brief overview of the events which had the most effect on the Far East.

EXPANSION AND THE QUEST FOR FUR

The speed and scale of the Russian conquest of eastern Siberia and the Far East was astonishing. After the first Russian explorers crossed the Urals in 1581, it took only 58 years for their successors to cover the thousands of miles to the East and reach the Pacific Ocean.

The driving force behind this frantic pace of exploration was the search for furs or "soft gold." Demand in Russia and Europe was so high that with a little perseverance and luck, a good trapper could strike it rich in a few months. As hunting grounds were depleted in Western Russia, Cossacks, hunters and trappers pushed increasingly eastward in search of lands rich in sables, fox and ermine, as well as local tribes to subjugate. As new tribes were encountered, a fur tribute, called *yasak,* was demanded in deference to the Tsar. The Cossacks "convinced" uncooperative natives to deliver this tribute by taking hostages or burning settlements. Once the natives were convinced of the Cossack superiority (at least in the military sense), they pledged allegiance to the Tsar and gave the amount of furs demanded. Divided ethnically and politically, the local tribes were subjugated one by one and, with the exception of the Chukchi and Buryats, could offer little organized resistance to the better-armed Russians. The Russian settlements and outposts served as collection points for the yearly native tribute, which then made its way back to Moscow. In such a manner the East was won.

The fur harvest reached enormous proportions and became a vital part of the Russian economy. By the mid-17th century, up to 500,000 furs a year were gathered and were responsible for 10% of the entire income of the Russian state.

EXILE

Although the fur trade opened the Far East, it was the exile system that populated it. Exile to Siberia first became an official form of punishment in 1649. By pursuing this penal policy, the Russian government hoped to accomplish two things: settle and develop the recently acquired eastern lands with Russians, and rid "civilized" society of its more loathsome elements.

Curiously, at that time banishment was considered an improvement over the current system of physical punishment, which included beheadings, hangings and mutilations. The exile system which was so hated and feared in the 19th century was considered liberal and progressive in the 1650's.

Exile could take three forms. The most severe was hard labor, in which case the prisoner was perpetually chained and worked in the mines or at other labor until the end of his term.

Afterwards, his sentence was converted to the second type of exile, that of a forced colonist. Colonists were sent to settle areas where the government thought the need for development was greatest. In some cases, like in Kamchatka, colonists even received land and support from the government. The third type of exile was that of mere deportation. Deportees were free to live and work where they pleased, but were forbidden to return to western Russia.

By the end of the 18th century nearly 500,000 exiles had been sent to Siberia. The silver and gold mines of Nerchinsk and Kara, the frozen exile of Yakutsk and the coal mines of the island "hell" of Sakhalin all were stocked with exiles who worked under appalling conditions. However, many Russians have noted that the labor itself was not as bad as the living conditions of the prisoners. Crowded into the dank, dark, vermin-infested blockhouses, underfed and inadequately clothed, death rates among prisoner exiles were high.

As outposts grew to settlements and more labor was needed to strengthen economic development, more crimes were made punishable by exile. In 1754, the death penalty itself was replaced with hard labor exile, and some people were sent east on the charge of being "incompatible with public tranquillity" or "prejudicial to public order."

Throughout the 17th and 18th centuries the flow of exiles continued, and the Tsar began to include political criminals in the lists of exiles, hoping to extinguish the reform movements gathering strength in western Russia.

Socially, cities in the Far East began to have alarmingly high percentages of resident convicts, and it is said that two-thirds of the Russian population in the area around Yakutsk was made up of exiles.[1]

From 1800 to 1899, when the exile system was abolished, approximately 1,000,000 prisoners were sent to Siberia and the Far East.

THE TRANS-SIBERIAN RAILROAD

The turn of the century played a significant role in the history of the Far East, as it marked the beginning of the construction of the Trans-Siberian railroad.

---

[1] *East of the Sun*, Benson Bobrick. p. 286

Long considered by Western Russia as not much more than a colonial base of natural resources, by the end of the 19th century, the Russian government began to devote more attention to Siberian matters. As the economy and population grew, it became clear that a railroad joining Siberia to Western Russia made military, economic and political sense. In 1891, a Tsarist decree authorized the construction of a railroad that would stretch from the Urals to Vladivostok, the longest railroad in the world: the Trans-Siberian. Although the project captured the imagination of the world, the cost was considered prohibitive, so to speed construction and cut costs, it was decided to use material of a lesser quality than those used in the West. This short-sighted decision was to cost Russia dearly during the war with Japan.

Labor, as always, was cheap in Siberia and up to 100,000 people were working on the line at any one time. Border towns such as Vladivostok, Khabarovsk and Blagoveschensk boomed, as thousands of Chinese and Koreans came to work on the railroad. Despite the scale and the extreme logistic difficulties of the project, the Trans-Siberian was built at an amazing pace. The project was divided into six sections, which were worked on simultaneously, and by 1895 almost 2000 miles of track had been laid. By 1898, despite floods, bandits and epidemics, the railroad stretched all the way to Irkutsk and the section from Vladivostok to Khabarovsk had also been completed.

The last section of the line to be completed was that circumventing Lake Baikal. Because of the harsh climate and the number of tunnels that had to be blasted out of the surrounding hills, the section around the lake was not finished until September, 1904.

In February of 1904, the Japanese, after months of tense relations with Russia regarding spheres of influence in the Far East, launched a devastating surprise attack on the Russian Fleet at Port Arthur in China. To Russia's (and the world's) surprise, Japan was victorious in battle after battle, and proved itself to be a major power in the Pacific. Because the rail section was not completed, Russian supplies and troops being transferred to the front bottlenecked around Lake Baikal. The poor quality of construction on the Trans-Siberian also made itself felt when Russia could afford it the least. "The equipment and rolling stock proved inadequate for moving heavy artillery and other modern war materiel; in addition, only a fourth of the bridges were of metal construction, the wooden bridges sagged, and the overlight rails... bent under the weight and strain of the trains.... One visiting engineer remarked that 'after a spring rain, the trains run off the track like squirrels.'"[2] The inability to shift large amounts of supplies and troops to the East in a timely manner contributed significantly to Russia's defeat, which gave Japan the southern half of Sakhalin Island, as well as its sphere of influence in Korea.

Regardless of the quality of the line or its effect on the outcome of the Russo-Japanese War, the Trans-Siberian sped the development of the Far East immensely. In areas around the rail line the numbers of Russian settlers rose dramatically, businesses flourished, and in general, the Far East developed and grew like never before.

THE CIVIL WAR

The Communist movement which found such fertile ground among workers and farmers in western Russia received much less support in Siberia and the Far East. There were many reasons for this. First of all, urban centers were smaller and the proletariats fewer than in European Russia. Secondly, on the whole, the Siberian peasants were richer and had more land than their western counterparts. Because the peasants were more prosperous, the shortages that plagued western cities and caused such unrest were relatively unfelt in the East.

After the fall of Tsarist power, the Bolsheviks tried to mobilize soviets (councils) of sympathetic workers and farmers to support their cause, but found that the moderate Mensheviks and right-leaning Socialist Revolutionary Party were much more popular among the masses. Popularly supported or not, the Bolsheviks had one major advantage over their opponents: their followers were united in purpose and ready to take power by force.

When the Bolsheviks did seize power in October 1917, it was a lack of a united opposition more than anything else that led to the establishment of their control throughout Russia. Although local resistance was fierce in some cities, within a matter of months the Bolsheviks were in control throughout the

---

[2] Ibid., p. 373

Far East. They would have stayed in power if it were not for the Czechoslovak legion.

Created from deserters and prisoners of war captured by the Russians during World War I, the Czech Corps was formed to continue the fight against the Central Powers in the name of the provisional government of Czechoslovakia. Despite the October Revolution and subsequent armistice declared between Soviet Russia and Germany, the Czech Corps declared that it would continue to fight the Central Powers regardless of Russia's agreement. However, realizing that it was useless to fight by themselves on the eastern front, the Czechs made an agreement with the Soviets that the Corps would be transported across Russia to Vladivostok, where they would then be shipped to France to continue the fight.

By March 1918, the first trains of soldiers were shipped East. But as the trains moved towards Vladivostok, the Soviets began to have misgivings about some 45,000 potentially hostile armed soldiers stretched throughout the length of Siberia. For their part, the Czechs were worried that they were being intentionally split up and delayed so as to be handed over to Germany.

In May an incident in Chelyabinsk started a fight between a Czech soldier and an Austro-Hungarian POW, and when some Red Army soldiers tried to intervene, they themselves were captured. Local Red Army units tried to help their comrades, but the Czechs were on a roll, and at the end of the day they had captured the rail station and over 1000 Red Army soldiers.

When news of this reached Moscow, Trotsky sent a telegram, ordering the local Soviets to disarm all the Czechs in the area, and that any Czech found with a weapon in his hands was to be shot on sight. Unfortunately for the Bolsheviks, this telegram was intercepted by the Czechs, who decided that their only option was to fight their way through to Vladivostok. After contacting the other trains of soldiers, the Corps proceeded to fight its way eastward with remarkable success. Within one month it had liberated most of Siberia, capturing Omsk, Novosibirsk and Krasnoyarsk. Although they fought fiercely in the Lake Baikal area, the Bolsheviks could not stop the Czech push eastward. By September, all Red resistance in Siberia and the Far East had been defeated, save for scattered bands of partisans, who took to the hills to continue the fight. With the

Bolsheviks defeated, an Anti-Bolshevik government was established with the self-proclaimed "Supreme Leader of Russia" Admiral Kolchak at its head. In the Far East, expeditionary forces from various countries landed in Vladivostok, ostensibly to protect their national interests, but more to help the Czechs and support the White cause by guarding transportation and supply centers, freeing up White Russian troops for the front. By the end of 1918, there were American, French, Canadian, British and Italian troops throughout the Far East. The Japanese, with hopes of annexing Russian territory, landed the most troops by far, with 200,000 soldiers in Manchuria and Russia.

Despite the allied intervention and initial White successes, the Bolshevik army gained in strength, and due to the excesses and dictatorial rule of Kolchak, the Bolshevik cause gained the popular support it originally lacked. The White Army's advance was first checked, then reversed. By 1920 the White forces were in complete retreat. Red partisan forces struck at supply stations, blew up trains, cut communication lines and created general chaos in the rear. Kolchak himself was caught up in the mass of the retreating forces and was turned over to the Bolsheviks, who promptly executed him. Seeing the writing on the wall, the allied forces pulled out of the Far East, with the exception of the Japanese, who occupied the Primorski and Khabarovski Krais, demanding that a democratic government be established in the Far East as a condition of their withdrawal. Not willing to risk a full-scale war with Japan, the Soviets agreed, and established the Far Eastern Republic, stretching from Lake Baikal to the Pacific. Although theoretically independent and democratic, the Republic was neither, as it was controlled and run by the Far Eastern Central Committee of the Communist Party. As soon as the Japanese withdrew the last of their troops from the mainland, the Far Eastern Republic was incorporated into Soviet Russia.

Alexander Vasilievich Kolchak

A brilliant naval commander, Kolchak was unable to transfer those leadership skills when appointed "Supreme Leader" of the Anti-Bolshevik forces in Siberia during the Russian Civil War. As leader of the White forces, Admiral Kolchak was a name long despised in the Soviet Union, but with the fall of Communism,

Russian historians are taking a new look at Kolchak's life and his role in the civil war.

Born in 1873 in St. Petersburg, Kolchak started his naval career after graduating from the Russian Naval Academy in 1894. By 1900, he had already sailed in two expeditions to the Arctic, for which he was awarded a gold medal by the Russian Academy of Sciences.

During the Russo-Japanese War, Kolchak was sent east to fight, where he first commanded a destroyer, and later was in charge of a battery inside besieged Port Arthur, which was later captured by the Japanese. Kolchak himself survived and was decorated with the Sword of St. George for his valor. A young talented officer, Kolchak was to prove his skills and worth again during World War I. Initially named as the Bureau Operations Chief of the Baltic Fleet, he was quickly promoted to head of the entire Baltic Destroyer Force. Here he showed his military talents in a series of engagements in the Gulf of Riga, for which he was promoted to Rear Admiral—the youngest Russian officer ever to receive such a rank. In 1916, Kolchak was named commander in chief of the entire Black Sea Fleet.

When the Tsar was overthrown in the first revolution of 1917, Kolchak quickly resigned and returned to St. Petersburg. Alexander Kerensky, the head of the Provisional Government, sent him to the United States to conduct a study of the American naval force, but Kolchak went quickly from there to Japan, where he offered to serve with the British. The British sent him to Siberia, and in Omsk Kolchak was appointed Minister of War in a new anti-Bolshevik government. This government was replaced in November by a new government, which nominated him Supreme Commander.

Unfortunately for the White cause, Kolchak was to prove a much less able political leader than military commander. His corrupt and dictatorial administration alienated the peasants, ethnic minorities and more liberal elements of the anti-Bolshevik camp. Although this divisiveness could be overcome while winning, Kolchak's military successes did not last and by the fall of 1919, the White forces were on the defensive. In retreat, the differences between the various groups became more apparent, and under pressure from the Red Army, the retreat quickly degenerated into a total rout. In January of 1920, Kolchak resigned, giving the command to General Denikin. Kolchak placed himself under the guard and protection of the Czech Corps, but they had had enough

> *of the Supreme Commander and turned him over to the Socialist government in Irkutsk, where he was promptly turned over to the Bolsheviks. The Bolsheviks, for their part, were happy to have the head of the White forces in their hands and on February 7, 1920, Alexander Kolchak was executed by a firing squad.*

THE STALIN YEARS

The years after the Civil War were hard ones. Trying to feed the cities, the government introduced a policy of forced farm collectivization and grain requisition. These policies were met with almost universal opposition by the peasants, and thousands of farmers from Buryatiya to Yakutia slaughtered their livestock rather than submit.

To crush resistance and to drive his grandiose plans of rapid industrialization and collectivization, Joseph Stalin, who succeeded Lenin as head of the Soviet Union in 1924, set up the now infamous State Department of Camps or *Gulag*.

Kulaks (rich peasants), Trotskyites, "wreckers," "spies," nationalists, workers who did not meet quotas, and the ubiquitous "enemies of the people" were all shipped to camps throughout the Far East to realize the breakneck pace of industrialization that Stalin demanded. Roads, factories, ports and even entire towns sprang up almost overnight, as prisoners slaved under conditions far more brutal than those of the Tsarist camps. Death rates of 20-30% were not uncommon, and new shipments of prisoners arrived on a regular basis to replace the dead. At the height of the terror (from 1937-38), it is estimated that some 7 million people were sent to the camps.

With the outbreak of World War II, the Far East was used as a production base for the western front. Prisoners of war, refugees and industries were shipped to the East; soldiers and military hardware were shipped back. German and Japanese POW's were sent to the camps and whole peoples were "resettled" within Russia; the Baltic nationalities and ethnic Germans living on the Volga were shipped eastward and ethnic Koreans in Primorski Krai were shipped to Kazakhstan, to name just a few of the major population resettlements of the era.

It was only after Stalin's death in 1953 that the labor camp system began to be dismantled.

RECENT HISTORY

During the mid-70's, the BAM, or Baikal-Amur Mainline, was planned to parallel the Trans-Siberian and speed development of the more northern regions. Designated a "hero project," the Soviet government called for young enthusiasts and "shock workers" to come and work on the railroad. Finally completed in 1989, the line proved to be a costly overestimate. Five years of repair work were needed before the first train could even travel on the rails and even now the BAM has not fulfilled the huge potential promised by its founders. However, the "hero" image of the rail line and the workers who built it is still very much a part of Far Eastern history and lore.

With *perestroika*, many areas of the Far East have been hard hit. Many cities whose industries were based on military production or resource extraction have had a hard time diversifying their economies. Tourism has increased dramatically over the last few years, but is not sufficient to stop the local economies from faltering. As contacts with China, Korea and Japan have increased, ties with Moscow have lessened, making the Far East once again a crossroads where East meets West.

Painfully aware of their current economic weakness and afraid of becoming economically "controlled" by the stronger Pacific Rim countries, most Russians are looking to take the best of both Europe and Asia to forge an independent future, based not on political and geographic boundaries, but on economic partnerships.

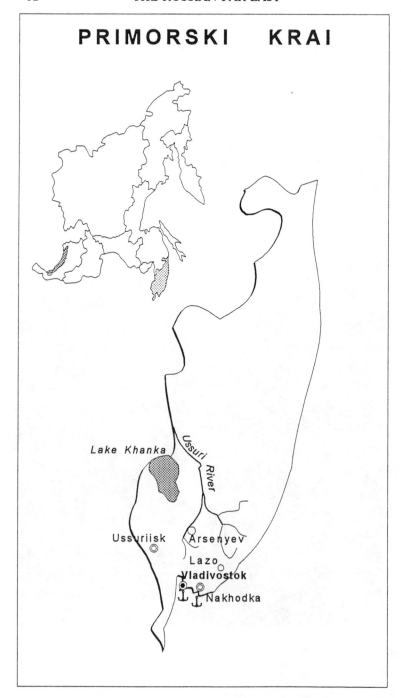

PRIMORSKI KRAI

CHAPTER 2

PRIMORSKI KRAI

In the southeastern corner of the Far East, bordered by North Korea and China, the Primorski Krai (sometimes called Primorye or the Maritime Region) has long been off limits to foreigners due to its strategic military importance. Today however, the krai has opened its door to the outside world and with its ports and relatively developed infrastructure, has been one of the most successful in attracting foreign investment and converting its defense industries. The area around Nakhodka is trying to regain its status as a Free Economic Zone, the northern towns of the region are involved in various lumber export deals, and Vladivostok (with a little help from foreign investors) hopes to become one of the major players on the Pacific Rim by the turn of the century. Currently, the krai's main industries are shipping, fishing and fish processing, and timber exports, while the defense and ship-building industries are in decline. The krai itself, although small, has a great abundance of wildlife, including the endangered "Siberian" tiger, and is home to Russia's only marine nature preserve, south of Vladivostok.

VLADIVOSTOK

INTRODUCTION

Home to the mighty Pacific Fleet and several military factories, and capital of the Primorski (Maritime) Region, Vladivostok was a closed city to both Soviets and foreigners until 1992.

Since then, Vladivostok has come a long way. Direct flights now connect the city to Japan and the United States, there are several consulates open, and an American cultural and business center has also opened its doors. Strengthening its cultural and economic ties abroad, Vladivostok has 6 sister city relationships around the world: Akita, Niigata and Hakodate in Japan; Pusan, Korea; Dalyan in China, and Tacoma and San Diego in the United States. The streets are filled with foreign cars and the kiosks are stocked with goods from China, Turkey, Japan, Hong Kong and Vietnam. Private stores and cooperative restaurants have sprung up all over the city and are flourishing. Unfortunately, as some have become richer, crime has grown accordingly and now a whole class of "*businessmeny*" wearing leather jackets or sweat suits count their ill-gotten dollars in the hundreds of thousands.

With its port, terminus on the Trans-Siberian Railroad and international airport, Vladivostok is hoping to become an international business center the likes of Singapore or Hong Kong. Although there are serious infrastructure problems to be dealt with before the city can attract the type of international firms that it hopes to, Vladivostok has the potential to be a serious player on the Pacific Rim.

HISTORY

On June 20, 1860, the military transport "Manchuria" with Ensign Komarov and 40 soldiers of the 4th Line Battalion dropped anchor in the Golden Horn Bay. As part of an expedition sent to map the eastern coast and to establish two outposts in the area, Komarov was drawn to the beautiful, peaceful bay with its overlooking hills, and founded the outpost which was to become present day Vladivostok. Coming from the Russian words meaning "to rule the East," Vladivostok staked Russia's claim to the Far East. This claim was officially recognized by the Peking Treaty, which transferred ownership of all lands east of the Ussuri River from China to Russia.

The first years were hard ones for the military outpost. In Russian tradition, the first building constructed was a barracks, the second a church. The outpost was cut off from the rest of the world during the winter months, so most of the needed food and supplies had to be obtained locally. Other difficulties such as tiger attacks and the harsh winter hampered growth of the post such that by the end of the year Vladivostok's population stood at 62 people, 78 horses. The first settlers to arrive in 1864 were exiles, sent from Siberia to help with the hard labor of building a settlement. In those early days, the post lived on its small ship-building and repair business, trade with foreign ships and the local Chinese, and sales of seaweed. Although the outpost was founded to secure a claim of a Tsar some 9000 kilometers to the west, it was Vladivostok's secondary role as a trading port that made it grow and prosper.

Located on the Golden Horn Bay, a natural deep harbor and warm water port, Vladivostok was ideally situated to serve as a link between the Orient and Western Russia. Foreigners, mostly Germans, Swedes and Americans, lured by the trading privileges and cheap land offered by the local administration, came to the outpost to live and work. The foreign companies of Kunst and Albers (German), the Smith Brothers, Cooper (American) and De Frize (Dutch) all did well in the free port. Today Cooper's Pass and De Frize Island are monuments to these companies' influence, and the Kunst and Albers building still stands in the middle of town.

By the end of 1868, the outpost had grown to a small village of 516 people, including both military and civilian inhabitants. From then on it grew rapidly. Within three years, the main Navy port and administration of the Far East was moved from the competing port of Nikolaevsk, instantly giving Vladivostok increased prestige and making it the preeminent port in the Primorski region. A Danish company linked the town by telegraph cable with Nagasaki and Shanghai, providing reliable communications with the outside world year round.

By 1878, the port had grown further to 8393 people, of whom 4163 were foreigners. The hotels Moscow, Vladivostok (both considered by contemporaries to be terrible) and the Hotel de Louvre (considered to be good but with expensive food), were built to accommodate the increasing number of visitors.

By 1880, the port city had grown to 13,000 people, and foreign ships were visiting Vladivostok at a rate of 60 per year. In 1889, the city was declared a fortress and the military began building the city's fortifications, which can still be seen today. The following year work began on the Ussuri railroad and plans were made for construction of a modern commercial port.

The city's population exploded as thousands of workers from China, Korea and Japan poured in to help build the railroad. These workers lived in whatever shacks they could afford to build, and the whole area where the Dinamo stadium now stands became a huge ghetto. The locals called the area "*millioniki*," presumably because it seemed as though millions of people were crammed in the desolate area. Crime and drunkenness rose sharply until the city forced these workers to move to an outlying area that became known as the Korean district, where present day Pyervaya Rechka (First River) is located. As this Chinese/Korean neighborhood grew, it became self-governing and had its own restaurants, theaters and temples. The Korean district was also notorious for its opium dens and houses of ill repute, which the authorities could never seem to eliminate.

That same year, in 1890, the famous Russian writer Anton Chekhov came to Vladivostok and wrote: "I was in Vladivostok. I can say only one thing about the Primorski Region: appalling poverty. Poverty, ignorance and insignificance that could drive one to despair." Despite Chekhov's words, Vladivostok grew, and its international community with it. By the turn of the century the city was an international trade center. The city had telephone and telegraph links to Japan, China and western Siberia. Businesses and trading houses prospered as the city grew, importing goods from the Near East, Australia, Europe and America. Foreign hotels and businesses were common sights and there were several consulates in the city. Reflecting Vladivostok's diversity, there were several Russian Orthodox churches, a Catholic and a Lutheran church, a Japanese Shinto shrine and a Korean Buddhist temple. (All were closed or destroyed during the years following the civil war). Chinese, Korean and Russian theater and dance troupes came and provided entertainment.

Vladivostok's international trade traffic all but came to a halt during the Russo-Japanese war of 1904-1905. Russia was soundly defeated and had to sign a peace treaty with the Japanese, ceding Port Arthur and the southern half of Sakhalin Island. Russia's loss was Vladivostok's gain, as it now became the undisputed leading port of the Russian Far East. With the war over, Vladivostok grew and prospered, until the outbreak of the Civil War.

In 1918 Japan sent a warship to Vladivostok to protect its interests in the Far East. Other countries soon followed, either to protect their citizens and property, or hoping to open up a second front against the Germans and/or Bolsheviks. The Expeditionary Forces, or "Interventionists" as they are called in Russian, finally came to include the Japanese, Americans, Canadians, French, English, Italians and the infamous Czech Legion that fought its way from the Ukraine all the way to Vladivostok trying to get home. The graves of some of these soldiers can be seen today at Vladivostok's Naval Cemetery. Largely due to the Czech's efforts, an independent Siberian Republic was formed, headed by the White Army General Kolchak. Vladivostok was a major lifeline for troops and supplies needed by the Republic and the Expeditionary Forces.

The Sukhanovs

The history of Alexander Sukhanov and his son Konstantin is a good portrait of Russia at the turn of the century and the years leading up to the revolution.

Alexander Vasilevich Sukhanov (a Buryat by nationality) was born in 1863 in Blagoveschensk in a family of priests. At an early age he, too, entered and studied in a seminary, but became lame and was unable to finish. At the age of 16 he entered government service. A dedicated monarchist, he hoped to one day earn a noble title for himself and his family. In 1894 Alexander, along with his wife and seven children, moved to Vladivostok where he became city councilman of the Primorski Administration. Due to his exemplary work with the roads, schools and hospitals of the city, he was personally congratulated by Nikolai II. Alexander was also decorated several times for his service.

Konstantin Sukhanov, born in 1894, was the youngest of the Sukhanov children. Sent to study at St. Petersburg University, Konstantin soon became politically active and was arrested for his political discussions with other students. In 1913 he joined the Communist Party and when World War I broke out, agitated against Russia's participation. Arriving back in Vladivostok, Konstantin founded the Vladivostok Initiative Group of Marxists and was elected chairman.

In 1916, police raided a workers' meeting organized by Konstantin's group and he was thrown in jail. Despite radical differences in political convictions, Alexander posted the bond to free his son.

> *On November 18, the Communists won a majority in the worker-soviet council and Konstantin was elected chairman of the executive committee. The soviet announced that it rejected the authority of the Provisional government and on December 12, took governmental power into its own hands.*
>
> *In January of 1918, Konstantin was named Commissar of Internal Affairs, in charge of suppressing all "counter-revolutionary" activity, a task he took to with cruel enthusiasm. However, he was not to hold this position for long. On April 5th, the foreign expeditionary forces landed and occupied Vladivostok. Later that month, Konstantin and the other leaders of the Vladivostok council were arrested.*
>
> *On November 17, Konstantin Sukhanov was shot "trying to escape" by members of the Czech legion. Alexander Sukhanov buried his son, and died 3 years later in an accident in the nearby town of Shkotova.*

Several bloody battles were fought in the area, first with partisans, then with the Red Army. The battle of Nikolsk is noteworthy in that it had Austro-Hungarians and Bolsheviks fighting together against the Czechs! In the end, the Bolsheviks defeated the White and Expeditionary Forces and "liberated" Vladivostok on October 25, 1922.

With the arrival of Soviet power, Vladivostok underwent the same changes that so many Russian cities did. Businesses and property were nationalized, political purges were carried out, churches were converted into warehouses or destroyed, and so on. During the 30's a transit camp was built here for prisoners being sent to Gulags farther north.

During the Great Patriotic War, the Russian name for World War II, Vladivostok was on the receiving end of American Lend-Lease aid. By the end of the war 2/3 of all the Lend-Lease aid given to the Soviet Union was delivered through the Pacific route. The United States provided over 90 ships and millions of tons of supplies while the Soviets provided the crews to pilot the ships. These brave sailors navigated convoys through Japanese-controlled waters to bring back much-needed supplies to Russia. In the last days of the war, Vladivostok was used as a staging area for the attack on the Japanese army in Manchuria. In all, twenty five ships were sunk and 30,000 Vladivostokians lost their lives during the war.

After World War II, Japanese POW labor was used to build apartment complexes and public works around the city. Many of the structures on Russky (Russian) Island as well as the interlocking system of tunnels and fortifications underneath the city were built by the Japanese. Some of these prisoners are buried at the Naval Cemetery.

For the next thirty years, Vladivostok worked and grew in secrecy. The city became exactly what its original founders intended; a fortress city. Since Vladivostok was in a strategic border zone, it was a closed city not only to foreigners, but to Soviet citizens as well. Those wishing to visit or work in the city needed a special invitation and authorization. The Pacific Fleet was based in the city, as were several defense industries. During the Korean War, Russian pilots flew sorties against U.S. planes from a nearby air base. In the nearby town of Shkotova-17, nuclear submarines were built.

In 1974, the city opened up a bit and Gerald Ford came to Vladivostok for a summit meeting with Leonid Brezhnev. A special negotiations hall (Dom Peregovorov) at Sanatornaya station was built in 1986 to encourage other meetings and is still in use today.

With Perestroika, the city opened further, allowing some student exchanges and a USIA exhibit in 1990. Finally, on January 1, 1992 the city was declared officially "open."

Vladivostok, 9200 kilometers and 7 time zones away from Moscow, has always felt a bit removed from the hectic pace and politics of the capital. Most in the area believe that the future lies in stronger economic ties not with Moscow and the western regions of Russia, but with the neighboring countries of the Pacific Rim. Plans include turning Vladivostok into a free economic zone like the neighboring port of Nakhodka and having the Primorski Krai apply for the status of an independent republic. In these plans Moscow is viewed as an interfering nuisance at best.

Vladivostok is a city with great potential. Although it is still plagued with blackouts and lack of hot water, it continues to grow in importance and relevance on the international scene. The next five years will be crucial to Vladivostok and Russia as a whole. The country is cautious, feeling its way forward, slowly but surely. Vladivostok, on the other hand, looks to the future with an impatience and confidence born from a desire to continue that growth so rudely interrupted some 70-odd years ago.

WALKING AROUND TOWN

The best place to start a tour of Vladivostok is from the **train station (*Vokzal*)**. Built in 1912 as the terminus of the railroad connecting Vladivostok to Ussuriisk, the train station was considered one of the best of its time. With restoration completed, the *vokzal* isl once again the pride of Vladivostok. The ceilings inside are a nice example of Socialist Realism and are worth a look. Recently restored, these paintings (called "Our Great Motherland") were originally done in 1956 and show strong, happy farmers, workers and soldiers looking to the future. The square outside the station was witness to a revolutionary demonstration in 1906 that was fired upon by Tsarist troops, killing 80 people.

Across from the train station is **Lenin Square.** Although Lenin was never in Vladivostok and only said one sentence about the city ("Vladivostok is far away, but it's ours"), it would have been unthinkable not to have a Lenin Square in any Soviet city. For our purposes, Lenin Square is important because it is the starting point for the city trams.

Crossing Lenin Square to the corner of Aleutskaya St. and Pyervaya Morskaya St., you will see a large yellow building. Before the revolution this building was the French Grand Hotel, one of the finest and most prestigious in the area. After the revolution it was converted into the Palace of Labor where unions gathered to hold meetings and discussions. It now houses the tax inspectorate.

Further up Aleutskaya St. on the right side is the **Primorski Art Museum.** At the turn of the century it was a French bank, and the old vaults are still used for the more valuable art pieces. Across the street from the museum at #15 is the **Brynner house** (of Yul Brynner fame). The Brynner family had a large trading business in Vladivostok before the revolution and their yellow house, built in 1912 and now in the process of being restored, is one of the prettiest in the city. It is followed by two huge, gray apartment complexes. The buildings were built by Japanese prisoners of war and are considered to be some of the best apartments in the city. Notice the roof of the building on the left is adorned with big, strapping farmers and workers.

Take a right onto Svetlanskaya at the corner. (If you are still on the left side of the street, take the underpass—Russians are notoriously dangerous drivers!) The large modern building on the right known as the "White House" or the "Wisdom Tooth" (because you never pay attention to it until it makes a pain of itself), is the **Primorski Krai Administration** building. Across from the White House an alley connects Svetlanskaya and Fokina. This is the **Flower Sellers' Alley**, where you can buy flowers in any season, day or night.

Passing the White House, you come onto the **Main Square** or, as it is officially called, The Square of the Fighters for Soviet Power in the Far East. On weekends, a band can usually be found playing in front of the monument, and on some weekends the square is the site of a bazaar. Standing on the square facing the sea one gets a good view of the Russian Pacific Fleet, quietly rusting away from lack of funds.

If you walk down the stairs and along Korablnaya Naberezhnaya Street you will pass on your left the tall building of the Pacific Fleet headquarters and the "friendship trees" planted by visiting foreign navies, and approach the **C-56 Submarine Museum.** Across from the submarine is the ferry station where boats leave for the local outlying islands, or to the other side of the bay. Although the other side is dirty, industrial and generally not very interesting, the ferry trip is. Not only do you get a nice view of the city, but also a mini harbor tour and a look at some obsolete submarines, abandoned and rusting at the piers. Ferries leave every 20 minutes.

Continuing up Svetlanskaya from the Main Square you will find **GUM,** the government department store. Originally owned by the German company Kunst and Albers, the building was built in 1882 with bricks brought especially from Hamburg to withstand the damp climate. The store of Kunst and Albers was said to have no rival in all of Russia and according to contemporaries, one could buy anything there from needles to a live tiger.

Further along Svetlanskaya at the tram stop "Lazo" burns the **eternal flame,** in memory of those sailors in the merchant marine service who died during World War II. Surrounding the monument and the flame are plaques with the name and description of each ship lost during the war. A bit further along is an impressive **monument to Alexander Nevelskoy,** one of the great Russian explorers of the 19th century.

V L A D I V

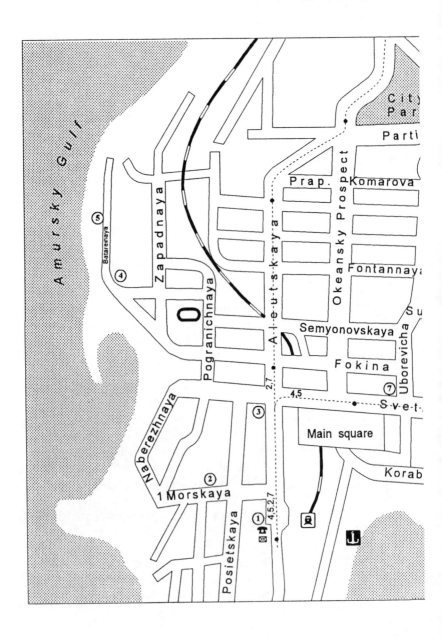

' O S T O K

Two great views of Vladivostok

View #1. Take tram #4 or 5 to the 4th stop ("DVTU" or "Universitet") and walk up to Pushkinskaya. Here take the funicular up the hill. If the funicular is not working (a distinct possibility), there are stairs that also lead all the way up the hill. When you reach the top, cross the street and climb the stairs to the gray building at the very top of the hill, the Far Eastern Technical University. If you walk around to the back of the building (facing the bay), the whole city and bay will be laid out before you. On a clear day the view is fantastic.

View #2. Look for the bus stop a half-block up from the Primorye Hotel on Posetskaya Street (in front of the Aeroflot office). Take bus #1 to its last stop, "Mayak" (lighthouse). The bus will travel down the length of the Egersheld Peninsula and leave you at a small overlook with a beautiful view of Russky Island and the lighthouse. At night the view is also impressive, with the moon and lights from passing ships lighting up the bay.

Svetlanskaya Street

Other sights

Across from the tram stop "Dalzavod" is a small park that hides an interesting **monument**. The column-shaped monument with the light blue ornament is dedicated to those who died on a Soviet civilian airplane that was shot down by an American fighter over China during the Korean War.

On Praporshik Komarova Street you can see Vladivostok's old **synagogue**. Closed in 1928, it was used as the club for the workers of the nearby candy factory, and now is an ordinary store. Take tram #7 to the third stop, "Kraevaya Bolnitsa." Turn right onto Komarova Street and walk up the hill one block. The old synagogue will be on your left, a pink building with rounded, arch-like roof decorations.

Across the Golden Horn Bay, up on the hillside is Vladivostok's **Naval Cemetery**. Located at the top of Churkin on the other side of the bay, this cemetery is best reached by car, as it is hard to get there by city transport. If you go by tram, take the #4 tram to the 2nd stop past Lugovaya and start climbing.

The Naval Cemetery is where the city's most prominent citizens are buried. A monument to the crew of the ship "*Varyag*," sunk during the Russo-Japanese War, stands near the entrance, and the captain of the ship is buried nearby. Vladimir Arsenyev, revered local author and scientist, is buried here, as well as some of the Canadian, French and Czech Expeditionary Forces from the Civil War. Some of the Japanese prisoners of war are buried in a common grave. The various graves trace the history of

Memorial to Czech Forces, Naval Cemetery

Vladivostok throughout its existence. One can see graves of those who have fallen in the Civil War, the Khasan conflict, World War II, the Korean War and Afghanistan.

Note:

Streets in Vladivostok   After the fall of Communism, several street names were quickly changed back to their original pre-Revolutionary names. The main street Leninskaya is now Svetlanskaya and the 25th of October Street (the date Vladivostok was "liberated" during the Civil War) is now Aleutskaya. Interestingly enough, the original name of Leninskaya, before it became Svetlanskaya back in 1873, was Amerikanskaya, named after the sail ship "America." Even though the names have officially changed, few of the signs have been changed and people use both the old (communist) and new (historical) names. For the sake of consistency, we will use the new names throughout the text, but have included a list of both names in Russian and English at the back of the city section.

PRACTICAL INFORMATION

Moscow time +7 hours.
Code for calling Vladivostok from outside the city: **4232.**
Information when calling from inside the city: **09.**
Information when calling from outside the city: **22-83-80**.
To order an operator-assisted international call: **21-00-17**.
United States Consulate U.S. citizen services Mon-Fri 2:30-4:00. 12 Mordovtseva St. (There are plans to move the consulate to Pushkinskaya 34 in the spring of '95, if their new building is built by then). Tel: 26-67-34, 26-84-58. Emergency number 21-58-54.
United States Information Agency Located in Olympeets Sports Hall, Battareinaya 2. Tel: 25-94-24.
United States and Foreign Commercial Service Office also in Olympeets, Battareinaya 2. Local tel: 25-46-61, satellite tel: (+7-509) 851-1211.
American Business Center A service of the U.S. Department of Commerce, this Business Center is scheduled to open shortly, and will offer office and conference rooms, photocopying, international phone and fax, word processing, interpretation and translation, and business appointments. Contact the U.S. Foreign Commercial Service Office, above, for details.
South Korean Consulate 45a Aleutskaya, 5th floor. Open Mon-Fri from 9-18, closed 12:30-14 for lunch. Tel: 22-78-22, 22-83-14.
Australian Consulate 17 Uborevicha St. Open Mon-Fri from 9-17. Provides visa application forms and sends them to Moscow for processing. Tel: 22-87-78.

Indian Consulate 14 Aleutskaya Street, 2nd floor. Open Mon-Fri from 9-17:30. Tel: 22-97-60.

Japanese Consulate 12 Mordovtseva St. Open Mon, Tue, Thu and Fri. Submission of visa documents from 10-12; pick-up of passports/visas from 16-17. Tel: 26-75-02, 26-75-13.

Pacific Law Center 2 Kapitana Shefnera St. 7th floor. Open Mon-Fri from 9-18. American-Russian joint venture specializing in commercial law. A great help for those who want to conduct business in the Russian Far East, these Russian and American lawyers can handle any legal problem you might have. Tel: 22-47-84, 22-41-43.

Business Center At this center you can make international calls and send or receive faxes or telexes; a boon to anyone who doesn't have an office, or who simply doesn't have an "international" line. Faxes to the States go through more quickly than if you are sending within Russia, but that is a common problem all over the former Soviet Union. Best of all is that the ladies are actually polite and helpful if you get frustrated. If you are expecting a fax, just look for your name on the list of faxes received that day. The charge to receive a fax is by the page, to send a fax is by the minute. 24 Okeanski Prospect. Open 8-19 (12-13 lunch) every day. Tel: 26-45-54, Fax: 25-38-41, 26-47-05 Telex: 213211 PTB SU, 213210 PTB SU.

Ricoh Copy Center Quick photocopies at reasonable prices. Okeanski Prospect 24. Open Mon-Fri 8-18, Sat 10-17. Tel: 25-69-32.

Main Post Office Open 8-20 every day, across from the train station. Long distance and international telephone center works 24 hours a day. Telexes, long distance phone calls, mail services.

CredoBank Currency exchange and cash advances on VISA in dollars/rubles. Open Mon-Fri from 9-18. 6 Aleutskaya St., in the Morskoi Vokzal (Maritime Terminal) on the second floor. Tel: 22-22-64, 22-49-54.

VostokInvestBank Currently the only bank which accepts traveler's cheques (Visa, MC, AX, Citibank). Large fee for cashing. Aleutskaya 45/A, 2nd floor. Open Mon-Fri 9-13. Tel: 26-55-88.

Fast Photo Fast Photo is one of the only places in town that offers next day film developing. Also sells Fuji film. Open Mon-Fri 10-18. Off Okeansky Prospect and up the block from

"Izumrud." 4 Krasnovoznameni Pereulok (not to be confused with Prospect Krasnovo Znameni).

Vladivostok News Vladivostok has one English language paper, the Vladivostok News, which comes out weekly and is mostly an English translation of the daily parent Russian paper "Vladivostok." Can be found at major hotels.

KGB building Just in case you wanted to know. The tall building is no longer operated by the KGB, but by the renamed democratic version of the KGB, the Upravleniye Kontra-Razvedki (Department of Counter Intelligence). 46 Aleutskaya.

DHL Express mail Khabarovskaya 27/B, 3rd floor. Tel: 25-52-26, 25-52-52.

UPS Express mail Tel: 22-45-52.

Russko Express mail Tel: 46-38-40.

EMS Garant Post Service of the Russian Postal system. Domestic deliveries only. Verkhne-Portovaya 3. Tel: 22-30-17.

HOTELS

Vlad Motor Inn Out at Sanatornaya Station, a stop on the *electrichka*, this hotel was shipped from the West in ready-built modules and assembled locally. The result is clean, comfortable rooms in a pretty area of the suburbs of Vladivostok. More importantly, this Russian-Canadian joint venture has a bilingual staff trained in the art of customer service. The hotel is surrounded by forest, and the beach is just a short walk away. Satellite communications available. Very expensive. Sanatornaya Station, 1 Vosmaya Street. Tel: 21-58-54.

Versailles The Versailles Hotel has recently opened in the heart of Vladivostok. Restored to its pre-revolutionary splendor by Japanese investors and Chinese construction workers, the Versailles has a restaurant, bar and casino with British croupiers. Unfortunately, the hotel's service does not reflect the elegance of the hotel itself. Very expensive, cost includes breakfast. Svetlanskaya 10. Tel: 26-42-01.

Hotel Gavan (Harbor) Not as well-known as other hotels in the downtown area, the Hotel Gavan on the Egersheld Peninsula deserves a second look. The hotel has a restaurant, a nice indoor swimming pool, and a business center replete with computers and fax machines. Each room comes complete with a VCR and videos available at reception. The Gavan also has that crucial element in Vladivostok: its own independent source of hot water.   Individual safe deposit boxes at front desk. Breakfast included with the price of the room.   Very expensive. 3 Krygina St. Tel: 21-95-73.

Acfes Seiyo A Russian-Japanese joint venture, this hotel is located in the Second River (*Vtoraya Rechka*) region of the city. Well-prepared for the business traveler, the hotel has its own hot water,   as   well   as   a   business   center,   international telecommunications, and satellite TV.   Payment by credit card or in cash, in dollars or in rubles at the current exchange rate. Very expensive, but popular with the Japanese.   100 Let Vladivostoka, 103. Tel: 31-90-00.

Pensionat   Clean, comfortable rooms with balconies, although not all rooms have telephones.   The Pensionat was formerly a hotel for CPSU members, and some of the Gerald Ford delegation stayed here during the summit.   Huge 2-room suites available with kitchens. Located at Sanatornaya Station, surrounded by forest and close to the beach.   Expensive.   14 Devyataya St.   Tel: 21-56-39 for general information and 21-58-40 or 21-53-12 for reservations.

Visit Small privately-run mini-hotel on the fourth floor of the Vladivostok Hotel.   The rooms cost more, but are better equipped (satellite phone lines and TV) and the service is much better. Expensive.   The bar works from eight at night to two in the morning. 10 Naberezhnaya St. Tel: 212-053, 21-20-63.

Vladivostok   Big, Soviet-style hotel overlooking the bay. The hotel's elevators hardly ever work, the prostitutes and black marketers hardly ever stop.   The staff gives you the service you expect from a state-run hotel.   On the other hand, the hotel is relatively cheap, centrally located, and has a nice view if you have a room facing the bay.   Moderate.   10 Naberezhnaya St. Tel: 22-22-08.

Hotel Vladimir Floating hotel moored in the Golden Horn Bay. Nice idea, but the rooms are very small and the area along the harbor is not well lit.   Noted hangout for Vladivostok's "tough guy" crowd. Restaurant and dance floor open from 7 at night to 3 in the morning.   Moderate.   Korablnaya Naberezhnaya. Tel: 22-33-92.

Amurski Zaliv   Soviet hotel management at its best (or worst). The good news is that the hotel is centrally located and the rooms are comfortable with a view of the bay. The bad news is that the hotel is the least "user friendly" in the city. To get to the front desk you have to go down two flights of stairs (the entrance to the hotel is through the top floor) and if you are lugging heavy suitcases, this is no mean feat. There also have been incidents reported of men knocking on women's doors at night, trying to get in. The restaurants are unremarkable. A written application is required from the organization that is stated in your visa. One bright spot is the hotel casino, which is open all night. Moderate. Naberezhnaya 9. Tel: 22-55-20.

Primorye Another previously state-run hotel, the Primorye is smaller and has a nicer staff than the Vladivostok. It also doesn't have seedy people lurking by the doorway. Two-room suites are available and come equipped with a refrigerator, television, telephone and a tea set. The buffet on the 2nd floor might have something in a pinch. Do NOT eat in the restaurant unless you are desperate. Inexpensive. 20 Posetskaya St. Tel: 22-51-22.

Ekvator Centrally located, but the surrounding streets are poorly lit. Near Okean restaurant. Intourist office located in the lobby. The hotel administration is not bad as far as state hotels go, but do not eat in the restaurant. Cheap. Naberezhnaya 20. Tel: 21-28-64.

RESTAURANTS AND CAFES

Vlad Motor Inn Restaurant As close to the West as it gets here in the Far East. This successful Canadian-Russian joint venture offers such fare as baby corn salad, steak sandwiches and real hamburgers. Desserts are a delight, especially the cheesecakes. Separate menus for lunch and dinner. Service is prompt and attentive, even refilling water glasses; rare for Russian service. The Vlad Motor Inn Restaurant is a great place to get away from it all, if only for a few hours. Expensive. Sanatornaya Station, 1 Vosmaya St. Tel: 21-58-54.

Captain Cook This Australian-Russian joint venture, located on the ground floor of the Pensionat at Sanatornaya station, offers a welcome escape from your hectic routine. The manager can often be found chatting with the guests, and piano music wafts over from the bar, offering a relaxed and friendly atmosphere.

The food is good and satisfying with a mix of Russian and Australian dishes. Try the mushroom blini appetizer for a Russian treat. Soups are hearty and flavorful. For the main course you can't go wrong with the steak, which comes with vegetables, even in winter! If you try any other dish (the grilled fish is also recommended), be sure to order vegetables on the side, well worth the extra.   Dessert is usually ice cream—if available, have it with fried bananas on top.

Service is usually attentive, although your table's main dishes might come staggered.   Reasonable prices in dollars, payment in rubles.   Sanatornaya station, 14 Devyataya St., Pensionat building. Open every day 7:30-23. Tel: 21-53-41.

Okean Restaurant   Located in the center of town overlooking the Amur Bay, the Okean serves good seafood in a relaxed atmosphere. Service is quick and the menu has a good selection. Daily specials are listed near the entrance. Moderate prices.   Open from 11 to 23 daily. Naberezhnaya 3.   For reservations call 26-81-86.

Volna (Wave)   A huge space on the top floor of the Morskoi Vokzal (Maritime Terminal), Volna provides a view of the harbor and tasty seafood.   Service is relatively quick and friendly and if you make reservations in advance, your appetizers will be waiting for you when you arrive. The seafood appetizers (in season) are your best bet.   The second course is more standard fare (meat cutlet and fried potatoes), though the "pot pie" is recommended. Open for lunch and dinner, however at dinner time the regulation blasting band plays, which effectively drowns out any conversation. Volna is also available to cater parties. Moderate. Maritime Terminal, top floor. Every day 12-17, 18-23. Tel: 21-93-40, 21-98-60.

Maranbon   North Korean-Russian joint venture.   Nice building, if you can ever get to see the inside of it. This restaurant is infamous for saying that there is no space available when the restaurant is obviously 1/2 empty. People joke that the Maranbon has two signs: "closed" and "no space." Having said that, service seems to have improved lately and the food is good. The cold crab is fantastic, and although offered as an appetizer, is a feast in itself. Expensive. Book in advance and hope they're in a good mood. Pervaya Morskaya St. 6/25. Open 12-17, 18-23. Tel: 22-77-25.

Nagasaki   Russian-Japanese joint venture.   Nice atmosphere and tasty food make for one of the better restaurants in the city. Service depends on the waitress, but is generally good. Try the "*Lapsha* Nagasaki" (noodles in beef broth), and the chicken curry. Expensive. 115 Svetlanskaya. Open every day from 11-16, 18-23. Tel: 26-97-48.

Sakura Restaurant Located on the lower level of the Vladivostok Hotel, the Sakura serves real Japanese food in a pleasant atmosphere. There is also Karaoke in the Fujiyama Bar. Expensive. Hotel Vladivostok, Naberezhnaya 10. Open 8-22 (closed 10-12, 16-17). Tel: 26-03-05.

Oasis Almost as nice as it sounds, Oasis is off the beaten track for restaurants, near the Aquarium. Circular booths in a circular restaurant make for a cozy atmosphere. The cold and hot appetizers are tasty and offer more variety than the main dishes. Order many appetizers for a satisfying meal. Particularly recommended is anything which comes "in a shell." Only 6 tables so reservations are advisable. Open from 12-20. Tel: 25-49-70.

Dary Morya (Gifts from the Sea) On the second floor of the red granite building that houses the store "Okean," this restaurant is big and Soviet in its atmosphere. At night the band will play Russian and American songs (especially Hotel California) loud enough to drown out any conversation. The cold seafood appetizers are good and the grilled salmon is a nice entree. For the adventurous, the sea cucumber stew is quite flavorful if you can get over the texture. 83 Svetlanskaya. Open every day from 12-17, 18-23:30. Tel: 26-61-83, 26-79-70.

Hingan Chinese Restaurant A decent variety of Chinese dishes, along with some Russian standards. Rice is hit or miss. Private rooms available for groups, or rent out the whole place for large parties. Popular with the muscle crowd and located in a desolate area; use caution when leaving late at night. Reservations suggested. In the Olympeets Sports Complex, Batareinaya 2. Open 11-23 every day. Tel: 25-37-11.

Laguna A cute wooden entranceway helps you find this cozy little restaurant. There is a surprisingly wide selection of food, and the interior decoration is tasteful and subdued. Portions are on the small side—order a few appetizers to fill you up. Nifty touch-lamps light each table. Some evenings an accordion player serenades you and in the summer outdoor seating is available. Slightly pricey, with a cover charge at all hours. On Svetlanskaya, between the tram stops "Tsirk" and "Dalzavod." Open 11-24 (15-16) every day.

Siliar This little cafe has a good house dish called "*lagman*": noodles in a thick beef gravy. A few small salads also available. Quick service. Okeanski Prospect 5. Open 10-19 every day. Tel: 22-80-16.

Sakura Cafe Not to be confused with the Sakura restaurant, this cafe has a pretty interior with plum flowers painted on the wall, but that is the extent of the Japanese theme. No Japanese food, but the Russian fare they have is decent. Very quick service—the waitresses are always in motion, a rarity in most restaurants. Svetlanskaya 4. Open 11-19:30 every day. Tel: 26-05-36.

Magic Burger Joint venture serving hamburgers, pizza and french fries. Although it's not the same fast food served in the West, the place is relatively clean and the service is fast. It's a good thing too, because there is usually a long line. If you don't see a line, run in and give it a try. Practically the only place in the city where you can get fed in less than 1/2 an hour. 42 Svetlanskaya. Open every day from 8-22.

Ldinka On the same block as the City Museum on Aleutskaya St., this cooperative (private) ice cream cafe is usually pretty crowded. However, you can get 2-3 different flavors of ice-cream (usually chocolate, green and pink) with nuts, cocoa powder or hot chocolate on top! Ldinka also serves juice, shakes and pastries—all for reasonable prices. A good place to relax after walking around town and eat your ice cream sitting down for a change. Open every day from 11-22. (15-16). Closed last Monday of every month. 23 Aleutskaya St.

Nostalgia See Nostalgia under shopping.

Hare Krishna A Hare Krishna vegetarian restaurant serving rice, curry, fried cheese, cucumber salads and the like. Total vegetarians should be aware that some of the food is cooked with sour cream. Okeansky Prospect 10/12. Open weekdays 10-19. The restaurant holds services on Sundays at 16:00. Tel: 26-89-43.

Chudesnistsa Little Russian co-op cafeteria at the end of Torgovaya Ulitsa. The staff is friendly, the atmosphere is. . . well, they try. The food varies from day to day but the goulash is recommended, as well as the cheese and garlic appetizer. A good place to rest after shopping along the Trade Street. 9 Fokina St. Open from 10-21.

Svetlana Lavishly decorated, the Svetlana serves good, Russian fare in a nice atmosphere at expensive prices. Good for banquets. Svetlanskaya 53. Open from 12-24 every day. Tel: 22-56-12.

Lesnaya Zaimka (Forest Castle) Exotic dishes prepared with wild game (boar, venison), served in a Russian cabin setting. 28th kilometer, across from the statue just outside the city limits. Tel: 21-58-05.

Flamingo Bar The gates are pink and there is actually a painting of a flamingo, but that is the extent of the atmosphere. There is a small patio open in good weather. Offers alcohol or coffee. Okeanski Prospect 26. Open 10-22 (16-17).

SHOPPING

Listed below are several stores that are good for shopping. Local buys are crab, honey, charoite (a purple stone which can be found only in Siberia), paintings, fur hats (in season) and wood carvings.

Izumrud (Emerald) Big state-run jewelry store selling gold and silver rings, necklaces, brooches and bracelets. Izumrud also has a good selection of watches, cutlery, stone boxes and amber. Prices vary but are definitely cheaper than in the United States. Even better bargains can be found in the crowd selling their wares in front of the store, but make sure what you buy is real. Three-line system in the store. Corner of Okeansky Prospect and Kolkhoznaya St. Open Mon-Sat 9-18, closed for lunch 14-15.

Amethyst Small private jewelry store down the block from Izumrud. Smaller selection than Izumrud, but some interesting buys, like seed pearl necklaces. 10/12 Okeansky prospect. Open 9-18 (13-14), Tue-Fri, 9-17 Sat. Closed Sunday and Monday.

Gzhel Small store selling the famous Russian blue and white ceramics of the same name. Mordovtseva 3. Open Mon-Sat 10-18 (13-14).

GUM The big state-run department store has come a long way. Before, all they had was the world's largest selection of shoe horns. Nowadays, it's the best place to go in the city for household needs, ceramic tea services, Russian records and tapes, huge Central Asian carpets or a chess set. The toy section is also worth looking at. Prices are in rubles, although there is a small hard currency section selling Japanese electronics and other Western goodies. 33-35 Svetlanskaya. Open Mon-Sat from 10-19. Closed Sundays.

Flotsky Magazin The Pacific Fleet Military Store, the Russian version of the American PX. Back in the old days the military stores were stocked with goods that were hard to get elsewhere. It was also the place where soldiers and sailors bought their caps, shirts, patches and insignia for their uniforms. However, although GUM has gotten better over the last few years, the Flotsky Magazin has definitely gone downhill. Nowadays, it has some interesting watches and a good selection of shoelaces (green, black AND brown), but not much else. The store has even been moved out of its previous building and now occupies a very humble space below street level next to the military book store (*Voennaya Kniga*). The uniform section still exists, and although technically they aren't supposed to sell military things to civilians, if you're really nice the sales lady might let you buy something. 11 Svetlanskaya. Open Mon-Sat 10-19, closed for lunch from 13-14.

Nostalgia Well worth a visit, Nostalgia is a cafe/restaurant/art salon. The downstairs shop offers lacquer boxes and trays, as well as brooches, dolls, scarves and other traditional Russian souvenirs.

Upstairs there is finely crafted jewelry, bone carvings, and paintings done by local artists. Find a scene of Vladivostok that reminds you of your trip, or buy a gift for a friend. A watercolor on birch bark (*akvarel na berestye*) makes a very unique souvenir. Shop hours are from 10-21.

If the rigors of gift-decision-making have worn you out, relax in the cafe downstairs. The decor recalls the pre-revolutionary grandeur of the elite, with draperies, flowers, and carved woodwork. The cafe offers coffee, tea, *kvas*, *blini*, homemade cakes and more. Breakfast is available in the mornings. Alcohol served after 7 pm. Karaoke in English and Japanese—just ask the barman. Cafe hours: 9-24.

If you are feeling hungrier, step through the doorway into the restaurant. There, under the gaze of the last Tsar and Tsarina, you may tempt your palate with such traditional Russian dishes as *borsch, pelmeni,* or *kvaldum* (a big dumpling stuffed with cabbage and meat). Restaurant hours: 12-24.

If you really want to step into another era, buy a ticket for one of the evening programs of "romances." Check with the management for times of these performances of classical Russian romantic ballads, gypsy songs, and White Guard melodies. The haunting melodies will stay with you long after your trip has ended.

Overall, Nostalgia is one of the better places you will find, both for shopping and for eating. Highly recommended. Pyervaya Morskaya St. 6/25. Tel: 26-78-13.

Torgovaya Ulitsa (Trade Street) This pedestrian street is the first block of Fokina St. and starts at the city beach. It is usually crowded and is completely lined with kiosks selling everything from Snickers to Chinese sex aids. The alcohol selection is extensive and there are also some good children's toys to be found. One can change dollars and yen here, either in the kiosks or with the people standing around with dollar signs pinned to their jackets. Changing money on the street is technically still illegal, and considering the preponderance of small exchange booths around the city, is not recommended. Corner of Aleutskaya and Fokina St. Most people have packed up by 5 or 6 pm.

Gastronom #4　This large state-run store in a pre-revolutionary building sells the standard meat, cheese and candy, but is worth dropping by just to check out the typical Soviet shopping experience. Three-line system for meat and dairy products. Some of the counters offer imported goods and take the money directly. Look at the ceiling to see remnants of a bygone age. 45 Svetlanskaya. Open every day from 9-21; closed for lunch from 13-14.

Antique Store see the Sukhanov Museum.

MARKETS

Pyervaya Rechka (First River) This general market is the place to find, meat, vegetables, pets, and assorted odds and ends. At the end of 1993 the city authorities made it illegal to sell anything but produce in this market, which essentially excluded all the Chinese merchants, but it is still a good place to pick up fresh fruit and vegetables and see a Russian market in action. Take the #7 tram to Pyervaya Rechka (5th stop). Everyday from 10:00 on. Wall to wall people on weekends.

Vtoraya Rechka (Second River) More organized than Pyervaya Rechka with more stalls and kiosks. Here, in addition to food one can buy all sorts of clothing, spare car parts and assorted knick-knacks.

Pokrovski Park Best place to buy stamps, coins and pins. Every weekend, rain or shine, about 15-20 regulars gather here to sell and trade their wares. For the rarer items, most dealers would rather trade than sell. Bargaining is expected. Take the #7 tram to Pokrovski (Gorodskoi) Park. Saturday-Sunday 10-15, depending on the weather.

MUSEUMS

The Arsenyev City Museum History, ethnographic and nature museum all in one. Traces the history of the Primorski region from ancient to modern times. The museum has good exhibits on Vladivostok, as it traces the city's growth from its founding in 1860 to the Soviet era, though the section on the civil war is being "updated." Interesting look at Vladivostok as it used to be, including a small exhibit on Yul Brynner and his family's house in the city. The museum also has exhibits on local minerals and the usual stuffed wildlife, as well as works by local artisans.

The museum also houses two stores. The first, directly in front of the entrance, sells paintings, jewelry, lacquer boxes and crafts made by the various indigenous tribes in the Far East area. The second store, found in the wildlife section of the museum, sells old coins, pins, paper money and various other collectibles. This store is actually a branch of the larger antique store found in the Sukhanov Museum. The director, Konstantin Petrovich, is a nice man and very helpful. Svetlanskaya 20. Museum hours are from 10-18:30, closed from 15:30-16:00 for lunch. Closed Mondays.

Wooden houses on Svetlanskaya

Border Guards Museum Located in the big bright blue building, this is a little-known but very interesting museum. Inside you will find the wet suit of an American-backed spy caught on Sakhalin, pictures of Soviet and Chinese guards having fist fights on the border, trophies of U.S. weapons from the Vietnam War and of course, the history of the border guards traced from the revolution till today. 17 Kolkhoznaya. Open from 9-17 Tue-Sat. Last Friday of each month closed for cleaning.

Krasny Vympel (Red Pennant) The "Aurora of Vladivostok," which helped bring Soviet Power to the Far East, is anchored in the harbor and open for tourists. Open Wed-Sat 10-18 (13-14). Buy tickets at the submarine, across the street on Korablnaya Naberezhnaya.

Sukhanov Museum Museum-house of Mr. Sukhanov, head of the city council in the early 1900's whose son, a Bolshevik leader, was killed by the Expeditionary Forces. Worth the climb, the house is furnished with period pieces and offers a great look at how the upper class lived at the turn of the century. It also offers a good view of the harbor and the city. Piano concerts are occasionally held in the museum; ask the director for more information. Also located in the museum is an antique store. One of the first and best antique stores in the city, one can find icons, paintings, engraved cigarette cases and all sorts of interesting things from before the revolution, including samovars with the imperial seal stamped upon them. The prices have gone up recently, but one can still find some reasonable buys. Be forewarned: it is illegal to take most silver articles and any icon out of the country. The general director, Konstantin Petrovich (usually found at his other store in the Arsenyev museum) is very helpful and will tell you what you can and cannot bring out of the country. 9 Sukhanova St. Open Tue-Sun from 10:30-19:00.

C-56 Submarine Famous submarine from Vladivostok that sailed in the Pacific and Atlantic Oceans, sinking 10 enemy ships during World War II. Interesting to walk around in, although the museum itself is nothing special. Outside, the sub is flanked by turrets of tanks that captured Berlin and an eternal flame burns for those killed during the war. Located on Korablnaya Naberezhnaya. Open Wed-Sat 9-18 (13-14).

Pacific Fleet Military Museum Housed in the old Lutheran church of Saint Paul the Apostle, this museum is easily recognized by all the tanks, guns and torpedoes in the front yard. Although under "government protection" as an architectural monument, the museum, done in the Late German Gothic style, is falling apart and discussions are underway to return it to the Lutherans. Some of the heavy artillery pieces were salvaged from Port Arthur before it capitulated to the Japanese in the

*On May 9, Victory Day, large crowds turn out to see
the military parade*

The Communists march, Victory Day

Russo-Japanese War. The collection, although not very large, is
an interesting one, tracing the local fleet's achievements from
Tsarist days up through the Cold War. Exhibits are labeled in
Russian. Pushkinskaya 14. Open Wed-Sun from 9:30-17:45,
closed for lunch from 13-14. Closed for cleaning the last Friday

of each month. Take trams 4 or 5 to the fourth stop: DVTU or "Technicheski Universitet."

ART GALLERIES

Primorski Art Museum A great little museum, situated in a pre-revolutionary French bank. Specializing in Russian icons and 19th century Russian Romanticism, the museum has over 5000 *objets d'art*, including a sizable Dutch collection and early works of Chagall and Kandinsky. The first paintings were given to the museum during the 30's by the world famous Hermitage, Tretyakov and Russian museums. The museum also has a gift shop where you can pick up some paintings, amber and other souvenirs. Excursions are available in English. 12 Aleutskaya St. Open Tue-Sat from 10-13, 14-18.

Art Etage Located in the White House, this large gallery has put on exhibits in the US and Japan and sells works by well-known local artists. Good changing exhibits on art from around the former Soviet Union and Primorski Krai. Also has handicrafts from local tribes on sale. Pricey, but good quality. 22 Svetlanskaya. Open Tue-Sun 11-18:30.

Primorski Gallery Sales exhibition of paintings by local artists. 12 Aleutskaya St. Open from 10-18:30, closed for lunch from 13-14. Closed Mondays, groups only on Tuesdays.

ENTERTAINMENT

Gorky Theater Vladivostok's main theater puts on concerts, plays and musicals in Russian. A nice way to spend the evening if your language skills are up to it. Occasionally there are performances by visiting theater groups from abroad. Tickets should be purchased during the day at the box office. Signs around town list what's currently playing. Svetlanskaya 49. Tel: 26-45-87.

Dvoretz Moryakov (Sailors' Palace) Dance festivals and concerts are held here. Announcements for upcoming shows are posted outside the hall. Take bus #1 from the stop at Posetskaya, one block up from the Primorye hotel, to the second stop.

Drama Theater Performances of classical pieces from Shakespeare to Chekhov. Ticket booth open from 10 to 16. Svetlanskaya 15a. Tel: 26-48-89.

Concert Hall The place to hear classical music and singers from around the Soviet Union. Announcements are posted around the city for upcoming concerts. Walk past the video games and slot machines to the box office to buy your tickets. Box office hours are from 13-21, closed for lunch from 15-16. 13 Svetlanskaya.

City Puppet Theater Nicely restored building in the center of town has children's puppet shows. Petra Velikova 8.

Green Lantern Small and plushly furnished, the Green Lantern used to be part of the Actor's Union Club but has now privatized and offers cabaret shows. Light snacks and drinks available. The show is quite good with a mixture of music, comedy and even some magic tricks. Buy your tickets in advance. The show runs from 9:30 pm till about 11:30 pm and the place closes at 2:00 am. Open Tue-Sun. 13 Svetlanskaya.

Blue Star In the same building as the Green Lantern, the Blue Star is a nightclub with a striptease show. Jacket and tie required. 13 Svetlanskaya.

Epicure Nightclub Out in the *Vtoraya Rechka* (Second River) district, the Epicure offers dinner until 9 pm, after which the place turns into a strip-tease. Stoletiya Vladivostoka 103. Tel: 31-97-09.

Nostalgia Evenings of musical "Romances." See Shopping, Nostalgia.

Casino Amurski Zaliv Offers the same fare as the other local casinos (blackjack, roulette), but has the lowest ruble minimum in town, so you can stretch out your losing streak longer. Seedy surroundings, just like the hotel. Naberezhnaya 9.

Casino Amherst Upscale, hard currency casino with British croupiers. Free drinks while playing. Cash advances can be taken on credit cards. Blackjack, roulette. Second floor of the Versailles Hotel. Svetlanskaya 10.

Casino Vladivostok First floor of the hotel of the same name. 10 Naberezhnaya St. Tel: 22-22-08.

Dance Boat Dead on weekdays, this grounded "boat" at the *Sportivnaya Gavan* (Sports Harbor) is hopping on the weekends. Dancing and drinking till dawn. Open in summer from 10 pm till 5 in the morning. Expensive cover charge.

City Circus When a circus comes to town it's a big event. Unfortunately, it's totally unpredictable when that will be. Long shows (up to 3 hours) have the standard tigers, bears and elephants. Sometimes you can have your picture taken with a live baby bear or stuffed tiger during intermission. When the circus is not in town, other animal acts can be seen. 103 Svetlanskaya. Tel: 26-56-50.

Baseball During baseball season, local teams battle it out on weekends at Stroitel Stadium. The teams wear Japanese uniforms and have only been playing for about 2-3 years, so play is at high school level, but it's still fun to watch. 30b Prospekt Stoletiya Vladivostoka. Weekends from 11 am.

Soccer Vladivostok's local team plays in Russia's second soccer league. *Luch* (Sunbeam) is struggling, but the games are exciting, the crowd is supportive and the stadium is right on the water with a beautiful view of the bay. The date of the next home game is shown on a wooden advertisement in the main square and at the stadium itself. Tickets can be bought at the stadium on the day of the game. Dynamo Stadium, 1 Admiral Fokina St.

Olympyeets Sports Hall Big red brick building on the Amurski Gulf shore houses a swimming pool, saunas and a weight room. Don't expect a modern health club. Private saunas must be booked in advance and easily accommodate 4-5 people. Batareinaya St. 8a . Tel: 25-84-67.

Across from the Olympyeets Sports Hall on the Amurksi Gulf are some **Beluga whales** in a holding pen. The whales are very friendly and do tricks at feeding time (sometimes you can buy some fish from the keepers). Unfortunately, feeding time seems to be whenever the fish are delivered, and changes every day. Modest entrance fee.

Okeanarium Vladivostok also boasts an aquarium. Out on the Amurski Gulf near the Oasis cafe, the "Okeanarium" has some interesting fish and sea animals but is suffering from a lack of funds. Batereinaya 4. Open 10-17:15 during the winter, 10-19 in the summer. Tel: 25-49-77.

PLACES OF WORSHIP

The Catholic Church has moved back to the original Catholic church building at 22 Volodarsky St. Closed in 1935 and used until recently as the Communist Party archives, the church building is now in the process of being restored to its previous glory. Take the #4 or 5 tram to the "Dalzavod" stop, walk uphill past Pushkinskaya to Shkipera Gecka St., turn left and look for a stone stairway leading up to the church. Masses are held on Sundays at 12 noon.

Russian   Orthodox Services   are   held   on weekends at St. Nicholas Church on Makhalina St. Check schedule outside for times.   Take the #4 or 5 tram   to   the   6th   stop ("Avangard")   then   walk uphill.   Named Our Lady Grieving, this church was built   in   1908   from donations and dedicated to the victims of the Russo-Japanese War.   Considered a small church of lesser importance   when constructed,   Our   Lady Grieving was left as the last Orthodox   church   in   the city center after the other churches were destroyed in

In 1994, an orthodox priest spoke at Victory Day for the first time

the 1930's.   Now lovingly restored, this church is one of the prettiest in the city.

Hare Krishna   Services are held in the Hare Krishna restaurant on Saturdays at 14:00 and Sundays at 16:00. Okeansky Prospekt 10/12.

The old **Synagogue** was converted into the municipal candy factory's workers club, but can still be seen at Prap. Komarova 5. Take the 7 tram to "Gorodskaya Bolnitsa" (city hospital) and take the street to your right about a block. The pink building, done in the early modern style on your left, is the synagogue.

TRANSPORTATION

Trams   Trams are old, crowded and frequently break down, but for the ordinary citizen who can't afford a car, it's literally the only way to go.   Trams #4 and 5 run along Svetlanskaya street, while the #7 heads up Aleutskaya Street. They all start from Lenin square, across from the train station (*vokzal*).

Trolleys and Buses start from Fokina street, between Okeanski Prospect and Aleutskaya, and go around the city and to its environs.

Long Distance Bus Station Located in *Vtoraya Rechka* (Second River), from here you can catch buses to the airport, Nakhodka, Arsenyev, Partizansk and other places throughout the Primorski Krai. Russkaya 2/a. Tel: 46-52-78.

Funicular Located on Pushkinskaya St., the funicular takes you to the top of Gogol St., next to the Far Eastern Technical University. It is frequently under repairs or closed for some reason or other, but gives a great view of the city.

Taxis are usually found waiting by the train station.

Train Station (*Vokzal*) Trains to Khabarovsk, Beijing or Moscow (Trans-Siberian), or local commuter "*electrichkas*" all leave from one of the prettiest and architecturally most interesting buildings in the city. 6 Aleutskaya St. Tel: 21-04-40. For train information dial 005.

Maritime Terminal (*Morskoi Vokzal*) Passenger ships for Japan, Korea and other international destinations leave from this terminal. Ships also leave from here to Sakhalin and the Kuril Islands. Ticket booths are inside, along with a myriad of stores, cafes, a bank and a photo developing outlet. For information, call 007.

Ferry Station (*Vokzal Priberezhnikh Soobsheniya*) The place to catch boats to the beaches and outlying islands. Ferries to the other side of bay (Churkin) also leave from here. Korablnaya Naberezhnaya.

Airport Actually in the town of Artem, (pronounced Ar-tyom) about 40 minutes from Vladivostok. During the summer, it's a pleasant green drive through the hills around the city. The airport is undergoing a massive facelift by an Italian construction company and should be finished in mid 1995. Direct flights connect Vladivostok with most cities within Russia and there are a few new international flights. The airport staff at the "International Hall" are some of the meanest in all of the Far East, quite an accomplishment. Look for Soviet bombers near the runway as your flight lands. Bus #101 makes trips between the airport and the bus station in *Vtoraya Rechka*, from there you can take a taxi or any city bus to the downtown area. For flight information, dial 006.

Aeroflot City Office All the loving care and service you've come to expect from Aeroflot. Currently the international flights offered by Aeroflot are to Niigata and Toyama, Japan, and Seoul, Korea. 17 Posetskaya. International section tel: 22-25-81.

Primorsky Klub Located in the *Vtoraya Rechka* district, this travel agency has friendly service and accepts credit cards for international flights, which is rare indeed in the Far East. Primorsky Klub offers its services for both international and domestic travel plans. 17 Russkaya, 4th floor. Tel: 31-80-37.

Alaska Airlines From spring to fall there are twice-weekly flights to Seattle, San Francisco and San Diego via Anchorage; fall to spring, once per week. Tickets can be bought at the airport office or at Primorsky Klub Travel Agency. The Alaska Airlines office itself is located at the airport in Artem, but has a phone number in Vladivostok: 22-76-45.

Korean Air Offers once a week flights to Seoul. Currently, tickets are available only at the airport or through Primorsky Klub Travel Agents.

OrientAvia A brand-new Russian airline and a welcome change from Aeroflot, as of October '94 OrientAvia offers daily flights to Moscow. Tickets available through Primorsky Klub.

Street Names

WAS	NOW
Ленинская (Leninskaya)	Светланская (Svetlanskaya)
25 Октября (25 Oktabrya)	Алеутская (Aleutskaya)
Дзержинского (Dzherinskovo)	Фонтанная (Fontannaya)
Колхозная (Kolkhoznaya)	Семеновская (Semyonovskaya)
Первая Мая (Pyervaya Maya)	Петра Великого (Petra Velikova)

Tram Routes

All trams start from Lenin Square. The number 4-5 trams split after Lugovaya. The "central city" stops are listed below, although the tram routes continue further.

#4, 5
Train Station (*Vokzal*)
Ploshad
Lazo
DVTU/Universitet
Tsirk/Dom Soyuzov
Dalzavod
Avangard
Gaidamak
Lugovaya

#7
Train Station (*Vokzal*)
Fokina
Krayevaya Bolnitsa
Pokrovski Park
Komsomolskaya
Pyervaya Rechka

AROUND VLADIVOSTOK

Islands: **Russky, Popov, Reiniky** Swimming in the summer, ice fishing in the winter—in any season the islands are pleasant getaways from the city. Boats leave from the Ferry Station, charter service also available.

Mys Peshanaya (Sandy Cape) Ferries leave twice daily to this nice beach outside of Vladivostok. On weekends an additional ferry makes the trip, allowing you to make a 1/2 day excursion. Ferries leave from the Ferry Station on Korablnaya Naberezhnaya.

Slavyanka Beach Hydrofoils leave twice daily from the ferry terminal to this beach, outside of Vladivostok. Less crowded and cleaner water than the city beaches, Slavyanka is a good summer day trip.

Sanitornaya Station Located at the commuter train stop of the same name, this area has a small park and a beach (with much cleaner water than the city beaches). During the winter, there is an ice skating rink. Skates can be rented on the spot, but you're better off bringing your own. A small wooden shack also rents cross-country ski equipment by the hour or for the whole day. Nearby are the restaurants Captain Cook and the Vlad Motor Inn.

Botanical Gardens A large preserve of the flora and fauna of the Far East. Unfortunately, most of the descriptive signs have been removed. Recommended is the "ecology walk," a 30 minute walk along a paved path leading up the forested hill behind the gardens and back. Modest entrance fee. Take trolleybus No. 6 from Fokina street to *Botanicheski Sad* (the stop right after the police checkpoint when leaving the city), about an hour ride. Most Russians do not bother with the front gates but enter through the many holes in the fence along the highway.

Scuba Diving with Valeri Darkin. One of the only PADI certified dive instructors in Russia, "Val" Darkin conducts snorkeling and scuba diving tours south of Vladivostok at the Far Eastern State Marine Reserve. Unique opportunity to explore some of the local sea life, including gray seals, octopus, king crab and more. Marine Technologies Dive Center #2772. P.O. Box 90-182. Tel/fax: 25-49-77.

Bannikov Adventure Expeditions A guide and photographer with over 25 years experience in the field, Leonid Bannikov provides nature expeditions for all levels of interest and experience. Among the more popular are his rafting tours, cross-country skiing, a walking tour of the waterfalls in the Primorski Krai or just a relaxing weekend in the countryside. For the serious nature buff, Mr. Bannikov can also arrange fishing and hunting expeditions, river rafting for all levels of difficulty, photo safaris of wildlife (July - August is the best time as bears trying to catch salmon are in abundance) and treks through Kamchatka and Yakutia. He has led expeditions of western journalists and Japanese film crews everywhere from Chukotka to Lake Baikal. Highly recommended. Rudimentary English. Tel: 29-46-26 (speak Russian). Messages by fax or e-mail can be in English. Fax: 26-45-89, e-mail: andrey@komet.marine.su.

Lazo A town northeast of Vladivostok, Lazo is known for its spectacular fall foliage, and for being at the center of "tiger territory." It's easy to get there by car—just four hours from Vlad, but a marathon day-long trip by bus. It's a five-hour trip to Nakhodka, then transfer to the bus to Lazo, another 3 1/2 hours. The museum of Lazo Preserve has stuffed animals and details of the conservation area. The ancient fortifications around Lazo are also interesting to look at. No hotel in town, so bring a tent. At the nearby town and resort of Chistavodnoe, small cabins or dormitories can be rented. About 15 miles down the road from Lazo towards the ocean is another resort, featuring thermal and radon (!) spring baths, as well as striking cliffs.

Sergei Lazo

Born in Bessarabia in 1894, Sergei Lazo is known for commanding the partisan forces in the Far East that helped defeat the anti-Bolshevik forces during the Civil War.

A strong disciplinarian, Lazo started his military career at the age of 22 when he entered the Alexeevian Academy in Moscow. Due to his revolutionary leanings, he was described as "democratic and unpatriotic" and after graduation Lazo was sent not to the front, but to a Siberian reserve division in Krasnoyarsk.

Lazo spent his time there agitating against Russia's participation in World War I, and when the February revolution broke out, against the provisional government. Popular with his men, he was elected as company commander and as a delegate to the local Krasnoyarsk Soviet (Council). After the second revolution, Lazo was sent by the Communist Party to Irkutsk to crush the "counter-revolutionary" forces there. This he did, and was consequently named commander of the Irkutsk Garrison. As anti-Bolshevik forces consolidated and the country was plunged into a full civil war, Lazo was promoted to commander of all forces beyond the Baikal region.

As front commander, Lazo fought successfully against the Cossack Ataman Semyonov until the Czech legion entered the battle versus the Bolsheviks. With apparent ease, the Czechs occupied Eastern and Central Siberia, smashing any forces the Bolsheviks could muster. It was at this time that Lazo asked to join, and was accepted into, the Communist Party. The front broken and his forces defeated, he went secretly to Vladivostok, where he was elected to the local leadership committee of the Russian Communist Party. In 1919, Lazo and other party leaders left the city to organize partisan detachments against Kolchak and the foreign expeditionary forces. Under Lazo's leadership the partisan groups were successful in interfering with supplies, blowing up trains and even driving back regular troops, including the Americans. In June of 1919, Lazo launched an operation against American, Chinese and Japanese forces guarding the coal mines in the Suchava region and was able to put the mines out of operation for 3 months.

By January of 1920, Kolchak's fortunes were on the wane and it was only a matter of time before he was completely defeated. An uprising was planned in Vladivostok and Lazo single-handedly convinced the naval officers' school in the city to stay neutral, ensuring the uprising's success. In March of that year the American, French and English troops were evacuated from Vladivostok. After the fall of Kolchak's forces, Lazo and other party leaders created a military council. This council was to organize the partisan detachments into a more regular force that could fight the Japanese troops that remained in the area, but the Japanese pre-empted them. On April 5, the Japanese troops took over Vladivostok and Khabarovsk and arrested all the members of the military council, including Lazo. Although he was never seen again, Soviet legend has it that Lazo was burned alive in the furnace of a steamship.

The Tiger Organization organizes tours for those who want to see a Siberian Tiger, or Amur Tiger as they are called locally. Located in Lazo, the most densely populated tiger habitat in the Far East, this organization offers 3 day interpretive hikes, and tiger photo hunts. Excursions include visits to archaeological sites, and arguably some of the best coastline in the Primorski Krai. They can arrange accommodation in rural homestays, or at the resort Chistavodnoe. 1-5 Nekrasovskaya St. Lazo. Tel: (277) 911-92.

Spassk-Dalny Small town of 61,000 whose claim to fame is that they produce 1/2 of the cement in the Russian Far East. It was in Spassk-Dalny that Alexander Solzhenitsyn served time in the Gulag (building the cement factory, actually), and is the basis for his book "A Day in the Life of Ivan Denisovitch."

*On Navy Day in Vladivostok, Neptune himself arrives by
seamonster to greet the crowds*

NAKHODKA

HISTORY

When the captain of the Russian sailship "America" landed in an unfamiliar gulf during a rough storm, he discovered a naturally protected deep water gulf surrounded by gorgeous rolling green hills. He named his newly found treasure "Nakhodka," the Russian word for "find," and later the gulf was named the Zaliv Amerika, "the Gulf of America." On June 29, 1859, the Nakhodka harbor was opened, and by the middle of the next century, Nakhodka had become the most important civil port infrastructure in the Russian Far East, the home of the Nakhodka Trade Port, the Fish Port, the Nakhodka Oil Terminal, and several bulk and break bulk ports, mostly built with labor from the local prison camps. More recently, in the early 1970's the Soviet government infused several million dollars into the construction of Vostochny Port, on the outskirts of Nakhodka. Vostochny Port has grown in size and volume, and is now the largest ocean container and bulk coal terminal in the Russian Far East. Though Vladivostok takes credit as the terminus of the Trans-Siberian Railroad, receiving the fabled passenger train in its central rail station, Nakhodka is in fact the terminus of the more important cargo aspect of the longest railroad in the world. Transit point for dozens of thousands of ocean containers annually and the bulk of Siberian raw materials exports, Nakhodka is the Pacific Rim gateway for the bilateral cargoes supporting the economies of Siberia and the Russian Far East.

A city of just under 200,000 people, Nakhodka suffers a climate similar to the windy one of Chicago. Hot and muggy in the summertime, Nakhodka becomes brutally cold during the winter months, despite limited precipitation. Though temperatures never approach the extremes of the northern tundra, the constant and fierce winter winds make the oceanfront weather thoroughly unenviable.

Nakhodka is the home of the original Soviet-American joint venture, which was called SOVAM, later known as Marine Resources Company International. Begun in 1977, the fishing venture recently moved its Russian office to Vladivostok, although the plaque bearing the venture's name can still be seen at 134 Verkhnaya Morskaya.

Also the center of some political and economic experimentation, Nakhodka for several of the last years boasted one of the only operating Free Economic Zones in the former Soviet Union. Though currently not operational, the local authorities, particularly the Free Economic Zone Administration, continue to lobby in Moscow and abroad to win support for the zone, which would have provided tax holidays to joint ventures comprised partly of foreign-owned investment. Nakhodka hopes to become home to both American and South Korean industrial parks within the next decade, in order to capitalize on the strategic value of the transportation infrastructure and the natural wealth of the region. Nakhodka has a sister city relationship with Oakland, California.

WALKING AROUND TOWN

Inasmuch as the city of Nakhodka encircles the bay around which the four ports are built, our walking tour will take you from the Nakhodka Hotel through the center of town, around the central part of the bay, and end at the Fish Port.

Start at the **Nakhodka Hotel.** If you are not already there, this landmark will be well-known to all taxi and bus drivers. The restaurant on the main floor will give you the energy needed for this 90-minute walk, even though the questionable service may extend your meal past the time it will take you to stroll across town.

As you exit the main entrance of the hotel, you will see a contemporary-looking building just to the right, the Nakhodka **wedding palace**. During the Soviet era, churches ceased to be the central authority in matters of marriage, and the fairly gaudy wedding palaces arose to take their place. If you are lucky, you may catch sight of the tail end of the ritual, complete with decorated cars and festive entourage. As you walk to the end of the access road, you will come to the main boulevard, called Nakhodkinski Prospekt. Turn right and head up the hill. On your right you will see the old **"Burevesnik" Theater**, which closed its doors two years ago and became a seedy and unsafe teen dance hall. Locals recommend keeping a safe distance from the "Burevesnik," despite its cultural roots.

Just beyond the theater is *Tsentralnaya Ploschad* (**Central Square**), where the city administration is located. City Hall is the sky blue building facing the bay, and it is flanked to the right by the tax authorities. Just behind City Hall is "Shkolnaya 7," the building which houses the Nakhodka branch of the reputable VostokInvestBank, as well as the most conveniently located of Nakhodka Telecom's several offices.

Across from City Hall you will find Nakhodka's remaining salute to **Lenin**, a statue which ironically was completed and placed in the square in 1985, the year Gorbachev began the deconstruction of the cult of Lenin with his policy of Perestroika. This small park offers a good view of the bay. If you face the bay from the statue, there is a road down the hill to the right, which leads to the administrative headquarters and entrance to the Nakhodka Trade Port. To continue to tour, face back toward City Hall and follow Nakhodkinski Prospect up the hill to the left.

You will walk about 10 minutes before coming to a three-pronged fork in the road. The Prospekt and our tour will continue to the left, but the two streets to the right, Red Army Street and Pogranichnaya Street, offer interesting asides. Down Red Army Street you will find the **"Portovik" Gymnasium,** where the Nakhodka All-Stars basketball team plays its games. If you are in town during the winter months, you might catch the team in action at Portovik, but don't attend a match unless you intend to root for the home squad.

Up Pogranichnaya, you will find "Cosmos," a small store on the left-hand side of the road, and directly across from it, a multi-storied brick building. Behind this structure is nestled the grounds of the **Dialog Hotel,** a small 10-room affair with a common dining room and good service. Back on the main drag, the Prospekt will take you further along the bay and up the incline. On the right you will find the city's tribute to its victims of World War II, honored by an **eternal flame**. Victory Day celebrations are centered around the monument, and all newlyweds make an obligatory stop at the flame on their wedding day, rain or shine.

As you ascend the boulevard toward the crest of the hill, you will pass two sites dedicated to Nakhodka by its Japanese sister cities. The second of the two monuments, a **rock garden** installed by the city of Maisumi, was dedicated to Nakhodka in commemoration of the 60th anniversary of the October

Revolution in 1978, and it bears an inscription written in the hope of eternal peace and friendship between the two seafaring cities on the Sea of Japan. Immediately across the street (be careful to look both ways, as traffic is brutally unruly), you will find a **bronze sculpture** called "Peace" by the Japanese artist Nayakawa Osumu, completed in 1991. The encircling small park overlooks the Trade Port's many-craned Second Pier, and offers an uninterrupted view of the two peaks known as **Brother and Sister**. Though there are several mountains in view from this side of the harbor, the Siblings are unmistakable, insofar as Brother was ignominiously mined for its valuable stone, and as a result had its tip lopped off. Local rumor has it that the destruction of Brother created a climatic stir which has continually ruined crops for the ten years since the mining was curtailed. Also in view here is the Nakhodka Can Factory, which is reputed to be the largest can factory in the world. Built in grand Soviet fashion, the factory had the capacity to supply 1 billion cans per year (say the locals), but it never quite realized its potential. Though production is reduced to a trickle these days, the 1 million square feet of factory floorspace stand as a monumental tribute to super industrialization.

The next stop on the tour is the **Central Rynok (Market)**, which is the center of all farmers', butchers', and traders' activities during the week and especially on weekends. Here you will find all types of produce, from the fruits flown in from Central Asia to the beef butchered on a daily basis. Nakhodka's Korean descendants occupy a section nearest the door of the covered part of the market, selling Korean foods including spicy calamari and *paporotnik*, made from the stem of the common fern. In addition to foods, you can find toiletries, books, flowers, clothing, shoes and many types of hardware at the Central Market. You will also find the largest concentration of moneychangers and voucher dealers in the city. Hold on to your wallet.

To the right and above the Central Market is the **Casino Spartak**, a Russian-South Korean venture which offers blackjack, roulette and slot machines. The building is the renovated Spartak Theater and even if you don't care to gamble, be sure to admire the turn-of-the-century Russian architecture. In the casino's upstairs dining hall, the kitchen offers light fare, and if you hit the right night, you may catch one of three loud local rock bands from 11:00 on.

Across the street from the casino, you will find the access road to the **train station**, where you can buy tickets to virtually any city served in Russia by rail. A short walk from the station is a pedestrian walkway over the tracks—the way to the new Italian-built Ocean Terminal (Passenger), complete with customs and passport control. If you are so inclined, it is here that you can purchase tickets on passenger vessels to Japan, Korea and China, depending on the likely variability of the week's schedule. From 12:30, the restaurant on the second floor serves what is arguably the finest luncheon available in Nakhodka with what is undoubtedly the best indoor view of the harbor.

As you continue past the Central Market, be sure to notice the gorgeous mosaic depicting agrarian and marketplace scenes from Nakhodka's past. Just beyond the market you will arrive at the **Pyramid Hotel**, also on the right. The building is identifiable by the crests of its various sister cities, Otaru, Maizuru and Tsuruga, molded into the facade. Though Oakland supposedly represents the United States' sister city organization in Nakhodka, its crest didn't make it onto the Pyramid. Next to the Pyramid is the local **art museum and gallery**, which generally fields traveling exhibitions which make their way to the Russian Far East. Thirty paces further along, the intersection of Leninskaya and Nakhodkinski Streets appears. Here you will find a wide selection of flowers from vending *babushkas*. At the start of Leninskaya Street, notice the two massive **anchors**, commemorating, respectively, the 100th anniversary of the opening of the harbor, and the Supreme Soviet's decree that Nakhodka's ascendance as a vital port made it an exemplary Soviet "working town," quite a compliment, on May 5, 1950.

If you choose to deviate from the boulevard, Leninskaya Street has the city's best collection of **stores and shops**. At the end of the street, you will find the Nakhodka Palace of Culture, in which resides the "Seamen's Club," ever popular with arriving sailors from foreign lands. Further up the hill is the Stadium, where the Nakhodka *Moryaki* (Seamen) play soccer against the toughest competition in the country. Even so, they usually sport a good record, though opposing teams complain often of the long journey and jet lag.

If you wish to continue along the boulevard, you will pass by the new Chinese hotel complex **Yuan Dong** on the left, and at the top of the next hill you will run across the "**Univermag,**" or "Universal Store," Nakhodka's answer to J.C. Penney's. Inside, you will find everything from soap to automobiles, though the selection may be a bit weak, depending on what you need.

At the bottom of the hill, the end of the tour arrives with the entrance to the Fish Port, the Okean Seafood store, and the **Zaliv Amerika Restaurant**. The third floor of the Zaliv boasts a bar with pirated MTV videotapes, which will help you to recover from your long trek. The number 2 and 5 buses will take you back to the Nakhodka Hotel, the Pyramid, or the Bus Station, should those be your final destination.

PRACTICAL INFORMATION

Code for calling Nakhodka from other cities: **42366.**
Code for calling Nakhodka from Vladivostok: **266.**
Information when calling from inside the city: **09.**
Information from outside the city: **266-** or **42366-40909.**
Main Post Office Nakhodkinski Pr. 43. Tel: 5-59-97.
Business Center Svyazi Nakhodkinski Prospekt 100. Tel: 4-35-84.
North Korean Consulate Vladivostokskaya 14 (Soon to move to Sedova 8). Open Mon-Fri 9-12, 15-18. Tel: 5-53-10, 5-84-61.
Vietnamese Consulate Sportivnaya 41, Kv. 34. Open Mon, Wed and Fri from 9-12, 14-16. Difficult to find, the consulate is located on the 4th floor of a residential building with no signs outside, in a new "micro-region" of Nakhodka. Tel: 2-76-46.
DHL International Nakhimovskaya 30. Tel: 2-15-10, fax: 2-14-45.

HOTELS

Pyramid Conveniently located at the southern entrance to the trade port, near the central market and the train station, the Pyramid is arguably the finest hotel in the city. Though the most expensive, the service is good, the rooms are clean and modern, with refrigerators and western-style plumbing. Bar and restaurant also tops in the city, and security guards and hotel administrator on duty round-the-clock. Very expensive. Ulitsa Vladivostokskaya 2/A. Tel: 5-98-94, 5-91-59, 5-77-60.

International: (+7-504-91) 5-22-09, international fax: (+7-509-91) 5-22-07.

Dialog Hotel   Operated by a Russian-American joint venture of the same name, the Dialog Hotel is a new two-story 10-room building with an enclosed compound. The rooms are comfortable, and although there is no restaurant, there is a cozy dining room, where breakfast is prepared and meals can be ordered. 24-hour security and international telecommuications. Expensive. Sovietskaya 1/A. Tel: 4-07-61.

Nakhodka   Formerly an Intourist establishment, the Nakhodka has made some effort at upgrading its amenities, adding new South Korean televisions and refrigerators within the past two years. Nevertheless, the service is poor and the single rooms are confining and uncomfortable, often with malfunctioning and smelly bathrooms. The larger semi-lux and full-lux rooms are more accomodating, some of which boast international phone lines and even pianos. The restaurant is one of the best in the city and the *banya*, when operating, is clean and cozy. Bar on the 4th floor. 24-hour administrator on duty. Moderate. Ulitsa Shkolnaya 1/A. Take bus number 5 or 2 from the center and get off at the stop "Gostinitsa Nakhodka." Tel: 4-71-88, 5-65-20.

Suan Yuan   Newly-built Chinese hotel in center of town. Moderate.   Bad service in restaurant and hotel as well. Malinovskovo 32. Tel: 4-09-77.

Vostok   Gorodskaya Ploschad (City Square). Tel: 4-50-58, 4-59-13.

Gorizont   Ulitsa Leningradskaya 10. Tel: 2-07-92, 2-07-70.

RESTAURANTS

Zaliv Amerika   In this newly-remodelled three-story building, you will find the finest nightclub atmosphere in the city.   There are two bars, two restaurants and several banquet halls. Loud, live music and an excellent, tasteful dance show. Though the remodelling was largely funded by the American partner of the joint venture Dialog, the management has since changed, and the quality of the kitchen is in decline. Yet it is still recognized as one of the better (and more expensive) dinners in town.   Located at the union of Nakhodkinski Prospekt, Gagarina Street and Verkhnaya Morskaya Street, across from the main entrance to the Nakhodka Fish Port. Open 12-24. Tel: 2-07-68.

Tedongon Newly remodelled, this ethnic Korean restaurant can have the finest food in town if you happen in on a fresh catch of shrimp or Kamchatkan crab. Frequented by international seamen and prostitutes, Tedongon may have the liveliest and most eventful milieu in town. DJ and discotheque-style dance floor. Mys Astafeva 0-34, Tel: 4-14-33, 4-13-95.

Pyramid Located in the Pyramid Hotel (see Hotels), the restaurant in the basement has the most expensive and best food in town on a consistent basis. Though the menu doesn't vary and the atmosphere is a bit bland, there is no better place for a quiet, comfortable (and safe) meal. The bar is generally the most well-stocked in town. Open 11-23.

Nakhodka Closed for repairs until last year, the new Nakhodka Restaurant (located on the first floor of the Nakhodka Hotel) offers reasonable fare at reasonable rates. Usually with a thin selection and poor service, the Nakhodka nevertheless offers a decent and economical alternative to the Zaliv and Pyramid restaurants. Dance floor and DJ on weeknights, live music on weekends. The Nakhodka also offers several private rooms for banquets and meetings. Ulitsa Shkolnaya 1/A. Open 11-23. Tel: 4-48-57, 4-53-07.

Morskoi Vokzal Restaurant Known to residents as the "*Novy MorVokzal*," the new Italian-built international passenger ocean terminal is a beautiful building with wide open, tastefully decorated spaces. Overlooking the inner harbor of the Trade Port, the *MorVokzal* is a relaxing and enjoyable way to dine. Dinner is by advance reservation only and usually requires a party of 10 or more, but lunch is served on weekdays to walk-in guests. Tasty food, expensive. Reasonably well-stocked bar.

Cafe Byelaya Gora With the exception of a few spicy dishes, this restaurant serves typical Russian dishes. Postysheva 27. Open 8-20. Tel: 4-02-39.

Vostok Reviews range from "average" to "really bad." Gorodskaya Ploschad. Tel: 4-59-17.

Chaika Average restaurant, seedy clientele. Timiryazeva 16. Tel: 2-28-63, 2-38-54.

Gorizont Leningradskaya 8. Tel: 2-18-65.

Riviera (Oriental) Pogranichnaya 30. Open from 12-16, 18-22:30. Tel: 5-64-35.

Cafe Luny Blues Malinovskovo 2. Tel: 4-23-00.

SHOPPING

Beryozka   Reasonable selection of liquor, canned goods, candies and gifts. Some electronics and other household commodities. Expensive. Leninskaya 17. Tel: 5-63-06.
Univermag   Largest department store in the city. Nakhodkinski Prospekt 62. Tel: 2-14-49.
Knizhni Mir (Book World)   Nakhodkinski Prospekt 50. Tel: 2-38-11.
Magazine #4 - Jewelry   Leninskaya 17. Tel: 5-55-59.
Art Salon   Vladivostokskaya 6. Tel: 5-64-26.

MARKETS

Central Market   The informal commerce hub of Nakhodka, the central market is the place to go to exchange money. Some kiosks are open 24 hours. Especially active during the weekend with traders of all kinds of goods, including all manner of foodstuffs, household commodities, garments, books, music, and selected hardware items. Open 8-17 every day. Nakhodkinski Prospect.
Barakholka   Most notably known for its used car trading, the *Barakholka* is the place to make the purchase of a used Japanese car with right-hand steering. Also available are car parts, hardware, and a mixed bag of other typically second- or third-hand items. Open Saturdays and Sundays. Located in the flats across from the central bus station.
Roadside farmers' markets dot the road between Nakhodka and Partizansk, particularly on weekends. For very reasonable prices, fresh eggs, yogurt, milk, vegetables, berries and some meat products are available seasonally.

ENTERTAINMENT

Interclub or International Seamen's Club   Located in the Palace of Culture at the end of the Pedestrian Mall on Leninskaya Street, the Seaman's Club is the original nightclub for visiting foreign sailors. Though the quality has deteriorated over the years, the bar is still one of the liveliest spots in town on any given night and there is a dance hall upstairs. Leninskaya 22. Tel: 5-62-50, 5-73-91.

Zaliv Amerika (see restaurants)
Puppet Theater Lunacharskovo 8. Tel: 5-79-79.
Philharmonic Nakhimovskaya 19. Tel: 5-99-40.
City History Museum Currently the main hall is closed indefinitley for repairs, but the hall for changing exhibits remains open. Vladivostokskaya 6. Tel: 5-53-90, 4-56-83.
Casino Spartak Blackjack and roulette from 8:00 pm to 4:00 am. Nakhodkinski Prospekt 32. Tel: 5-52-51.

PLACES OF WORSHIP

Orthodox Church (Christ is Risen Cathedral) An active church for the last 10 years, the Christ is Risen Cathedral recently had a fire and is in the process of being restored. Services are held on Sundays and holidays. To get there, take bus number 5 to the stop "Briz" and head to the left. Ulitsa Veselaya 1. Tel: 4-52-23.

SPORTS

"Portovik" Sports Hall Home of the Nakhodka All-Stars, a semi-professional basketball club, Portovik has the largest court in the city, which is used alternately for basketball and soccer, as well as other athletic play and instruction. Krasnoarmeiski Pereulok. Tel: 4-42-69.
"Spartak" Sports Hall Regular aerobics classes, sauna, full-size basketball court, and a variety of athletic instruction. Outdoor tennis courts and lessons. Verkhnaya Morskaya. Tel: 2-18-04, 2-01-19.
"Vodnik" The biggest stadium in Nakhodka and home to the local soccer team "Okean." Although they play in Russia's second league, the fans are always up and the games are fun to watch. Cheap tickets. Mayakovskovo St. at the end of Leninskaya.
"Primoryets" Leningradskaya Street. Tel: 2-34-53.
"Olimpyeets" Leningradskaya St. Tel: 2-05-88, 2-05-10.

TRANSPORTATION

Aeroflot Agency Nakhodkinski Prospekt 18. Tel: 5-72-25.
Taxi stand is located in front of the bus staion. To order a taxi call 4-34-90.

Bus Station *(Avtovokzal)*   Ticket booth 4-33-21, advance tickets 4-34-88.

Train station *(Vokzal)*   For ticket info. call: 5-32-2-72, 5-32-2-80.

Getting to Nakhodka:

As Nakhodka does not have a civil airfield, the only means of accessing the city are by train, by road and by sea.   Until 1992, there was a regular commuter hydrofoil that connected Vladivostok and Nakhodka by a two-hour, comfortable and scenic journey.   Due to rising fuel costs, this service has been intermittent at best over the last two years.   Also intermittent, though wonderfully convenient when operating, is the helicopter service that connects the cities.   Operating twice daily, the 10-seater makes the trip in half an hour.

If a tight schedule dictates your means of transport, a taxi or bus (No. 206) from the Vladivostok bus station is the best alternative.   The road winds through green hills, valleys and small towns where cows still have the right of way.   Although the road is partly unpaved and comprised of 180 km of alternating torturous bumpiness and stunning beauty, the trip rarely exceeds 3 hours by car, and is usually completed in under 5 hours by bus.   The train, though reliable, is a local one, making all the stops, and it runs at inconvenient times—early in the morning and late at night.

For the military inclined, the Nakhodka-Vladivostok road passes through several towns which were formerly off-limits due to their military bases and industries.   Bolshoi Kamen produced nuclear submarines, while Tikhiokeanski and Shkotovo-17 were considered to be so important that they were not even shown on local maps.

Getting out of Nakhodka:

It is easier to leave Nakhodka than it is to get there.   Taxis and buses can be found at the bus station across from the Nakhodka Hotel, and a ride to the airport (2 1/2 hours) or to Vladivostok can be negotiated down to $50-75.   The "Tikhiokeanski" (Pacific Ocean) train station is located next to the Marine Passenger Terminal, newly built by an Italian construction company.   The overnight train to Khabarovsk is very convenient, departing at 7:50 pm every night and arriving at around noon the following day in Khabarovsk.   The train is comfortable, and though passenger tickets increased in price practically every month during 1993-94, it is still less expensive than flying, and infinitely more convenient and comfortable.

If you have a hot summer day to kill on your return to Vladivostok, there are several nice beaches along the road from Nakhodka. Though the local taxi drivers would charge an arm and a leg if charging hourly, the buses all stop at the beaches, and they run hourly to Vladivostok.

As you enter or leave the city by car, there is a large fishing trawler named Nadezhda (Hope), which is creatively situated atop the big hill overlooking Nakhodka Bay. The boat was dragged there years ago in pieces and it served as a public restaurant until last year, when it was purchased by a group of local businessmen and remodelled into an elite businessmen's club.

ARSENYEV

Originally called Semyonovka, the town of Arsenyev came to prominence during Soviet times due to its defense industries. In 1938 two factories; "Progress," an aircraft factory, and "Askold," an avionics factory, were built. Because of these factories, Arsenyev (pop. 75,000) became known for its civilian and military aircraft production and had more highly trained engineers, managers and technicians per capita than most cities in Russia. The Progress factory manufactured the helicopters used in the Afghan war, and the sophisticated "Black Shark" anti-tank helicopter, as well as a world-class acrobatic plane, the Yak-55.

Today, Arsenyev is struggling with defense conversion, but is still known as a quiet town where people come from the city to get away from it all. Averaging 265 days of sunshine, Arsenyev is surrounded by large hills which make for a much drier climate than the coastal areas of the region. The hills overlook the valley and the surrounding taiga, and offer great hiking in the summer, when they are covered with wildflowers, or fall, when the leaves are turning.

There is an excellent sky-diving club sponsored by the Progress factory—some of its members have made thousands of jumps. There is also a sportsman's club which maintains a downhill ski run on the 2500 foot mountain slope which overlooks the town. Plans are underway to develop the slope into a modern ski base, with a cafe, rest house and sauna, but these are only in the preliminary stages. At present, skiing can be arranged through the hotel, given advance notice.

PRACTICAL INFORMATION

Code for calling Arsenyev from outside the city: **261.**
Information when calling from inside the city: **09.**
Information from outside the city: **261-249-50.**
Post Office 45 Leninskaya.
Militzia (police) 4 Zhukovskovo. Tel: 225-78.
Bus/train station Both services in one building. For train information, call 293-42, for bus information 241-02. Corner of Vokzalnaya and Devyatovo Maya (May 9th street). Trains leave twice daily from Vladivostok and take approximately 5-6 hours to reach Arsenyev.
Hotel Tayozhnaya The only hotel in Arsenyev, the Tayozhnaya is a large comfortable hotel with reasonable prices. The staff is friendly and makes a genuine effort to accommodate guests. Inexpensive. 5 Gostinni Proezd. Tel: 232-14.
Usadba Planned tourist agency that will work with the town's administration to attract tourism to the area. Should be operational by spring of 1995. When in service, Usadba plans to organize horseback riding, fishing and hunting excursions, helicopter tours, picnics in the taiga or just visits to an old-style Russian house for tea with a friendly *babushka* (grandmother). Located in the Tayozhnaya hotel.
Dolina (Valley) Restaurant Located in the Tayozhnaya hotel, this small restaurant has nightly live entertainment. Private rooms are available. Both the service and the food are recommended. Food is standard Russian fare at inexpensive prices.
Grot (Grotto) Bar Although the food and service are very ordinary, this bar-restaurant is tops for atmosphere. Located in a redecorated bomb shelter, the interior has been redone to resemble a cave (or a dungeon), complete with dinosaurs. Music and dancing four nights a week. Closed Fri and Sat, but available for private parties. Open 21-2. The Grot Bar is next to the main market. Tel: 222-60.

Rynok (market)   Selling an assortment of food and clothing, you can find a variety of goods here, from frozen crab legs and locally gathered honey to Chinese jeans and Russian fur hats. Corner of Ostrovskovo and Zhukovskovo.

Winter ice sculpture, Arsenyev

Arsenyev Museum The museum features, naturally, a display on Vladimir Arsenyev, but also includes exhibits on the local wildlife and artifacts from nearby archaeological sites. Artwork from local artists also displayed. Open 9:30-17, closed Mon. Kalininskaya 13. Tel: 239-29.

Russian Orthodox Church One of the few churches allowed to operate during the Soviet era, the Arsenyev church has been active for the last twelve years. 11v Zoya Kosmodemyanskaya Street. Tel: 201-52.

Arsenyev Monument Overlooking the town there is a monument to Vladimir Arsenyev, the famous Russian explorer and naturalist for whom the town was named, and Dersu, Arsenyev's native guide. Local legend has it that the monument is placed on the site where they camped. The statue was paid for with donations from the citizens of Arsenyev and erected in 1972.

Japanese Memorial During the years of the civil war, the Japanese army had some 70,000 troops in the Far East and one of their camps was in Arsenyev. In 1993 a memorial was erected by the Japanese to those who died during their service in Russia.

Vladimir Arsenyev

One of the first to fully explore the Primorski Krai and study its indigenous peoples, fauna and flora, Vladimir Arsenyev was one of the few outstanding personalities to be honored both during Tsarist and Communist times. Vladimir Arsenyev was born in 1872 in St. Petersburg to a large family of 9 children. He attended Military Cadet School and joined the Army as a young officer, a topographer. Always fascinated by stories of the Russian Far East, Arsenyev requested and was granted a transfer to the area, arriving at Russky Island outside of Vladivostok on August 5, 1900. Here he began his lifelong studies of the Primorski Region and became a member of the Russian Geographical Society. His studies of the flora and fauna of the region were extensive: his personal butterfly collection had over 14,000 specimens. Although Arsenyev had many talents and interests, including taxidermy (he preserved many animal species from the region), his strongest interest was ethnology.

His most famous book, Dersu Usala, *is published in over 60 countries, and is presented as a biography of his native friend and guide of the same name although in fact, the main hero is a compilation of all the traits of the native people that he knew during his travels. He worked on several films about the Udege, a tribe of hunters, gatherers, and fishermen. Arsenyev met Dersu in 1906 and worked with him until 1927. Together they covered tens of thousands of kilometers on foot, exploring the Primorski Krai and southern Khabarovski Krai. The life of Mr. Arsenyev was one long expedition to the taiga, but he found the time to be a lecturer and writer, leaving more than 70 scientific articles and books about his studies. Some of his personal collections can be found in the National Museum in Washington, DC.*

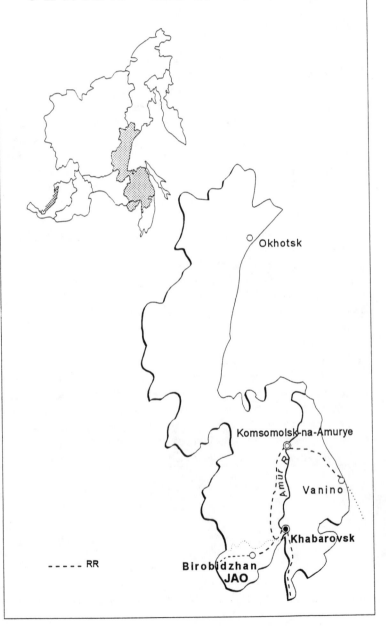

KHABAROVSKI KRAI
JEWISH AUT. OBLAST

CHAPTER 3

KHABAROVSKI KRAI

The third largest region in the Far East, Khabarovski Krai rivals Primorski in development and foreign investment. Crossed by both the Baikal-Amur and the Trans-Siberian railways, the southern half of the krai has a relatively well-developed infrastructure. The Port of Vanino serves as a terminus for the rail ferry to Sakhalin. The northern half of the region is known more for its pristine forests and salmon harvests than heavy industry.

With internaional flights to the U.S. and countries on the Pacific Rim, the region has succeeded in attracting both foreign tourists and investment. July to September are considered the best times to visit the krai.

KHABAROVSK

INTRODUCTION

Khabarovsk is a quiet village. No, Khabarovsk is a bustling industrial capital. Actually, it is both, depending on your interests. Tourists will find quaint 19th century buildings of wood and brick, quiet tree-lined boulevards, shops filled with native crafts. Businessmen will find services geared to Western travelers and industry eager to attract foreign investment. Many international companies have opened offices here, and the number is increasing monthly. Almost 3/4 of the work force is engaged in industry, but most of this activity is located in the newer parts of town, the "micro-regions" where factories sprang up, along with ugly Soviet pre-fab panel apartment blocks to house all the workers.   However, the central part of town still retains its pre-revolutionary charm.   A flourishing tourist industry is also developing, and with its new international airport and international ties (Khabarovsk has a sister city relationship with Portland, Oregon),   Khabarovsk looks to become the gateway to the Far East.

HISTORY

Khabarovsk (Kha-BA-rovsk) was founded in 1858 by order of Muravyov, governor-general of Eastern Siberia, to strengthen Russia's hold on the territories newly acquired from China by the Treaty of Aigun. The outpost was named after the explorer Yerofey Khabarov, who headed the first Russian expedition down the Amur River in 1651, razing settlements and killing natives in such numbers that they appealed to the neighboring Chinese to protect them from the Russian menace. Khabarov's cruelty and excesses were such that the Tsar, who usually turned a blind eye to any "liberties" taken by pioneers conquering in his name, had Khabarov arrested and demanded an accounting of his activities. Despite his excesses, Khabarov was cleared of any wrongdoing and was subsequently promoted.

Situated on the hills overlooking the Amur River, Khabarovsk grew quickly as a trading outpost. In 1868 the town had telegraph communications with its southern sister Vladivostok, and in 1872 the river port was completed, increasing the town's importance as a fur and trade center. In 1880 the town received official city status, and replaced Nikolaevska as the capital of the region. In 1884 the city's population reached 5,000. In 1897 the railroad link was completed between Vladivostok and Khabarovsk, with trains taking 2 days to make the trip. Not only did the new train line widen the trade lanes between the Amur and the Sea of Japan, but it also greatly increased the number of immigrants who settled in Khabarovsk. By 1899 the population had tripled to 15,000.

After the Russo-Japanese War, settlers increased further as the Tsar ordered more peasants to colonize the Far East as a way to lessen the land problem in the west.

In the fall of 1918, Khabarovsk was occupied by the Japanese, overturning the local Communist administration. Khabarovsk remained "White" until 1920, when it became part of the Far Eastern Republic, a buffer zone between the Japanese and the Bolsheviks. This "independent" republic did not last long, and in 1922 a decisive victory at Volchaevsky (45 km from Khabarovsk) sealed the fate of the anti-Bolshevik forces. In October of that year the last Japanese troops left the Far East and within a month the Far Eastern Republic was annexed to the Soviet Union.

In 1924 the city was named the capital of the Far Eastern Region, and remained so until 1938, when the region was divided into Khabarovski and Primorski Regions.

After World War II the city developed its industrial base and is now a major machine-building and repair center for the Far East. Although Khabarovsk is the center for the Far Eastern Military Command, it was also one of the few cities in the Far East that was always open to foreign tourists, and today the city enjoys a regular flow of visitors from Japan, South Korea, and China, making it the tourist center of the Far East. Today, with a population of 700,000, Khabarovsk's future looks bright and if economic ties continue to expand at the rate that they have been, the city will be one of the leading business, transport and administrative centers for the Far East going into the 21st century.

WALKING AROUND TOWN

Khabarovsk was laid out along the tops of three ridges, with two boulevards in the valleys between. The three main streets now run along the tops of those three ridges. Russians delight in renaming things, and the center street has gone through many versions. Originally Khabarovskaya, in 1880 it was changed to Bolshaya, or "Broadway." At the turn of the century it was renamed Muravyova-Amurskovo, in honor of the former Far Eastern Governor. Under Communism it had a stint as Karl Marx, but is now once again Muravyova-Amurskovo (but only as far as Lenin Square). The signs have even been changed, unlike in most other cities in the Far East. The sidewalks are broad and airy, and in summer open-air cafes appear all over. Side streets off the beaten track are quiet, and water pumps and laundry on the line beside 2-story wooden houses add to the village feel.

K H A B A

① Market
② Hotel Amethyst
③ Hotel Lyudmila
④ Drama Theatre
⑤ TSUM
⑥ Aeroflot
⑦ Main Post Office
⑧ #17, Tainy Remesla
⑨ Geological Museum
⑩ Sapporo Hotel,
   Japanese Consulate
⑪ Innokentevski Cathedral
⑫ Intourist Hotel
⑬ Military Museum
⑭ Krai Museum
⑮ Art Museum
⑯ Tower Cafe
⑰ Glory Square
⑱ Ferry Station

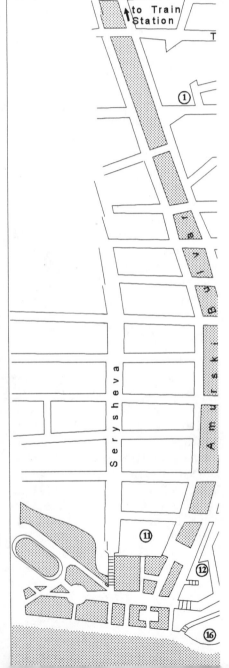

R O V S K

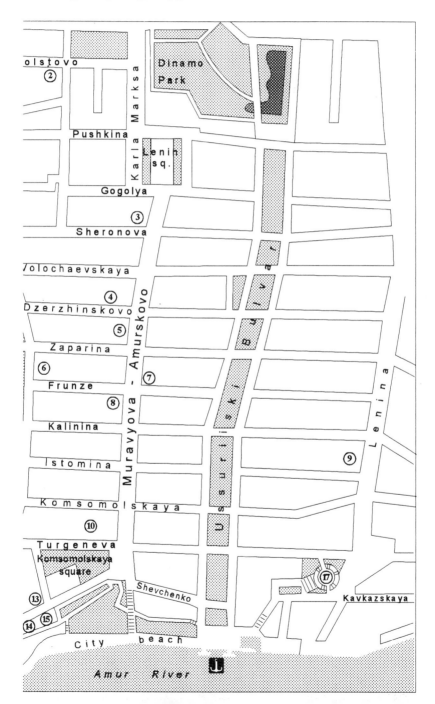

The boulevards are also pleasant places to walk. In the winter, undisturbed by the noise of cars, you can listen to your footsteps crunching through the snow. In summer the trees and grass turn them into cool shaded oases from the heat. Both boulevards will lead you to the banks of the Amur, which in summer has beaches clogged with sunbathers, and in winter is a haven for ice fishermen.

Another plus for walking around Khabarovsk is that many streets are one-way, and the drivers are actually polite, allowing you to cross the street without being honked at or run down.

The best place to start a walking tour is **Lenin Square**, beside the modest-sized Lenin statue. With your back to the **Tsentralnaya Hotel**, you will be facing Lenin Square, which has gone through many names: Nikolaevskaya (after the Tsar), Respublikanskaya in 1917, Freedom in 1918, and then Lenin. It was originally used as a parade ground. Now it is usually empty, but in summer is filled with flowers and around New Year's there are some ice slides and children's carousels. There is also a **monument** to soldiers who died in 1929 in a dispute with the Chinese over the Northeast Chinese Railway.

The first street after you cross Lenin Square and head down Muravyova-Amurskovo will be Sheronova. If you are interested in the old architecture of the city, turn to your right down Sheronova, and on the right are four old **wooden buildings**, slightly varying in style and stages of dilapidation. Despite the Soviet zeal for standardization and construction of identical housing complexes, in Khabarovsk many old buidings remain which show the style of architecture of a bygone age. These buildings look to be under reconstruction, and with the proper sort of restoration could once again be lovely.

Returning to Muravyova-Amurskovo, one block along on the right-hand corner of Volochaevskaya is the old office of the Governor-General. This building now houses the Krai Council on Landmark Preservation.

Between Dzerzhinskovo and Zaparina is **TsUM** (*Tsentralni Universalni Magazin)*, the Central Department Store, and a good place for souvenir shopping.

Continuing along Muravyova-Amurskovo you will come to **#17**, at the corner of Frunze. This lovely building has gone through many incarnations: originally the City Duma, also a Pioneer Palace (Children's Center), it now houses some of the nicest shops in the city: souvenirs, flowers, etc. Right across the street at #26 is another pretty building which was also the store of a prosperous merchant, Mr. Kishali, who had a paper store. Now it is simply **Bread Store #226,** which has a small stand-up cafe, but the main attraction is the bakery, which on a good day has had as many as 5 different types of bread with names like Podolski, Saratovski, Snezhinka, etc. (Open 8-20 (14-15), Sun 8-18).

Between Istomina and Komsomolskaya is **Mercury Gastronom**. This used to be owned by Kunst and Albers, a German trading company which was one of the most famous foreign merchants in the Far East around the turn of the century. Kunst and Albers had huge stores with a wide selection of imported goods in most of the cities of the Far East. The Mercury Gastronom has not yet regained the stature and selection it had in its previous life, but it is one of the best stocked stores in town, and has retained some pretty interior decorations as well.

At the corner of Komsomolskaya is the restaurant **Lotos**. In 1912 this was the home of Mr. Takeuchi, the representative of the Japanese community in Khabarovsk. It also had a hotel and shop. Nowadays the Japanese Consulate is located in the Sapporo Hotel, on the other side of Komsomolskaya.

Across Muravyova-Amurskovo is the **Hotel Dalni Vostok**. At present it is under restoration, and perhaps it will be restored to its former grandeur, when it was the Hotel Esplanade, a gathering place for the well-to-do.

Back on the right side of Muravyova-Amurskovo, No. 3 used to be the shop of the "wine king" of Khabarovsk, Mr. Pyankov (Pure chance or an ironic twist of fate that Pyankov sounds a lot like "*pyanni*," the Russian word for drunk?). This pretty building now has the ignominious fate of being a fish store.

Continuing along Muravyova-Amurskovo to Komsomolskaya Square you will pass the Sapporo Restaurant, which has tastefully attempted to blend in with the older buildings which surround it. Within the Sapporo are two restaurants and a souvenir shop. Next door is the **Krai Library**, which was built by the Plyucin family, one of the most wealthy and powerful merchant families in Khabarovsk at the turn of the century. The Plyucins also built the brick building which now houses the Geological Museum on Lenin Street and the **Uspenski Cathedral** which used to stand in Komsomolskaya

Square (then called Cathedral Square), which unfortunately was destroyed in 1930.

The Tower on the Cliff overlooks the Amur, which is a favorite with ice fishermen in winter...

From Komsomolskaya Square you have many choices. You can walk straight ahead, down the stairs to the shore of the Amur. Or a turn to the left onto Turgeneva will take you down into the valley of Ussuriiski Boulevard and up the other side to **Glory Square**. This square also offers a view across the other side of the hill, across some wooden houses towards the more industrial areas of Khabarovsk and the curve of the Amur. Not exactly a beautiful view, what with the smokestacks and industrial areas, but perhaps educational. Or take Shevchenko street to the left, which will lead past the AIDS research center to the **rechnoi vokzal** (ferry station), for ferries

...and with bathers in summer

along the Amur. However, the most relaxing choice is to follow Shevchenko street to the right, which will take you first to the

Art Museum, then the **Krai Museum**, and if you follow the path up into the park, you will come to the **Tower on the Cliff**, which affords a view over the Amur and hides a small cafe where you can drop in for refreshment after your long walk.

PRACTICAL INFORMATION

Moscow time +7 hours.
Code for calling Khabarovsk from outside the city: **4212.**
Information when calling from within the city: **09.**
Information from outside the city: **4212-21-65-03.**
Address Bureau Tel: 34-57-61.
Japanese Consulate Komsomolskaya 79, in Hotel Sapporo. Tel: 33-26-23, 33-78-95.
Chinese Consulate in Lenin Stadium. Tel: 34-85-37, 39-98-90. Open Mon, Wed, Fri 9-12 for visas. Takes a week.
United States and Foreign Commercial Service Office Turgeneva 69. Tel: 33-69-23.
American Business Center A service of the U.S. Department of Commerce, this business center is scheduled to open shortly, and will offer office and conference rooms, photocopying, international phone and fax, word processing, interpretation and translation, and business appointments. Contact the U.S. and Foreign Commercial Service Office, above, for details.
The Pacific Law Center A Russian/American joint venture. Turgeneva 69. Tel: 39-86-34.
Vneshtorgbank (External Trade Bank) Kim Yu Chen 15. Tel: 33-89-40.
Credobank Kim Yu Chen 45. Tel: 21-04-06.
Kombank "Bison-Kapital" A Peace Corps volunteer works with this bank. Turgeneva 68. Tel: 33-46-74, 33-47-87.
Main Post Office/Telephone Upstairs there is a post office, where you can send a fax or telegram, and there is also a credit card phone which may or may not work. Downstairs you can order an inter-city or international call. For international, you will have to order your call at the desk, then wait until your call is announced. The weary looks on your fellow call-makers will give you an idea of how long this takes. For inter-city calls you can also order through the desk, or for certain cities you can buy *zhetoni* (tokens) and dial direct. Whatever method you choose, calling from the post office or a *peregovorni punkt* is always

cheaper than calling from your hotel room. Muravyova-Amurskovo 28 (corner of Frunze). Tel: 33-13-03.

Telephone/Telegraph Station Karla Marksa 58 (corner of Pushkina). Tel: 33-69-41. Telegraph: 33-54-36, or 06 to charge it to a home phone.

Peregovorni Punkt Same idea as at Main Post Office for ordering calls or using *zhetoni*, but less crowded. Open 8:30-22. Pushkin 52, right below Hotel Tsentralnaya.

Parus Business Center A Russian/Japanese joint venture catering to the needs of businessmen. Open 24 hours, you can make calls or send and receive faxes by satellite at the going hard currency rate. Helpful service. Shevchenko 5. Tel: 33-44-14.

Daltelecom Business Center You can send faxes or make international calls, and they also offer installation of international lines in offices. Courteous service. In the White House (administration building) on Lenin Square. Tel: 33-18-96, 24 hours: 33-84-76.

DHL International Muravyova-Amurskovo 4. Open Mon-Fri 9-18. Tel: 33-08-57, 33-09-49, 38-84-78, 38-84-98. Satellite Tel: (+7-50901)-600053.

UPS Ussuriiski Bulvar 2, office 310. Tel: 22-21-21.

EMS Garant Post A Russian Postal System quick delivery service. Muravyova-Amurskovo 28. Tel: 33-47-86, 33-45-61.

HOTELS

Hotel Sapporo A neat and clean hotel, just around the corner from Muravyova-Amurskovo and the Sapporo restaurant. The rooms are pleasant, the staff is polite and helpful. There is a sauna, a small souvenir booth, exchange office. Tours of the city can be arranged in Japanese or English, there is a small room for conferences, and car and driver can be arranged. Reservations recommended. Very expensive. Komsomolskaya 79/3. Tel: 33-27-02, Fax: 33-28-30.

Hotel Amethyst A fairly new establishment (opened in January '94), run by the Krai Geological Department. The service is friendly and helpful at this small hotel, and the rooms are spacious and comfortable. Single rooms have double beds, double rooms have single beds. There is satellite TV, and each room has its own little hot water heater for tea, etc. You can order a car and driver through their service desk. There is a small bar (open 8 am to 1 am), which is currently being converted into a small cafe. A reservation is recommended, since there are only 16 rooms which book up quickly, but if there is space available, you can get a room without having a *zayavka*. Expensive. Lva Tolstova 5. Tel: 33-46-99.

Hotel Intourist This used to be the only hotel open to foreigners. Now that you have a choice, the Intourist is actually putting effort into improving service and comfort. All the rooms are carpeted and have wooden cabinets. There are two restaurants, a bar, and souvenir shops. Alaska Airlines tickets can be ordered at their service desk (major credit cards accepted). City tours or Amur cruises can be arranged, cars with drivers and interpreters hired. A Fuji shop in the basement develops film quickly. The Korean Times (in English) is available in the newspaper kiosk. Expensive. American Express accepted. Pereulok Arseneva 7. Tel: 33-63-95, 33-65-07, 39-93-13.

Hotel Lyudmila With no sign outside, this small hotel is unobtrusive, but centrally located right on the corner of Muravyova-Amurskovo and Sheronova. All the rooms are two-room suites, some with double beds, some with two singles. Amazingly, each room has an air conditioner! The bathrooms have been recently remodeled. Service is polite. There is a small restaurant on the third floor, open 9-22 (16-18). One disadvantage is that all calls go through a switchboard. The lobby has interesting wood carvings on the walls. Expensive. Muravyova-Amurskovo 33. Tel: 38-86-49.

Hotel Tourist (do not confuse with Intourist, above) A regular tourist class hotel with standard (brusk) service. If your room faces the front, you'll get a good view of the *Slava Rabochemu Klassu* (Glory to the Working Class) sign on top of the nearby apartment blocks. Has a fax "center" in lobby where you can send or receive a fax (open 8-20), an open air cafe, a restaurant with decent food and service, and an evening bar. There is also a casino. The hotel has moderate prices. Ulitsa Karla Marksa 67. Tel: 37-04-17, 37-23-23.

Hotel Tsentralnaya The only good thing about this hotel is that it is centrally located. Rooms are ok, but you'll have to beg to get toilet paper. Service is more brusk than usual. Restaurant is not recommended. The buffet on the first floor is ok, but surprisingly expensive. Moderate. Pushkina 52. Tel: 33-47-59.

Hotel Amur The lobby was recently remodeled, and is now comfortable and inviting. The staff, however, remain indifferent. Pleasant rooms. There is a *banya* where you can have private sessions (see under Banyas). Inexpensive. Lenina 29. Tel: 33-50-43, 39-43-73, Fax: 22-12-23, Sauna: 39-43-12.

Hotel Zarya A no-frills establishment on a side street. No restaurant. Inexpensive. Kim Yu Chena 81. Tel: 33-70-75.

Dalni Vostok Under renovation, scheduled to reopen fall '95. Muravyova-Amurskovo 18. Tel: 33-14-34, 38-84-21.

RESTAURANTS

Pyonyang (North Korean) A scenic restaurant with a striking mural in the entranceway, a waterfall (which rarely works), and a latticework ceiling with dangling plants. The menu sometimes includes reindeer meat or rabbit, and they cook it at your table. Ulitsa Karla Marksa 108. Open 12-23. Tel: 37-16-25.

Sapporo Restaurant The first and second floors of this Russian/Japanese joint venture offer Russian food, served by polite staff at reasonable prices. The third floor serves real Japanese food, Japanese-style. Very expensive, cash only. Muravyova-Amurskovo 3. Open 8-23 (16-18). Tel: 33-08-82 (Russian food), 3rd floor (Japanese food) 33-51-75.

Niigata Restaurant Real Japanese food and a Karaoke bar combine for a tasty and potentially interesting evening. Lenina 32. Open 11-23 (16-17). Tel: 21-53-33.

Regent Restaurant Owned by Koreans, but serving Russian food. There is a band and often Karaoke in the evening. Meat cooked at your table. Amurski Bulvar 43. Tel: 34-28-22.

Okean Recently remodeled, this seafood restaurant has a nice atmosphere and friendly service. A band plays in the evenings. Lenina 45. Tel: 33-16-11.

Business People's Club Restaurant (*Klub Dyeolviye Lyudi*) A pleasant place for a business meal. Reservations suggested. Zaparina 82. Tel: 33-26-97, 33-98-21.

Harbin (Chinese) Real Chinese food, with either great service, or terrible service. In order to share, make sure you order enough portions for all. Reasonable prices. Volochaveskaya 118. Open 11-23 (16-18). Tel: 33-13-56.

Parus Excellent service, good Russian food at this Russian/Japanese joint venture. By reservation only. Shevchenko 5. Tel: 33-72-70.

Intourist Breakfast, lunch and dinner served in this standard hotel restaurant. On weekend evenings there is a loud band and lots of dancing. Pereulok Arseneva 7. Open 8a-2a. Tel: 39-93-26, 39-90-81.

Unihab Expensive Japanese restaurant on the top floor of the Intourist Hotel. Open 8:30-10, 12-15, 18-22. Tel: 39-93-15.

Restaurant Rendez-vous A small restaurant on a side-street. Pleasant atmosphere, polite service. Open 11-23 every day. Dzerzhinskovo 36. Tel: 33-32-25.

Rus Restaurant Best to avoid, as it is known as a Mafia hang-out, but the cafe Rus next door is good for a quick bite. Muravyova-Amurskovo 5. Tel: 33-28-98.

Ussuri Roast chicken specialty. Open 11-23 (16:30-17:30). Muravyova-Amurskovo 32. Tel: 33-64-74.

The cafe Rus is topped by a tower

V Gostyakh U Natali (At Natalya's) Friendly service. Open 14-23 (18-19) every day. Muravyova-Amurskovo 2.

CAFES

Ramen Small cafe right at the entrance to the market. The specialty is a huge bowl of miso soup with noodles, ferns, a piece of beef, and half a hard-boiled egg. They may only do one dish, but they do it right! This will warm you up in winter, and fill you up any time. Pay the cashier by the door for a soup and *napitok* (fruit drink), give the ticket to the waitress at the counter

and she will bring you your bowls. Tolstova 19. Open Oct -
Apr 8-18, Apr - Oct 8-20. Tel: 33-69-45.

Bistro Niigata Another small cafe about a block from the
market, it doesn't have much to remind you of Japan except for
a kite in the corner. However, the food does have more variety
than a regular Russian cafe. Decent pizza, curried rice and large
bowls of ramen noodle soup. The 4 small tables fill up quickly
at lunch time, but there are standing tables available as well.
Pushkina 64. Open 8-20 (16-17). Tel: 33-29-31.

Pizzeria This is unabashedly the best pizza we have found
(so far) in the Far East. There is a choice of 3 or more pizzas,
all with the basic requirements of a tomato base and cheese
topping (not guaranteed in most other places offering so-called
pizza). Various toppings include sausage, olives, mushrooms.
Pizzas are plate-sized and filling. Table service is polite and
quick. You can also get take-away (wrapped in paper). There
are fresh donuts (*ponchiki*) for dessert. Open 11-23 every day.
Dzerzhinskovo 36. Tel: 33-32-25.

Cafe Sapporo Nice atmosphere, popular with young
people. Has various salads, and even a "Clinton Cutlet."
Komsomolskaya 77. Open 11-23 (16-17:30). Tel: 33-13-92.

Utyos (Cliff) Cafe This cafe is in the tower precariously
perched above the Amur River, affording a lovely view both
summer and winter. Red frilly curtains give the interior a
decadent feel. A good place to stop in after a walk along
Muravyova-Amurskovo or through the park. Coffee, pastries,
ice cream. Grumpy service. Reasonable prices. Open 10-22
(16-17). Tel: 38-93-52.

Buterbrodnaya A stand-up cafe offering quick
snacks—open-faced sandwiches and coffee.   Popular with
students. Komsomolskaya 79. Open 9-21 (14-15) every day.

Khinkali *Khinkali,* a traditional dish from the Republic of
Georgia, are giant *pelmeni* (meat-filled dumplings), and that is
what you can get here, with various sauces (soy, sour cream,
butter or ketchup), plus a few small salads. The interior is quiet
and quaint with wood carvings on the walls, but the tables are
greasy, the floor is dirty, and there is an air of indifference.
Inexpensive. Kalinina 82. Open 9-21 (15-16). Tel: 33-38-45.

Dauria Large windows onto the street allow you to check
out the clientele at this cafeteria before stopping in. Food is so-
so, but is already out on the counter, so you can see what you

are getting before you commit yourself. Usually a hang out for young people. Muravyova-Amurskovo 25. Tel: 39-94-95.

Rossiyanka A stand-up cafe whose specialty (read: only dish) is *pelmeni*, with a variety of sauces. Quick but gruff service. Inexpensive. Muravyova-Amurskovo 15. Open from 9-20. Tel: 38-88-69.

Russki Kvas Step down into a cave-like cafe with fancy wood carvings and a fake fireplace. Small sandwiches available, ice cream, "shakes." Inexpensive. Muravyova-Amurskovo 40. Open 9-21 (14-15). Tel: 33-83-57.

Snezhinka Good pastries. Muravyova-Amurskovo 25. Open 9-21 (15-16) every day. Tel: 33-84-00.

Cafe Pogrebok ("The Cellar") A beer bar. Ussuriiski Bulvar 9. Open 11-23 (11-17). Tel: 33-89-98.

Golden Fish and **Gamburger** Two fast food joints, with the quality you expect from fast food. Serysheva 7. Tel: 34-08-78.

SHOPPING

One of the best buildings for shopping is #17 Muravyova-Amurskovo. About 5 stores occupy the ground floor of this lovely old building. Among them you can find souvenirs, books, computers and cosmetics. The following four shops are all at #17:

Tainy Remesla (Secret Arts) Run by the Khabarovsk Culture Fund, this art salon and souvenir store is a "must-see." Full of paintings, carved birchbark boxes, stone jewelry, painted balalaikas, and native crafts by Nanaitsi and other local ethnic minorities. Slightly pricey, but lovely work. Downstairs there is a hall with

#17 houses some of the best souvenirs in the city

changing exhibits. Also planned are literary and cultural evenings. The Khabarovsk Culture Fund has had successful international exchanges, and welcomes the opportunity for wider intercultural understanding.   Svetlana Yurievna Cherepanova, the director, is polite, helpful and courteous, as are the rest of her staff. There is a small coffee bar where you can sip espresso and examine the crafts. Muravyova-Amurskovo 17.   Open Tue-Sun 10-18:30 (13:30-15:00). Tel: 33-10-68.

Anyuta Tsveti (Flowers)   Flower arrangements, both live and silk, gzhel porcelain, ceramics from Kazakhstan, small jewelry section.   Open Mon-Sat 9-21 (14-15).   Muravyova-Amurskovo 17. Tel: 33-68-16.

Xerox Store   Copiers, supplies, computers, TVs, Sony appliances,   old   American   magazines,   exchange   office. Muravyova-Amurskovo 17. Open Mon-Sat 10-19 (14-15).

Sony/Toshiba Handicams, TVs, small jewelry section and souvenirs, imported beauty supplies. Muravyova-Amurskovo 17.

Other stores are:

Tsentralni Univermag (TsUM)   You'll find a diverse selection of goods here, including records, electronics, clothes, sports equipment, imported toiletries, children's toys, etc. There is a souvenir section on every floor, and although the selection is not nearly as nice or as large as at the art salons, most items are less expensive. Some Russian versions of American records can make interesting gifts. There is a photo shop which can develop foreign film quickly (3 or 4 days). Also a desk for ordering tickets to concerts, shows, etc. Muravyova-Amurskovo 23. Open Mon-Sat 10-19. Tel: 33-17-20.

Art Salon Outside: wrought iron window frames. Inside: a wide selection of carved items: ivory figures, wooden brooches, intricately carved wooden boxes.   Also paintings, jewelry of amber and local stones, and a stuffed iguana (go figure). Expensive. Muravyova-Amurskovo 15. Open Mon-Sat 11-18. Tel: 33-21-31.

Okruzhnoi Univermag (Military Department Store) Trying to have something for everyone in a small space, they end up with small departments of everything: American packaged food, clothes, military patches, stand-up cafe, sports equipment, carpets. Serysheva 8. Tel: 34-47-25, 39-51-85.

Start (store No. 31) This camping store has everything for the intrepid outdoorsman.   Unfortunately, not everything is available at the same time: skis but no bindings, boats but no paddles, etc. But if you have the time, be persistent: eventually every element appears.   Inflatable boats, fishing gear, cooking sets, etc. Muravyova-Amurskovo 40. Open Mon-Fri 10-19 (14-15), Sat 10-18. Tel: 33-09-14.

Gastronom Mercury (Central Gastronom)   Called "Mercury" due to the grand statue of Mercury which crowns the building.   Lots of space inside.   There is a wide selection of imported foods, as well as the regular local supplies.   The building itself is quite fancy with stained glass, chandeliers, glided mouldings and a central staircase.   A small cafe on the top floor serves "*koktaili*"—no, not cocktails, but ice cream and juice "shakes."   Muravyova-Amurskovo 9. Open 8-20. Tel: 33-16-91.

Knizhni Mir (Book World)   As the name implies, this is a large multi-department bookstore.   The current fascination seems to be Russian translations of American detective, science fiction, and romance novels, but you might also find some Russian classics here. Good for maps, too.   Karla Marksa 37. Tel: 33-33-51.

Filatelia (Stamp Store) Has sets of stamps, old and foreign coins, and Tsarist money.   Collectors also meet on Sundays at the Chess Club (*shakhmatni klub*) at Amurski Bulvar 40, near the market (Tel: 33-39-79).   If you can't find them (while the club is being repaired) you can ask the guy at the stamp store. The old proprietor is friendly and helpful.   The sign outside just says "*magazin*," but take the outside stairs (with no railing) up to the second floor. Zaparina 65. Open from 10-19 (closed Sun). Tel: 33-82-65.

DalArt Gallery Art and jewelry by local artists and native craftsmen. Expensive.   In Art Museum, Shevchenko 7.   Tel: 39-93-12.

The Amber Room An exhibit of exquisite amber jewelry (not for sale), plus the best selection in town of amber for sale. **Note:** one floor above the Amber Room is an art and souvenir shop which trades in endangered species (on more than one occasion it has offered for sale the skins of Siberian Tigers, whose estimated population is 250-500 individuals).   Poaching is a major cause of the tigers decline, and patronizing such shops only encourages this illegal activity. Do not confuse the Amber Room with the "souvenir" shop.   In the Military Museum, Shevchenko 20. Open Wed-Sun 10-18.

Globus Book Store This corner store has a small foreign language section. Zaparina 55. Open Mon-Fri 10-19 (14-15), Sat 10-18. Tel: 33-49-56.

Bukinist　Has collections of old and rare books (along with lots of modern stuff). Karla Marksa 49. Open Mon-Fri 10-19 (14-15) Sat 10-18. Tel: 38-55-11.

Almaz (Diamond)　The largest state-run jewelry store in Khabarovsk. Gold and silver, amber, watches and clocks. Muravyova-Amurskovo 13. Tel: 33-78-70.

Granat　(Garnet)　Small selection of jewelry. Amurski Bulvar 3. Open Tue-Fri 9-17:30 (14-14:30), Sat 10-17 (no break). Tel: 34-85-71.

Yantar (Amber)　Small selection of jewelry. Lenina 33. Open 10-19 (14-15), closed Sun, Mon. Tel: 22-18-21.

Agat　More jewelry. Lenina 44. Tel: 33-30-47.

Melodia　Russian records and CD's from the States (rarely have Russian CD's). Serysheva 74. Tel: 35-73-71.

Market AMI　Business travellers who find they've forgotten some item of clothing can drop into this store to buy slacks, skirts, shirts, blouses and jackets, even undies, all imported from the West, but sold at reasonable (western) prices. Turgeneva 68.

MARKET

Anything (food-wise) available can be found here. Fruits from the Caucasus, Korean salads in little tubes, cooked chickens, raw pork and cow heads, vegetables, flowers, you name it. Out the back you can find knitted baby booties, light bulbs, and other miscellaneous items. The back of the market used to be a bustling area full of Chinese merchants selling down coats, boots, dresses, etc., but the "powers that be" decided that it was too crowded and chaotic (and there was a general crackdown on all Chinese), so everyone was moved out to a spot halfway out of town (on the road to the airport). Now the back of the food market is mainly manned by babushkas. Tolstova, at Amurski Bulvar. Open summer 6-19, winter 7-19.

MUSEUMS

Military Museum　Traces the history of the Far Eastern Army, with models, documents and displays of arms. Tanks in the back yard are in good condition. Has a dramatic diorama of the battle with Japan in 1945. Also has a hall of changing exhibits. Recently the exhibit was of paintings of the siege of Leningrad. Tours are available and the lady "guards" in the halls are knowledgeable. Modest entry fee. Also has a small souvenir shop called "The Amber Room." Shevchenko 20. Open Wed-Sun 10-18. Tel: 33-11-50.

Geological Museum This museum is housed in a quaint old building built in the 1800s by the merchant family Plyucin (who built the Krai Library and the Cathedral). The ground floor covers basic geological history, including volcanos, fossils, and moon rocks from Soviet moon bases which you can examine under a microscope. The second floor covers local geology. A must if you like rocks and geological maps. Modest entrance fee. Small gift shop. Lenina 15. Open from 10-18. Tel: 21-53-70, 33-04-91.

Kraevecheski Museum The ethnographic and history museum. Founded in 1894, it has a stuffed tiger, archaeological remains, local native cultures and history. At time of writing it was closed for remodelling, but scheduled to reopen in '95. If still closed, visit the Youth Museum (below), which has some exhibits from this museum. Shevchenko 11. Tel: 33-08-64, 38-93-54.

Youth Museum (formerly Museum of Komsomol Glory) This museum traces the glorious history of the Communist youth organizations ("Pioneers" for younger children, "Komsomol" for teenagers). Not much of interest here in the regular halls, but the revolving exhibits are sometimes intriguing. While the Kraevecheski Museum is closed some of the exhibits are housed here, including a display on Shamanism. There are occasionally lecture series on the history, ethnography, archaeology, etc. of the krai. Call for current info. Turgeneva 86. Tel: 33-19-36.

Art Museum *(Khudozhestvenni Muzei)*, **Exhibit Hall** *(Vystavochni Zal)* This art museum was originally founded with contributions of paintings from the Tretyakov and Pushkin museums in Moscow. Put slippers over your shoes before entering to keep the marble and wood floors of this grand building from getting scuffed. There is a fine collection of icons, 19th century Russian portraits, statues, the art of "Peoples of the Far East," including carved ivory and fish-skin clothing, and changing exhibits. They now have so much art that half of it is stored in the basement and a new art museum is being built at Frunze 45 to house it. The new museum is projected to open in '95. There are two shops—a jewelry shop and an art shop with native crafts, paintings, carvings, etc. Both shops are very expensive. The entrance fee to the museum is significantly higher for foreigners than for Russians.   Shevchenko 7.   Tel: 39-93-12.

ENTERTAINMENT

Gorky Drama Theatre   Tragedies and comedies by such authors as Tolstoy, Francoise Sagan, and Schiller. Dzerzhinskovo 44.   Tel: 33-02-55.

Musical Comedy Theatre   A grand and fancy theatre with performances of classics by Cole Porter, Strauss, and modern Russian composers.   Karla Marksa 64.   Tel: 33-48-21.

Kino Center   Housed in one of the old red brick buildings left over from before the revolution, this small film center doesn't want to be considered "intellectual," yet it shows avant-garde and foreign films (sometimes dubbed, sometimes with subtitles) and has cultural evenings with musicians and representatives from the Writers' Union.   Other organizations can rent the hall for special events. Films are advertised in the local papers, or stop by and ask during the afternoon (go around to the side door).   The organizers are friendly and helpful. Espresso available at the cafe before the film. Frunze 69a. Tel: 33-37-61.

Pantomime Theatre "Triada"   Good for non-Russian speakers!   They are building their own theatre at Lenina 27, scheduled to open in '95. Till then they usually perform at the Children's Theatre. Tel: 21-59-02.

Philharmonic   Check with the administration here to find out what concerts will be performed around town.   Symphonies usually appear at the concert hall (see below).   Muravyova-Amurskovo 8. Tel: 33-89-51, 33-14-11.

Movie Theatre _Gigant_   Usually shows American films, well-dubbed, which means that there are many voices, not just one guy in the projection room doing all the voices, as is often the case. Muravyova-Amurskovo 19. Tel: 33-09-02.

Molodyozhni (Children's Theatre)   Performances geared to children. Very popular—get tickets in advance. The pantomime theatre occasionally performs here as well.   Muravyova-Amurskovo 14. Tel: 33-40-63.

Concert Hall   Concerts by local and visiting artists. Shevchenko 7. Tel: 33-79-71 (_kassa_).

Chess Club Drop by any time to play chess with the members. On Sundays the coin and stamp collectors meet here to trade their wares. Amurski Bulvar 40. Tel: 33-39-79.

Casino Tourist Reputed to be the best casino in town. At night a free casino taxi can take you home. Open 17-5. At the Hotel Tourist, Karla Marksa 67. Tel: 37-04-73, 39-15-25.

Casino Amur (and Art Shop) In the words of the sign on the door: "We welcome you every day from 21-7 am with happy thoughts and evening dress." Shevchenko 15 (in park). Art shop open 15-21. Tel: 33-47-82.

Disco Boat Every night during the summer there are 1 1/2 hour cruises along the Amur, with drinking and dancing. There is a bar on board or you can bring your own. Currently cruises leave at 19:30 and 21:30. Check at ferry station for more details.

Circus Performances have become less frequent due to lack of city funds. Performances only in summer. Tolstova 20. Tel: 33-38-93.

Banya in Hotel Amur Private and small group sessions available. Day and evening rates. Book well in advance for popular times like evenings and weekends. Pay at front desk. Lenina 27. Tel: 39-43-12.

Public Banya No. 6 Open 15-20, each session 1 1/2 hrs. Zaparina 97. Tel: 34-88-39.

Botanical Garden (*Dendrarium*) A beautiful place to roam around. Take bus No. 29 from Komsomolskaya Square to "Ussuriiski" stop, continue walking in the direction of the bus, then turn right. Open 9-17. Tel: 22-34-01.

SPORTS

Park of Culture and Rest (*Park Kulturi i Otdykha*) Along the banks of the Amur, this is a pleasant place to stroll or jog. For the energetic there are tennis courts, a swimming pool, and sports stadium.

Lenin Stadium in the Park of Culture (by the Amur) is the site of ball-hockey games (*hokei s myatchom*). Signs around town tell the schedule of upcoming games. Tel: 39-98-85.

Tennis Lessons are also available at Lenin Stadium. Tel: 39-98-85.

Open-air swimming pool (*otkryty plavatelni bassein*) This pool is open year round. Unfortunately, when the city hot water goes off the pool closes, which means that it is closed much of the summer. But for an interesting winter experience, go swimming while it is snowing! Steam rises from the heated water, creating an eerie effect. Keep dunking your head so it doesn't freeze. The water isn't hot, like at a hot springs, but is warm enough to be comfortable in any weather. Also offers classes for children, and lifesaving classes for adults. Near Lenin Stadium in the Park of Culture, you can't miss this large building with columns, rotunda on top, and statues of bathers. Tel: 39-73-09.

Swimming Pool (indoors) Shevchenko 18. Tel: 39-75-80.

City Park "Dinamo" In winter there is ice skating on the ponds, and sometimes the paths are frozen and you can skate through the park. In winter this is also the place for large ice sculptures and ice slides. In summer there are tennis courts available, there is lots of greenery and a haven from the city. From Karla Marksa to Ussuriiski Bulvar, just beyond Lenin Square.

Dinamo Stadium Dinamo soccer team plays here. Check billboards around town for schedule of games. Karla Marksa 62. Tel: 33-86-48, 33-86-46.

Children's park "Gaidara" named after the beloved children's author (not the famous economist). Has lots of swings, cosy corner benches, and Far Eastern flora. Karla Marksa 69 (right across the street form the entrance to Dinamo park). Open 10-21, closed Monday.

PLACES OF WORSHIP

Innokentevski Khram (Cathedral) In 1964 this cathedral was taken over and converted into a planetarium and, in the words of a 1988 guidebook, "center of propaganda of natural sciences and atheist knowledge." Recently reclaimed, there is still discussion as to which is more "useful," a cathedral or planetarium. The cathedral is still undergoing reconstruction, but services are held Saturday and Sunday at 9am. Turgeneva 73b (set back from street). Tel: 34-05-75.

Russian Orthodox, Church of Christ's Birth Built in 1901, it has a beautiful interior with striking icons and a golden altar. Leningradskaya 65. Tel: 38-06-71.

Alexander Nevski Temple Yasnaya 24. Tel: 27-70-49.

Presbyterian Services: Sun 14:00, Weds. 17:00. Muravyova-Amurskovo 17 (in former Dom Pionirov).

Evangelical Church of Grace (Korean Christian) Ul. Serysheva 22. Tel: 34-36-29.

Seventh Day Adventists Sovkhoznaya 3. Tel: 35-78-82.

TRANSPORTATION

Airport Khabarovsk is one of the few cities in the Far East which has international flights, although more cities are slowly receiving international status. Flights now connect Khabarovsk with Anchorage, Seoul, Singapore, Beijing and points in Japan. To befit its status, the airport has recently completed a new terminal, so far the best in the Far East. The airport is now a sprawling complex.

To the far right is the brand new terminal for domestic flights. This new terminal has a couple of restaurants, souvenir shops, a really quick photo developing shop—all extremely expensive. In the middle of the complex the old domestic terminal now stands abandoned, but plans for remodelling are in the works. To the far left is the modern international terminal, very clean and efficient, which charges about a $20 registration fee for international flights.

In the center, fronted by classic columns, is the "International Sector," for international passengers taking domestic flights. They also charge a large "service fee" for registering you for your flight. However, since you are foreign and therefore an international passenger, you are ONLY allowed to go through the international section. Take trolley #1 to the airport, about a 20 minute ride. Airport info: 006.

Airlines which now have flights into Khabarovsk:

Alaska Airlines Spring to fall there are twice weekly flights to Seattle, San Francisco and San Diego via Anchorage; fall to spring once per week. Tel: 37-88-04.

Air Koryo Flights to Pyongyang once per week, summer only. Tel: 37-83-73.

Asiana Airlines Flights to Seoul once per week. Tel: 37-83-73.

China Northern Airlines Flights to Harbin twice per week. Tel: 37-34-40.

Japan Airlines (JAL) Once per week flights to Niigata, June through August. Tel: 37-06-86.

Russian Executive Air Currently offers flights to Irkutsk, Vladivostok, and Yuzhno-Sakhalinsk. Ussuriiski Bulvar 2. Tel: 22-35-28, 22-36-00.

Eurasia Trans Inc. Tel: 33-60-67.

Evergreen International Airlines (Cargo) Tel: 34-69-03.

Aeroflot City Office for international flights or non-Russian travelers.   A brand new building, new sidewalks, new landscaping. Amurski Bulvar 18 (corner of Frunze). Open Mon-Sat 8:30-20 (13-14), Sun 9-17 (13-14:15). Tel: 37-87-58.

Aeroflot kassa at Tsentralnaya Hotel. Tel (but don't expect them to answer): 39-34-06.

Train Station Trains leave twice daily in the evening for the overnight trips to Vladivostok or Komsomolsk-na-Amure, or the 7-day journey to Moscow. Tickets can be bought here for same-day trains (if available). Leningradskaya 11. Tel: 34-21-92, 38-35-30, Intourist Hall 33-97-77.   Take trams # 1,2,6 from Sheronova St. (one block from Lenin square) to the train station.

For **advance train ticket** sales go to Leningradskaya 56/v, about a 5 minute walk from the train station. Inside you will find a green electric sign saying whether tickets are still available for particular routes during the next 7 days. If you are going long-distance, look for "K" (for *Kupe* or compartment).   Tel: 38-31-64, 38-33-50.

Bus Station Voronezhskoye Shosse 19. Take bus #6 from train station. Tel: 34-39-09.

To order a **taxi** call 004. There is also a taxi park at Kim Yu Chen 44. Dispatcher 33-10-44.

Car Rental Some hotels offer car-with-driver rental as one of their services. Other organizations which can provide cars or minivans by the hour or by the day are: Parus Business Center, tel: 33-72-70, and EurasiaTrans, Inc., tel: 38-44-48. A couple of days notice is usually a good idea.

Helicopter tours Russian Air Services offers tours over the Amur, and a "Champagne sunset flight." Tel: 22-40-31.

Rechnoi Vokzal (Ferry Station) When the river is not frozen, ferries go back and forth across and up river, carrying citizens heading to their summer gardens. A trip on the ferry is still relatively cheap, and affords you a nice escape from the city. If you have limited time, make sure you don't get on one of the 2-hour ferries! More information on destinations and schedules can be found at the station. There are also evening "cruises to nowhere." Shevchenko 1. Tel: 39-88-32, 39-86-90.

River Port

Nikolai Muryavov-Amurski

Nikolai Muravyov-Amurski is one of the great figures in Russian Far Eastern history. He was a controversial forward-looking politician, and although his contemporaries accused him of being out for personal power, it cannot be denied that he obtained huge tracts of land for Russia.

Muravyov came from a family of explorers, military men, and politicians. His great-grandfather had explored the Arctic, his grandfather was governor of Archangelsk, and his father was governor of Novgorod. Born the eldest of 17 children (9 of whom lived), Muravyov was sent to military school at an early age. His military career included a stint in the Russo-Turkish War and engagements against the Poles and mountain tribes of the Caucasus. While his superior officer was away, Muravyov struck an agreement which quieted the mountain men, for which he was decorated with the Order of Stanislav.

However, despite his military successes and promotions, he wasn't satisfied in the military life, and twice he retired due to "health reasons". It was at a health spa in Cologne that he met his future wife, the French Catherine DeCastri, in 1845.

In 1846 he was named governor of the city of Tula. In this post he finally "found himself." He took his job to heart and took it upon himself to carefully inspect every aspect under his jurisdiction, from prisons to agriculture, and found matters to be in a terrible state. He gave a truthful accounting of his findings to Tsar Nikolas I, and went so far as to declare that serfdom was a hindrance to progress, putting forth the idea of emancipation of the serfs. He was the first governor to propose such a radical concept (17 years before it was passed), and his boldness was noted as a liability.

In 1847 at the age of 36 he was named governor-general of Eastern Siberia, a huge territory which stretched from Siberia to the Pacific. Most of his contemporaries hadn't anticipated that he would receive such a promotion, and they speculated that either the Tsar wanted to keep him as far away as possible, or that he had somehow mixed Nikolai up with a relative of the same name, a military commander of long record. In any case, Muravyov headed out to Irkutsk and in 1849 made a grand tour inspection of his territory. During his years as governor-general of Eastern Siberia he traveled more than 120,000 versts, which is more than three times around the world.

He traveled by river to Yakutsk, overland to Okhotsk, by boat to Petropavlovsk, and returned to Irkutsk in the winter. During this time he actively evaluated the advantages and disadvantages of each city or settlement he went to. Noting that the port town of Okhotsk was poorly chosen, he saw that Petropavlovsk had a better harbor and directed the fortification of that port. (His calculations were proven correct in 1854, when the English and French invasion force was repulsed by a meagre battalion of defenders.)

Muravyov encouraged colonization, and ordered the construction of new military outposts. Among his opinions was that the Pacific would become strategically important, and that Russia needed to have an exit on the Pacific. The Amur river provided that exit, but was controlled by the Chinese. At first the Tsar was more interested in gold prospects and trade than in the Amur, and as no one wanted to stir up trouble with the Chinese, Muravyov's suggestions were ignored. However, as the Crimean War approached, and the English and French encroached upon Kamchatka, the Tsar realized the importance of the Amur, and gave Muravyov full authority to try to negotiate a new treaty with the Chinese.

Each year Muravyov sent a flotilla down the Amur—a show of strength as well as an influx of Cossacks and colonists. The Chinese were overwhelmed with internal struggles of their own at the time, and in 1858, under pressure from Muravyov, signed the Treaty of Aigun, ceding all lands north of the Amur to Russia. For this achievement Muravyov was made a Count, and the title "Amurski" was added to his name.

Despite this great honor, resentment had been growing against him among the nobility for his abrasive character and liberal tendencies. In 1848 when a charge had been brought against him that he associated too closely with the exiled Decemberists, Muravyov had answered that it was better to educate people than to continuously eke out vengence. However, when this charge appeared again in 1861, the new, more conservative Tsar Alexander II, saw Muravyov as a liability. Muravyov further fell out with the governemnt over whether to divide the Eastern Siberian Territory into two governorships.

In 1861 Muravyov retired and returned to St. Petersburg. There he was elected to the Government Council, but went with his wife to live in Paris, only rarely returning to St. Peteruburg for particularly interesting Govenment Council meetings. He died in Paris in 1881.

After his death there were plans to bury him in the Far East but, while details were being worked out, he was buried in the De Castri family plot outside Paris. In fact, it was only in 1991, 110 years after his death, that Muravyov's remains were finally returned to Russia, brought to Vladivostok and re-inturred amid great ceremony.

Nikolai Muravyov-Amurski was a pioneer and a patriot, whose contribution to the development of the Russian Far East and expansion of the Russian empire was immeasureable.

AROUND KHABAROVSK

There are many opportunities for unique travel experiences around Khabarovski Krai. There are caves for spelunkers, rivers for rafting trips, fishing trips, or cruises, and scenic woodlands for hunting and camping, cross-country skiing, you name it!

For those who want to strike out on their own, the Khabarovski Krai offers miles of untouched coastline and a variety of climatic zones and natural environments. Below are listed some of the areas worth visiting:

Dzhangi, a Nanai village in the south of Khabarovski Krai is in a known tiger habitat. Tours can be arranged with the Wildlife Foundation, Institute of Wildlife Management. Ulitsa Tolstova 15a. Tel 21-12-98.

About two hours south of Khabarovsk is the **Khekhtsyr State Park**, best known for its cross-country skiing. At the park there is a *tourbaza* (tour base), where you can rent equipment.

The **Ulya River** is one of the better rafting rivers offering good rapids (Ulya is a 3rd category river) and great scenery, especially in July and August when the bears are active but content and well fed.

Southwest of Pereyaslovka are the **Proschalnaya Peshera.** These large honeycomb caves are great for spelunkers, but as they are not well-developed, should only be attempted in groups with an experienced guide. For more information, call the Spelunker Club in Khabarovsk at 331-140. Ask for Oleg Shadrin.

Festival of Indigenous People and Ethnic Minorities (*Festival malykh narodnostyei*). Every two years (even years) in August this festival occurs in Nizhne-Khalbe (about 100 km below Komsolmolsk-na-Amure). This is a festival of all indigenous peoples in Khabarovski Krai (Evenki, Udeghe, Ulchi, Nanaitsi, Nivkhi, Nedigaltsi, Orochy). They gather to participate in native songs, dances, and sports competitions. For more information, ask in the Kraevecheski Museum in Khabarovsk.

The following local travel agencies can arrange trips to suit any taste. For hunting or fishing, for which you need a license, a couple of weeks advance notice is necessary.

Far East Co., Ltd. This company offers hunting and fishing tours, rafting trips, geological or ornithological trips, and so forth. The best season for camping is summer, till mid-September. Zaparina 67. Tel: 33-83-63, 37-87-44.

Dalreo Travel Agency This agency can also organize trips around Khabarovski Krai, including river trips on the Amur. Fishing and camping trips are also available. Moskovskaya 7. Tel: 33-27-41, 33-07-98.

JEWISH AUTONOMOUS OBLAST

In the bottom southwest corner of Khabarovski Krai, on the border with China, is the Jewish Autonomous Oblast, a district set up in 1928 to settle the "Jewish question." Its history is an interesting one. In the 20's the Soviet government made several efforts to found Jewish homelands in the Ukraine and Crimea where Jews could work and live without fear of repression. These met with such local resistance that the projects were quickly abandoned. In March of 1928 the Soviet government allotted an area in the Amur River Basin for "settlement by working people of Jewish nationality." By creating a special area for the Jews in a sparsely populated region in the Far East, the Soviet Government hoped to accomplish several things. First, they would create a "homeland" for working Jews in an area where there would be no local backlash. Second, by devoting resources and land to the Jews, the Soviets hoped to attract Jewish money and settlers from abroad. Third, the region selected bordered on China, and settling and developing the area would be a strategic step in strengthening Soviet control of the area.

Soon after the declaration, the first migrants arrived and over the next 10 years a total of 35,000 Jews came to the area, mixing with the Cossacks and Koreans already there. Conditions were terrible: the land was swampy and winters harsh. Although some migrants stayed and built the settlements of Waldheim, Tikhonkaya (later Birobidzhan), Amurzet and others, even the most conservative sources cite that of the arriving settlers, 20-30% returned home each year, and in some cases up to 70%. By 1934, although 22,000 Jews had come to the region, few more than 5,000 had stayed to work and live. That same year the authorities gave the region the status of "Jewish Autonomous Oblast."

In the post-war years, Jews again became the subject of persecution in Russia and all Jewish institutions were shut down. In the JAO, migration came to a standstill. Thousands were imprisoned or killed. Afterwards, the region became "Jewish" and "Autonomous" in name only. Economically, the JAO became the light industrial center of the Far East, known for its clothing, factories and treaded combines.

In the late 80's less than 5% of the population was Jewish, and there was a one-room synagogue for the capital city of Birobidzhan. However, in the last few years this figure has grown to 16% as some residents are now less afraid to announce their Jewish background, while others look to use their Jewish nationality as a way to emigrate to Israel.

BIROBIDZHAN

Founded in 1912 as a railway station while constructing the Amur railroad, Tikhonkaya received its first major group of settlers in May of 1928, as Jewish migrants traveled east to settle the new Jewish homeland. Whatever their expectations, they were probably disappointed by what they found. A few wooden buildings surrounded by low-lying marshy ground and forests was to be their new home. But harsh climate and primitive living conditions notwithstanding, the settlers drained the swamps, cleared the forests and built a town. In 1931 Tikhonkaya was renamed Birobidzhan after the Bira and Bidzhan rivers which border the Jewish Autonomous Oblast. In 1934 it became the capital of the JAO and in 1937 received official city status.

Today Birobidzhan (pop 90,000) is rediscovering its Jewish roots and reaching out to make international cultural and business ties. It has a Jewish folk ensemble, and a theatre group as well. Groups have also been started which teach about Judaism, Hebrew language, and Israel. Birobidzhan has a sister-city relationship with Beavertown, Oregon.

PRACTICAL INFORMATION

Moscow time +6 hours.
Code for calling Birobidzhan from other cities: **42162.**
Information from inside the city: **09.**
Information from outside the city: **42162-60610.**
Airport (tickets) Tel: 715-35.
Aeroflot City Office Open 9-17 (12-13). Kalinina 25. Tel: 692-06.
Train Station 1 Tel: 670-42. Birobidzhan is 3 hours from Khabarovsk.
Train Station 2 Tel: 646-61.
Bus Station Kalinina 2. Tel: 695-39.

RESTAURANTS

Birobidzhan Corner of Gorkovo and Lenina. Tel: 684-19.
Elita Prospekt 60 Let SSR 14. Tel: 697-18.
Freid Dzerzhinskovo 6. Tel: 648-50.
Solnechni Ostrov Bumagina 8. 686-49.
Vostok (in Hotel Vostok) Tel: 652-20.

MISCELLANEOUS

Hotel Vostok Inexpensive. Sholom-Aleikhema 1. Tel: 653-30.
Market Sholom-Aleikhema 3. Tel: 663-68.
Kraevecheski Museum Open 9-17:30 (13-14). Lenina 25. Tel: 645-39.
Philharmonic Prospekt 60 Let SSSR 14. Tel: 656-79.
Synagogue Mayakovskovo 11.
Russian Orthodox Church Kirova 4. Tel: 135-55.
Intour-Birobidzhan Sholom-Aleikhema 55. Tel: 615-73.

KOMSOMOLSK-NA-AMURE

Referred to as "What a Soviet City should look like," Komsomolsk-na-Amure was founded in the 1930's by thousands of enthusiastic young communists (*komosomoltsi*) trying to break the 5-year plan targets and establish an industrial base in the Far East.

Within five years the city was already building ships. To help development of this wonder city, labor camps were constructed around the area to provide the needed labor for the ambitious plans of the party leaders. These prison camps existed all the way up until the 1970's. A refinery, a port and several factories were also built in short order.

Today the founders of the city are honored by a statue in town and a memorial on the rock upon which they first landed. Trams run along wide, tree-lined streets with large pastel-colored buildings. The city itself, with its strategic military industries (nuclear attack submarines and Sukhoi fighter planes) and the largest steel plant in the whole Far East, was a showcase Soviet city in regards to production and politics. Unfortunately, the industries that made Komsomolsk so important a few years ago are now struggling with conversion of their production lines to consumer items.   More importantly, Komsomolsk is struggling to convert its conservative thought, where defense conversion is seen not only as difficult, but wrong.

PRACTICAL INFORMATION

Moscow time +6 hours.

Code for calling Komsomolsk: **42172**.

Airport   The airport is located about 30-40 minutes from city.   Make sure someone is meeting you, because getting into town is not convenient.   Bus #1 goes to the city, but stops about 500 meters from the airport building.   No public phones available—the only telephones are at the Police Station.   Airport closes often due to lack of fuel.

Train Station   It is an overnight trip to Khabarovsk, approximately 24 hours to Vladivostok.   Vokzalnaya 46.   Tel: 38-22-91.

River port The Amur-Port "Turist" organization (in room 2 of the port) is the place to go to organize a trip on a river boat. Naberezhnaya. Information: 431-09.

HOTELS

Voskhod   Centrally located on the main street.   A very Soviet hotel, with an average restaurant.   Pervostroitelei 31.   Tel: 303-36.

Otel Inostrannykh Grazhdan (Foreign Citizen Hotel) Sidorenko 17. Tel: 353-09.

Amur Hotel   Cheap hotel, with a bar on the top floor. Prospekt Mira 15. Tel: 430-74.

Lyudmila Hotel   Has a sauna and bar, neither of which work if there are not enough guests.   Cheap.   Prospekt Lenina 22. Tel: 430-70.

FOOD

U Konstantina   Friendly service at moderate prices. Pionirskaya 17. Open 9-17, 20-24 every day. Tel: 442-67.

Daker Pervostroitelei 20. Open 12-16, 19-24. Tel: 333-87.

Voskhod Typical hotel restaurant.

Kafe Tri Shampura (Three Skewers Cafe) Pr. Lenina 36.
Kafe Tsentralnoe (Central Cafe) Pervostroitelei 19.
Central Market Ulitsa Kirova.

MISCELLANEOUS

Kraevecheski Museum Prospekt Mira 8.
Art Museum Prospekt Mira 16.
Labor Museum Kalinina 7.
Drama Theater Alleya Truda. Tel: 321-34.
Proizvodstvo Kombinat Banya Separate days for men and women. General admission, or private rooms for up to five people available. Take tram #2 from Hotel Voskhod to "Komsomolskaya" stop, cross the tracks, then walk straight. Kirova 36. Open 13-20:30.

Banya #2 Separate days for men and women. General admission, inexpensive. Orekhova 57. Open 13-21. Tel: 229-18.

"Ekzotur" Experienced eco-tour company arranges various tours throughout Khabarovski Krai. Trips include cross-country skiing, mountain climbing, fishing and river rafting as well as ethnographic/archaeological trips. Ul. Mira 43. Tel: 42-196.

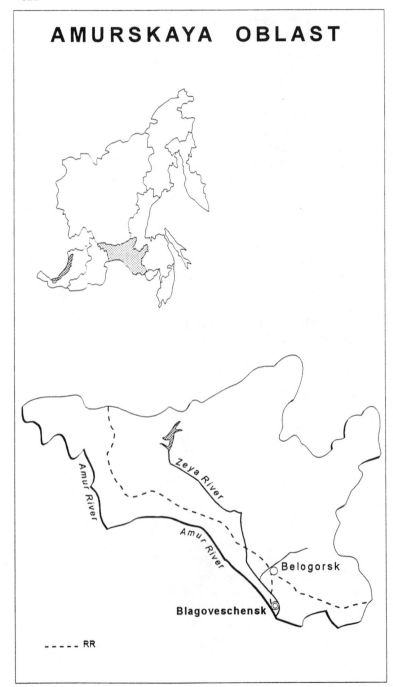

AMURSKAYA OBLAST

Blagoveschensk

Belogorsk

Amur River

Zeya River

Amur River

- - - - - RR

CHAPTER 4

AMURSKAYA OBLAST

The Amurskaya Oblast is somewhat of a paradox. Located on the border with China, crossed by both the BAM and Trans-Siberian railroads, bestowed with large coal deposits as well as good arable land, the region has the potential to be one of the richest in the Far East. However, it has been left behind by its neighbors in commercial and industrial development. Cross-border trade has been limited by restrictions placed by the Russian authorities, afraid of being overrun with cheap Chinese goods and illegal immigrants. The coal industry is struggling in the new market economy, and foreign investment has been lower than expected. Long a sensitive military border zone, the Amur region is still unsure whether to open its doors fully to the outside world. With its mining, railroad and military industries, the Amurskaya administration is more conservative than most, and contacts and trade with China have fluctuated depending on the political atmosphere. Physical proximity and mutual benefit should make an Amurskaya-China trading relationship inevitable, but how and when remain to be seen.

HISTORY

The Amur Region was a target for exploration as far back as the mid 17th century. Russian explorers, having founded outposts in the harsh conditions of Eastern Siberia and the far north, looked for regions in southern areas with a milder climate. The Amur river valley was such an area, but was nominally controlled by the Manchu Empire. Nevertheless, Russian groups began exploring the area and building outposts. However, the Russians' cruelty to the natives made the latter ask the Manchus for protection, and in 1652 the Russian outpost of

Achansk was besieged, its defenders forced to retreat. Two years later the Russians were again defeated in Kumarsk, forcing them to abandon the entire Amur region and retrench in the Transbaikal area. In 1689 the Treaty of Nerchinsk was signed, which fixed the border between Russia and China (not in Russia's favor) and established an official trade agreement between the two countries. This treaty ushered in a 170 year period of relatively peaceful and profitable relations between the two powers, with neither of the two really trusting the other.

After China's defeat in the Opium War of 1839, the weakness of the Manchu Empire was exposed to the outside world and the colonial powers rushed to extract concessions from the defeated power. Russia was no exception, and began sending expeditions into Chinese territory around the Amur. They met no opposition and soon began crossing the territory at will. In 1858 the outpost of Ust-Zeyski on the Amur was renamed Blagoveschensk and became the base for future settlements. In the same year, Count Muravyov forced the signing of the Aigunski Treaty, which made China give all lands north of the Amur River to Russia. After World War II, the Amur region developed its two main industries, agriculture (soy bean production) and mining (lignite). The construction of the BAM, the Baikal-Amur Magistral, also made the region into a transportation center. Relations have changed over the years, from armed conflicts in the 20's and 60's to warmer relations in the 70's. Currently, Blagoveschensk is looking south with a cautious optimism, hoping to have profitable border trade without being overrun.

BLAGOVESCHENSK

INTRODUCTION

Capital of the Amurskaya Oblast and located on the border with China, Blagoveschensk (Blago-VEH-shensk) is a place where one can get a glimpse into another world, one which the Russians are afraid will come sweeping across their border at any moment. Before, the Russians were afraid of an armed invasion; today they are worried about an irresistible economic and cultural invasion. Although you can receive two channels of

Chinese TV, surprisingly little else of Chinese influence is seen in Blagoveschensk, probably due to the strict border regulations. There is one Chinese cafe, a couple of Russian cafes with Chinese names, and only an occasional Chinese person in the street.

HISTORY

Founded in 1856 as a Cossack fortress at the confluence of the Zeya and Amur rivers, Blagoveschensk (or Ust-Zeyski, as it was then called) grew quickly to become a trade, commercial and administrative center in the Far East. Placed in an area that physically belonged to China at the time, Russia hoped to quickly populate the rich Amur valley area and present China with a de facto Russian region. China was in no condition to dispute its northern border with Russia, as it was divided internally and threatened by both the English and French demanding concessions in the south. On May 16, 1858 the Aigunski Treaty was signed, ceding to Russia all lands north of the Amur River.

In July, Emperor Alexander II renamed the outpost Blagoveschensk in honor of the church which began construction that same year, and in December formed the Amurskaya region with Blagoveschensk as its capital. Needless to say, the settlement's livelihood was its trade and ties with China as shown by the fact that when the first typograph was founded in the city in 1862, it had both Russian and Chinese types.

By 1865 the population stood at 2341 people and in the next years academies, factories and theaters were built, as well as the usual churches and trading houses. In 1896 the city had its first telephone station, and in 1900 its own electric power station.

In 1900, popular resentment against foreigners in China led to the rise of a reactionary group called the Boxers who went throughout the land attacking and killing foreigners. Rumors circulated that the Chinese in Blagoveschensk (at that time more than half the population) had been given orders to kill all the Russians and take over the city. The local Russian commander ordered all Chinese to leave the city immediately and on July 14, drove all the remaining Chinese into the river at gunpoint. Those that resisted were killed, while most of those forced into the river died by drowning in the swift current. The body count rose into the thousands. Shortly thereafter, Russian troops invaded Manchuria, burning villages as they went.

After the 1917 Revolution and ensuing civil war, Blagoveschensk became the watchdog of China. Border incidents were common and in the late 1920's the city was shelled and was almost witness to a full scale war over the Chinese eastern railroad conflict. During the height of the Stalinist repression many churches were destroyed or put to non-religious uses. The city became known less for its Russo-Chinese trade status and more as a railroad, mining and agricultural center (Amurskaya region provides some 70% of Russian soy production).

Today Blagoveschensk is undecided where its future lies: to western Russia and Moscow as it has for the last 60 years, or to its giant southern neighbor: China.

WALKING AROUND TOWN

Walking around Blagoveschensk is a pleasure. There are many beautiful old buildings which have been kept up or recently restored. Streets are broad and tree-lined. There are many cafes where you can stop for refreshment. A walk down Lenina is your best bet for shopping, but a walk along the Amur gives you a view of China, beaches in the summer, and some monuments.

If starting from the **Hotel Zeya,** turn right onto Kalinina Street and you will hit the river Amur. In the winter buses travel on the frozen river to China (the border crossing points are not directly across from each other—the entrance to China is a few kilometers farther up river). The Amur is one of the great Russian rivers, affectionately called "*Batushka Amur*" or "Little Father" in literature. Turn left on Krasnoflotskaya Street and continue along the river. The lovely red and white building to your left used to be a **trading house**, but is now a research institute. A little farther along there is a **PT-boat**, in honor of those who died in World War II. Yet farther along is a statue to **Count Muravyov-Amurski**, governor-general of Eastern Siberia under the Tsar, who was responsible for getting the Chinese to agree to the Amur as the border between Russia and China, thus obtaining huge tracts of land for Russia and a border more easy

BLAGOVESCHENSK

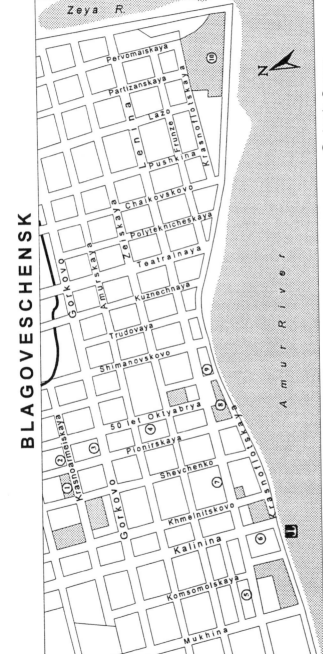

① Market
② Chinese Cafe
③ Russian Orthodox Church
④ Univermag Dept. Store
⑤ Aeroflot office
⑥ Hotel Zeya
⑦ Krai Museum
⑧ Lenin Square
⑨ Hotel Yubileinaya
⑩ Pyervomaiski Park
🄻 Ferry Station

to secure.   For this achievement the title "Amurski" was bestowed upon Count Muravyov and added to his name.

If you prefer to shop, then when you leave the hotel you should turn left, and then right onto Lenina.   Blagoveschensk was once called "the New York of the Far East," and Bolshaya Ulitsa was its Broadway.   Renamed Lenina under Communism, as in most Soviet cities, Lenina is the main street of Blagoveschensk, and a walk along it will take you past most shops, hotels, the museum, theater, and many pretty buildings. The first fancy building you go past on your right used to be the main store of **Churin and Co.**, one of the largest Russian trading companies at the turn of the century.   In front of it was a huge trade square.   The whole thing has been turned into a **"Children's Palace,"** that is to say a children's center where cultural events take place and after-school classes are held.

Across the street on the left is **ZAGS**, the government marriage bureau.   On weekends cars decorated with ribbons, bells, and often dolls strapped to the front bumpers are lined up outside, waiting for the blushing brides to emerge.

The **Krai Museum** is ahead on your left, at the corner of Internatsionalni   and   Lenina.   Although   nowadays Internatsionalni Alley (*pereulok*) is so insignificant that it isn't even shown on modern maps, in the early days of the city it was an important artery leading to the river port, and it was named Americanskaya, after the sailship *America*, which explored much of the Amur and the Far Eastern coast.   The Krai Museum is housed in what used to be the main store of **Kunst and Albers**, the German merchants who were so active in the Far East at the turn of the century.   By 1914 there were a total of 28 Kunst and Albers branches throughout the Far East, many of which are still the prettiest buildings in the city.

If you continue past the **drama theater** and **gastronom** you will come to Shevchenko Street.   Shevchenko is a good side-street to walk up, since it leads to the market.   Along the way, just around the corner from Lenina there is a small **Kvas store**. Unfortunately it only rarely has kvas, but drop in just to look at the murals inside.   They depict village scenes: greeting guests, nature, etc.   The chandeliers are also holdovers from an age when the store was more elegant.

A modern vegetable store not much farther up Shevchenko on the left hides a small cafe upstairs, decorated with carved wood and stained glass. It seems like Blagoveschensk puts more effort into making things nice.

After a block or two, old **wooden houses** begin to mingle with the modern buildings on Shevchenko. Fancy carved wood around the windows adds a pretty touch to otherwise shabby houses, with run-down sheds, gardens and occasional outhouses.

After four blocks you will come to Krasnoarmeiskaya Street and the **open air market**. The **puppet theater** is a bit farther along Shevchenko, but if you are not trailing children, struggle through the crowds at the market until you find something to buy. If you are hungry by now, you are only one block along Krasnoarmeiskaya from the **Chinese cafe**. After satisfying your hunger you can turn down Pionirskaya one block to Gorkovo, then left to the **Orthodox Church**. In the early days of Blagoveschensk when churches abounded in the city (there were 5 or 6 at one time for a population of about 16,000), this was the Catholic Church. Most churches met their demise in the 20's and 30's. Yet somehow this one survived, and since 1945 it has been Russian Orthodox. Filled with paintings and icons, it has been well-maintained by a crew of *babushki*. You are welcome to visit, as long as you don't interrupt any services.

Continue to 50 Let Oktyabrya, and past the **Univermag** (department store) you will come to **Lenin Square**. The square covers territory where the Blagoveschenskaya Cathedral used to stand. Alas, there is no trace of the wooden structure.

"Our Policy is the Policy of Peace" and "Glory to Labor"; such vestiges of Communism still grace many buildings

If you are not too tired and want to look at more wooden architecture, head down Lenina, past the peach-colored Teacher's Training Institute to 103 Lenina at Kuznechnaya (Blacksmith) Street, one of the few streets that has maintained it's pre-revolutionary name. These **wooden houses** look as if they have stood there forever unchanged. They stand across from a hideous unfinished modern monstrosity, supposedly planned as a theater. There are no construction materials or cranes around it, so it is uncertain when/if it will be finished.

A walk to the river will get you back to the Zeya if you turn right. For the truly energetic a turn to the left will head you towards **Pyervomaiski park** and the confluence of the Amur and Zeya rivers.

PRACTICAL INFORMATION

Moscow time +6 hours.

Code for calling Blagoveschensk from outside the city: **41622.**

Information when calling from inside the city: **09.**

Information from outside the city: **416-99-09-111.**

Main Post Office on Pionirskaya, just before Amurskaya.

DalvneshtorgBank 36 Shevchenko. Tel: 2-56-35, 2-56-53.

Central Bank of Russia This pretty blue building with the wrought iron fences has been a bank since before 1900. Internatsionalni Prospekt 17 .

Intourist Can arrange small city tours. Tel: 2-14-46.

CHINA!

As previously mentioned, Russia and China have kept themselves as separate as possible, despite the fact that you can see across the border. You can, in fact, take a trip across the border into Hei Hei, but you'll have to be prepared well in advance. It cannot be a spur of the moment decision. For one thing, everyone, including Russians, must have a Chinese visa, which (at time of writing) can only be obtained from the Chinese Consulate in Khabarovsk or Embassy in Moscow. If you do plan to cross at Blagoveschensk, make sure that it specifically says Blagoveschensk in your Chinese visa as your border crossing point, otherwise you may have problems. Another important fact to keep in mind is that if you have a simple single entry/exit Russian visa, your stay in Hei Hei may be extended when you discover that the Russian border guards will not let you back into Russia! Make sure you have a multiple-entry visa before attempting to leave the country!

Furthermore, there are differing opinions (at the Chinese consulate, at Intourist, and at the border) as to whether anyone besides Russians are allowed to cross into Hei Hei at all. Before attempting a visit, confirm the current regulations with the Chinese consulate or embassy, and, if possible, get a letter of permission.

If you arrive in Blagoveschensk with a multi-entry Russian visa and a Chinese visa burning a hole in your pocket, getting across the river seems fairly simple. In the winter, there is a bus that makes eight trips across the frozen river. The first leaves at 8:45 and the last at 17:30. There are also eight return trips from the Chinese side between 9:45 and 18:20. In the summer there is a hydrofoil that makes twelve trips between borders. Blago-Hei Hei runs from 9:15 to 15:20 and the return trips go from 8:45 to 16:30. Prices change rapidly, but at time of writing the cost of a round-trip ticket was approximately $50.

To get to the border crossing (*perepravka*) take the K bus from the center and get off at Chaikovskaya stop. From there walk down Ulitsa Chaikovskovo toward the river, about 1/4 mile. The customs building is clearly marked. There you can buy tickets and get current schedule information.

There are also plans to build a bridge between Blagoveschensk and Hei Hei. These plans have been in the talking stage for years, but there are finally investors, and the current plan projects the bridge to be finished by October 1995.

HOTELS

Hotel Zeya The rooms are simple but pleasant. Most rooms have stand-up showers with no curtains: be prepared to make a mess. Luxes (suites) have 3 rooms and direct-dial telephones (within Russia). Buffets on two floors are open from 8-20, varied selection, brusk service. Moderate. Kalinina 8. Tel: 2-11-00.

Hotel Yubileinaya Centrally located on Lenin Square. Has Aeroflot booth. Inexpensive. 108 Lenina. Tel: 9-38-96.

Hotel Amur Inexpensive. Lenina 122. Tel: 2-11-13.

Hotel Druzhba (Friendship) Has a Chinese/Russian restaurant. Inexpensive. Kuznechnaya 1. Tel: 9-05-40.

FOOD

The main restaurants tend to be in the hotels. Although they are not the nicest places (often loud, crowded, with indifferent service), they will most likely be the places you will end up having dinner. However during the day there are many cafes which are available for lunch and snacks.

Kitaiskaya Kukhnya (Chinese Cuisine) This is the real thing! Run by Chinese, this cafe serves Chinese food like you expect it: a variety of dishes are available, different sauces and tastes, pork dumplings, chopsticks. The menu is in Russian, hand-written and hard to read, but if you need a recommendation, the harried waitress (the only worker who speaks Russian) will advise you. The cafe is very small and tends to fill up around lunchtime, but dishes are served quickly and there is rapid turnover. They work hard, are friendly, and this is the only   place you can get completely non-Russian food. Definitely worth a stop.   Located on the corner of Krasnoarmeiskaya and Pionirskaya (one block from the market). Open 10-17 daily.

Morozka   This small corner shop mostly sells milk products, but also has a cafe which offers ice cream with toppings and "*kokteili*" (a sort of ice cream shake mixed with juice). Pretty murals adorn the walls. Corner of Lenina and Shevchenko. Open 7-21 (13-14).

Cafe Otdykh A small cafe upstairs from the **Kolosok** bread store. On the ground floor there is a small display of fancy breads in the shapes of squirrels, hedgehogs, rabbits and more. Upstairs the cafe serves cakes, pastries and coffee. 106 Zeyskaya (at Pionirskaya). Open Mon-Sat from 9-19 (14-15), Sun 9-18 (14-15).

Gastronom Cafe   On the third floor of the Central Gastronom there is a cafe which offers "pizza" (actually more like a roll with a light cheese topping), ice cream, light sandwiches and juice. Large windows overlook Lenina Street. 161 Lenina.

Kvas Store   Rarely has kvas, but does have interesting murals inside.   On Shevchenko, just up from Lenina.   Open 8-20 (14-15), closed Sun.

Many old buildings have been maintained and restored in Blagoveschensk

Hotel Zeya Restaurant The waitresses are harried and the bands are loud, but if you want to get up and dance, this is the place for you. The food is ok, IF they have what is on the menu.

Hotel Amur Restaurant Much quieter crowd than the Zeya, although when the band starts up...

Grill Grill This non-descript place from the outside is actually a pretty happening bar in the evenings. Located on Krasnoflotskaya, just off Kalinina. Open late.

Druzhba Restaurant (in Hotel Druzhba) Chinese and Russian cuisine. Open from 18-2. Tel: 9-05-35.

Yubileinaya Hotel Restaurant Open from 18-24. Tel: 2-85-49.

SHOPPING

Univermag The main department store, with everything from imported cookies, candies and chocolates, to fur hats, fabrics, clothes, toys, electronic equipment, etc. 50 Let Oktyabrya Street #20.

Gastronom This huge food store is housed in two buildings: one is a lovely old building which used to be a credit society at the turn of the century. The other building is an ugly modern structure. The outside of the old brick building has decorated tiles, added or at least repainted in 1986. Go in the front door and turn right to check out the chandeliers and stained glass from a previous era. The second floor is pretty, too. Cafe on the third floor of the modern building. 161 Lenina.

Knizhni Mir (Book World) As the name suggests, a big varied bookstore. This is where you can find city maps. There is also a Xerox store here where you can buy a machine, or just make a few copies. 3 Pionirskaya. Open Mon-Fri from 9-18 (13-14), Sat 8-16.

Melodia Small selection of Russian and American records. Very small selection of pirated cassettes. 5 Pionirskaya. Open Mon-Fri 9-18 (13-14), Sat 9-17.

Amurski Passage From the outside this looks like a small suburban shop. Unfortunately, it is not yet finished. So far there are two stores in it, both run by a Russian/Singapore joint venture called Dzhesnina. The left store has TVs, VCRs, handi cams, and other electronic equipment. Open 9-21 (13-14), Sat 9-19, Sun 9-18. The right store has clothes and crystal. Open 9-21 Mon-Fri. A porcelain shop is preparing to open up in the middle store. 159 Lenina.

Vesna The outside of this building has gryphons on it. The inside is less exciting, however some jewelry and pretty painted trays can be found among the household items and furniture. Don't neglect to check upstairs, too. 157 Lenina. Open Mon-Fri 9-18 (13-14), Sat 9-17.

Artist's Board (*Upravleniye Khudozhnikov*) Has an art salon selling the work of local artists, and a small cafe. At the Exhibition Hall (*Vystavochni Zal*), 50 Let Oktyabrya 2A (near Lenin Square). Tel: 2-75-14, 2-46-46.

Yantar (Amber) Government jewelry store with a wide selection of gold, silver and precious stones. 112 Lenina. Open Mon-Fri 9-18 (13-14), Sat 8-16.

MARKET

The main market is at the corner of Krasnoarmeiskaya and Shevchenko streets. Here you can find just about anything: clothes, household goods, fur hats, car parts, etc. The "things" market is outdoors, food is indoors. Surprisingly few Chinese, although most of the goods themselves are from China. The recent border restrictions have limited the flow of traders across the border, but the supply of goods continues!

ENTERTAINMENT

Kraevecheski Museum The museum is housed in a beautiful old building, and much love and attention has gone into the upkeep of both the outside and inside of this historic edifice. The museum collections include a natural history section with stuffed animals, birds eggs, and descriptions of the flora and fauna of different regions of the Oblast, a section on native history, including a couple of shaman's outfits and an Evenk tent, a large informational section devoted to the history of the city, with room reconstructions, ancient maps, photographs and models of the original fort and early buildings. Upstairs there is information on the Soviet period, with documents of partisans, weapons, etc. The second floor also has changing exhibits. Recently there was the work of a local artist, a section on the Art of the East, with carved elephant tusks from China, embroidery from Japan, and many more beautiful items, and an exhibit entitled "Secrets of Grandmother's Trunk," on ladies fashions at the turn of the century. Tours available. 165 Lenina. Open 10-18 (closed Mon). Tel: 2-40-86, 2-24-14.

Drama and Comedy Theater A list of all upcoming performances during the month is posted outside the theater, and also on signs around town. Classics as well as modern plays are performed, and there are afternoon matinees for children. 163 Lenina. Tel: 2-42-58.

Movie Theater Amur Used to be Shadrinski Cathedral, but they took off the spires before conversion. Lenina 58, corner of Chaikovskovo.

Philharmonic Pionirskaya 1, corner of Lenina. Tel: 2-42-05.

Puppet Theater (*Teatr Kukol*) 62 Shevchenko St. Tel: 2-73-37.

Movie Theater Rossiya 171/179 Zeyskaya. Tel: 2-47-76.

City Beach The main city beach is right on the Amur, where the bank widens (starting near the end of Trudavaya St.), although locals recommend sandier beaches along the Zeya (see Around Blago). The Amur has a very swift current, so be careful when swimming!

PLACES OF WORSHIP

Russian Orthodox Church Originally founded as the Catholic Church, it was reconsecrated Russian Orthodox in

1945, and has been open and maintained since the war.   The iconostasis is beautifully painted, with candles lighting the faces of icons.   A sign outside lists the times of daily services. Gorkovo 133 (just off Pionirskaya).

TRANSPORTATION

The **airport** is only about 20 minutes from town.   At present it is very small, with rudimentary facilities and no international section.   However, a new wing is being built, anticipated to be completed in 1995, so expect services to improve (and prices to go up!). Bus No. 101 goes to the airport from in front of the Univermag. Airport info 2-50-02.

City Aeroflot Office Lenina 193. Open 8-19 (13-14). Tel: 2-59-02.

Aeroflot booth in Yublieinaya Hotel Tel: 9-35-85.

Bus Station (*Avtovokzal*) corner of 50 Let Oktyabrya and Krasnoarmeiskaya. Take bus Nos. 1, 5 or 7, or trolley No. 1. Tel: 2-69-15.

Train Station (*vokzal*) Overnight train to Khabarovsk takes about 17 hours.   Stantsionnaya St. and 50 Let Oktyabrya. Station: 2-24-07. You can also order tickets by phone for home delivery, for an extra 5% service charge.   To get to the train station take bus No.1 or trolley No.1.

River Port (*rechnoi vokzal*) This is a small green floating building, which is usually "parked" on the Amur near the end of Kalinina.   Various boats and ferries leave from here: ferries to small villages on the Zeya and Amur rivers, and a larger ship takes a 2-week cruise to Nikolaevsk-na-Amure, where the Amur enters the Sea of Okhotsk.   Schedules change, so check out current times and destinations at the dock. Tel: 2-46-95.

AROUND BLAGOVESCHENSK

Blagoveschensk is so small that you can quickly "do" the town, but in order to really appreciate the region you should make the effort to get out of town and into the surrounding countryside.   The northern half of the region is covered in permafrost and offers a contrast to the southern regions with the milder climate. There are pine forests, lakes and meadows, not to mention the sandy beaches along the Zeya. It is easier to get anywhere by car, but since most Russians cannot yet afford that luxury, most spots can be reached by bus.

Vladimirovski Lakes   Only about half an hour from the city, the Vladimirovski lakes are a series of 4 lakes set in lovely meadows. If you want to stay for a while, there is a *dom otdykha* (rest house) by the first lake. Locals tend to favor the 2nd and 3rd lakes for picnics and summer outings.

Mukhinka   Hills surround this lake area and there is a *dom otdykha* here as well, providing a nice retreat from the city. About 1 hour from town, it can be reached by bus from the main bus station.

Tourbaza Snezhinka   In winter you can take bus No. 13 to its last stop, which is this cross-country ski base.   There is a small building where you can rent skis.   The area around the *baza* is lovely during the summer as well, and there is a spot called *Peschannaya Ozero* (Sandy Lake) which is especially picturesque. Ask for directions at Snezhinka.

If you don't want to go too far afield, but still want to feel like you are away from the bustle of the city, there are **sandy beaches** along the Zeya. The best are on the other side of the Zeya from the city, across the bridge.

The **Muriyovka National Park** is the first non-government national park and is home to many animals that are in the Russian Red Book of endangered species, including cranes and storks.   Groups interested in visiting the park should contact Yuri Darman in Blagoveschensk, Relochnii pereulok 12-510. Yuri can be contacted by email at amur@glas.apc.org.

BELOGORSK

Founded as Alexandrovskoye in 1860, Belogorsk is a sleepy town of 75,300 on the Tom River. Known mostly as a railway stop on Trans-Siberian Railroad with a connection to Blagoveschensk (108 km away), and for its 18 meter high silo, Belogorsk's main industries are agricultural machinery, building materials, and food production.

Code for calling Belogorsk from outside the city: **24101.**

Hotel Zarya   The only hotel in town.   Very cheap. Partizanskaya 23. Tel: 2-37-50.

CHITINSKAYA OBLAST

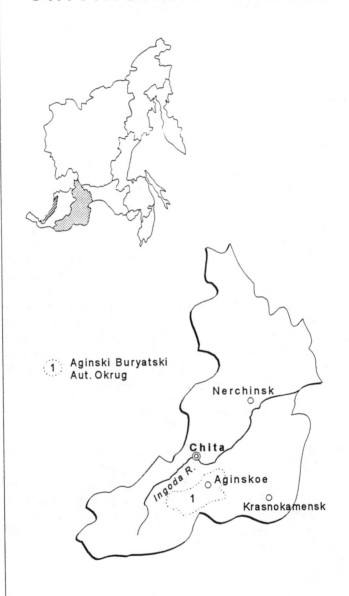

CHAPTER 5

CHITINSKAYA OBLAST

Interest in the Chitinskaya Oblast first arose due to the silver mines of Nerchinsk. Today the area is still known for its mining, but agriculture and the railroad also play a central role in the economy. Unfortunately, subsidies are now harder to come by and the mining and agricultural industries have fallen on hard times. Currently adjusting to unemployment and the sharp decrease in financial support from the federal government, the Chitinskaya Oblast is struggling to reshape its identity in the new market economy, but with its natural resources and strategic location is looking to become one of the leading industrial and commercial areas in the Transbaikal (or Zaibaikal) region.

For the traveler, the region offers mountains and rolling hills, medicinal resorts and large stretches of untouched forests. Chita is best visited in the spring when the *bagulniki* (purple rhododendrons) are flowering, and summer when the trees are green and one can go swimming in the various lakes of the area. In the winter, the region is subject to bitter cold fronts.

Although it shares a long border with Mongolia, Chita does not share the same cultural ties with its southern neighbor as Buryatiya does. With the exception of the Aginski Okrug, Chita is thoroughly Russified.

<u>CHITA</u>

HISTORY

In the middle of the 17th century Russia was in the middle of fulfilling its "manifest destiny," its push to the east. Cossack detachments in search of land and glory pushed eastward, bringing the territories they found under the rule of the Tsar.

Chita was founded in 1653 by Pyotr Beketov, a noble's son, as a wintering spot on the banks of the river Chita for his Cossack detachment.

There are many theories as to where the name Chita comes from. Some say it is from the Evenk word "*chata,*" meaning clay, others claim it comes from the Uigur word "*chyt,*" meaning water. Whatever the case may be, it is clear that the name of the river and subsequently the town was borrowed by the Russian pioneers from the local population.

The outpost served as a military base to further explore and conquer new lands, but civilian traders and settlers also came to Chita, albeit very slowly. By 1690 the population stood at "4 residents and 65 head of cattle." Most newcomers chose to settle in other places along the river and by 1710 there were 18 trading and military outposts stretched along the Chita and Ingoda rivers. In 1726 Chita became a station on the pony express mail service to western Russia. Later, the long arm of the Tsar was extended and a customs and taxation office was set up.

Chita fortress in 1798 (Reconstruction by V. Nemerov)

In 1762, more than a century after its founding, Chita's population stood at only 73, testimony to the harsh living conditions found there. The city and region continued to grow slowly, bolstered infrequently by exiles and criminals, and the occasional merchant. By 1823 Chita had a population of 300 people with the whole region numbering 3000 spread among 44 settlements. Chita would have continued to be known as a backwater trading and military post, were it not for the Decemberists.

The failed uprising of December 14, 1825 in St. Petersburg resulted in the exile of 85 revolutionaries, or "Decemberists" as they came to be known, to the Chita region. Some of the exiles were followed by their wives, who were stripped of their noble titles and privileges by the Tsar. Although this did not dissuade them from following their husbands, it did go a long way to ensuring that the Decemberists would become a romantic legend in Russian history. The majority of the exiles were of noble extraction and well educated and did much to raise the cultural and educational level of the local inhabitants by teaching various classes, organizing musical parties, introducing new ideas and so on.

In 1851 Chita received another large boost to its growth when it was named the capital of the Transbaikal region. This region was separated from the Irkutsk administrative region and Chita became an essential communication, transport and administrative center. In the next 10 years Chita grew from 650 to 3140 inhabitants, of which 1/4 were soldiers and government officials. By 1876 the number of soldiers and government officials had grown to 1/2 the total population.

Although an administrative/population center, Chita was still in most respects a frontier town. The *Asian Rus* newspaper described Chita as having "wooden, monotonous, homely houses and long unpainted fences, gray with age, which give the town a dirty look. The unwashed streets, wide ruts and holes make walking or driving at night impossible. Livestock and dogs walk freely, dirtying the streets..."

Despite the grim description of Chita, the town grew and slowly added new institutions. In 1865 a high school was built. By 1887 Chita boasted 5 churches, a synagogue, city social club and 3 private libraries. In 1894 a city park was founded, in 1895 a public library. In 1899 the first train arrived in Chita.

By 1905 Chita numbered 42,795 citizens, and as one of the larger cities in the Transbaikal region, the social unrest which swept through Russia did not leave the city untouched. On January 9, 1905, a demonstration of workers was fired on in St. Petersburg and in response, the Social Democrat Party in Chita organized protests and demonstrations. These demonstrations continued throughout the year, intensifying in character. By November, arms were being distributed among the workers in preparation for an uprising against the local administration. On November 22 the revolutionaries struck and overthrew the city authorities, gaining control over the city.

Government forces were immediately sent from the east and west to crush the uprising. When they arrived, the revolutionaries decided not to fight the regular troops with their hastily formed militias and on January 27, 1906, the "Chita Republic" fell. The ringleaders were shot, the other activists sentenced to hard labor camps. As throughout all of Russia, the flame of the workers movement would lie dormant, but not extinguished, to burst forth anew in 1917.

After the events of 1905, Chita became a city of contrasts. The city boomed in trade and production, as companies from around Russia and the world came to Chita to do business. One could buy fish from Vladivostok, bananas from China, toys from Hamburg and even coconuts from southern climes. There were representatives of banks and trading houses from as far away as New York, Greece, Paris and Vienna.

On the other hand, despite its economic growth, Chita still lacked many amenities that cities half its size had acquired long ago. The first hospital opened only in 1904 with 50 beds, and a second was built which had space for 30 patients, but for a city of more than 40,000 inhabitants, it was a far cry from what was needed. Only in 1906 did Chita receive electricity to light the streets and houses at night and as late as 1920 Chita was described as a "dusty, dirty city with dead cats and dogs in the streets, with holes and trash piles on the sidewalks."

After the October Revolution and the establishment of Soviet power, all banks, transport, communications and gold mining operations were nationalized. Supported by a local Cossack regiment, the Soviets ruled for six months until the arrival of the Czechoslovak legion which entered the city in late August 1918. For the next two years Chita either "lived under the White terror" or was "defended from the Red devils," depending on which side you were on. Ultimately the Whites were defeated, and Chita became a Soviet city.

In 1920 Japan agreed to withdraw her troops from the Russian Far East if the area from Lake Baikal to the Pacific was set up as a democratic government, to act as a "buffer zone" between Soviet Russia and Japan. Not willing to risk an all out war, the Democratic Far Eastern Republic was duly set up, with

Chita as its capital. When the last of the Japanese troops left the Primorski Krai, the Far Eastern Republic united with Russia and Soviet power was extended all the way to the Pacific.

In the 1930's Chita was made capital of the Transbaikal Military District and construction of several factories was completed. However it wasn't until 1938 that construction of pipes for bringing water to Chita began; till then this city of almost 70,000 people had relied on wells. During World War II Chita, like many Siberian cities, provided the industrial power to supply the front, pumping out countless tanks, trucks, and other military hardware.

After the war, Chita was closed to foreigners due to its military industries and proximity to the Chinese border. Today, Chita (population 379,000) has opened its doors once again and is looking to regain its international status, lost after the revolution. A proposal to set up a free economic zone in the area to attract foreign capital is being considered, while sister city relationships have been established with Boise, Idaho and Chita, Japan.

The Decemberists

In the first part of the 19th century, popular dissent was growing rapidly against the Tsar. Although Alexander I had started his reign with promises of democratic reform, his regime grew increasingly repressive. Young military officers who had traveled to France and the West during the Napoleonic Wars brought democratic ideas back with them to Russia and became disillusioned when faced with the repressive regime of the Tsar. Secret societies and political parties were formed, based on ideas ranging from introducing reforms to the current system to overthrowing the Tsar and introducing a purely democratic government.

Two such groups of officers and nobles with similar aims joined together into a secret society which pledged to overthrow the ruling government and give Russia a constitution. The group was divided into two factions; the first intended Russia to become a free republic, while the second group, headed by Nikita Muravyov and Kondraty Rylov, planned for a constitutional monarchy. In 1825, Alexander I died and on December 14, the coronation day of his successor, Nicholas, the conspirators struck. The Decemberists, as they came to be known, led some 2000 soldiers to occupy Senate Square in St. Petersburg with the hope of inciting a general revolt. However, the popular uprising did not occur and loyalist troops soon surrounded and crushed the revolutionaries.

The leaders were arrested and sentenced. Five were executed, some were imprisoned, but the majority were sent into Siberia to hard labor exile. The exiles were sent to various regions in Siberia and the Far East, but the majority were sent to Chita. In all, 82 Decemberists were sent to the Chita region to build new prisons and work the Nerchinsk silver mines. Their fame was heightened by the fact that some were followed by their wives into exile, leaving riches, noble titles and even their children behind.

The Decemberists' cause of working for the people did not end with their exile Some taught classes on various subjects to the locals, some helped finance local city projects, and all generally contributed to the societies they lived in. After two years, their leg irons were removed and the famous exiles were able to expand their activities. Some did research on the native flora, fauna, and indigenous tribes, one compiled a Russian-Buryat dictionary, one published a newspaper, and so on. This injection of "Western Russian intelligentsia" is credited with greatly advancing the level of culture and education in Chita and the Transbaikal region in general.

WALKING AROUND TOWN

Chita was laid out in a grid pattern by the Decemberists, supposedly following the grid pattern of St. Petersburg. The resulting regularity of the streets allows you to orient yourself quickly. In general, the points of interest are centrally located, and you could circumnavigate the center of the city in about an hour or so, if you didn't stop off at cafes or shops.

With its wide tree-lined streets and turn-of-the-century architecture, Chita is a pleasure to walk around, no matter where you go. However, if you are looking for a specific "theme" route, then your choice of walking tours can be summarized as follows: for shopping, along Lenina; for historical buildings, along Anokhina or Kalinina; for cafes, along Kalinina; for nature, along Gorkovo. Buses and trolleys run along both Lenina and Kalinina.

A logical starting place for any walking tour is **Lenin Square**. Right in the heart of town, Lenin Square is built on what used to be Cathedral Square, where the Alexander Nevski Cathedral once stood. The stone cathedral was built in the Russian-Byzantine style in 1899, but apparently there were miscalculations in the building measurements and cracks soon appeared. The fate of this cathedral is best summed up by a 1981 Chita guidebook: "In 1924, the movie theater "Atheist" opened in the former cathedral. In 1935 the cathedral was dismantled, and from the bricks of the Cathedral of Obscurity the Soviet people built a Cathedral of Enlightenment—high school No. 4." High school No. 4 can still be seen on Chaikovskova Street, on one side of Lenin Square.

Alexander Nevski Cathedral at the turn of the century

Lenin Square is not only the physical but also the cultural heart of Chita. For parades, concerts and demonstrations, Lenin Square is still the location of choice. A group of honored military pilots was buried here in 1944. In summer the square is filled with trees and has a long series of fountains which cool the air. In winter it is decorated with a New Year's tree and traditional holiday decorations including ice slides.

Lenin Square is bounded by 4 streets—Leningradskaya, Lermontova, Butina and Chaikovskovo. On Butina some older buildings are still preserved. Number 37, a small wood and brick building, was and still is the **main post office**. Built in 1893, it is the only building in Chita which still fulfills its original function.   The post office itself is set back from the street and there is a pleasant little park in front with benches.

You might note that No. 39 across the street, a low gray building, has the arched windows and small tower that you will see on many buildings around town. This building was commissioned by Dmitri Polutov, one of the wealthy merchants in town at the turn of the century.   Born into a merchant family outside Chita, he and his brothers continued their father's trade, expanding into gold mining, coal

Dmitri Polutov

extraction, timber and more. Upon moving to Chita, Dmitri Polutov became an integral part of the city, serving as a member of the bank auditing commission, assisting charities including the Russian Red Cross, serving on various committees, and even founding a church. For all his activities he was awarded medals by the Holy Synod and was one of the few Chita residents listed in the "Honor Book" (Who's Who) of Russian Citizens, issued on the 300th anniversary of the Romanov line.   He was an active member of his adopted city and made sure that all buildings he commissioned harmonized with the historic center of the city. The building at 39 Butina was built in 1907 by F. Ponomarev, an architect whose work is seen throughout the town. At the present time it is the **headquarters of the City Administration**, including the Mayor's office.

City administration building

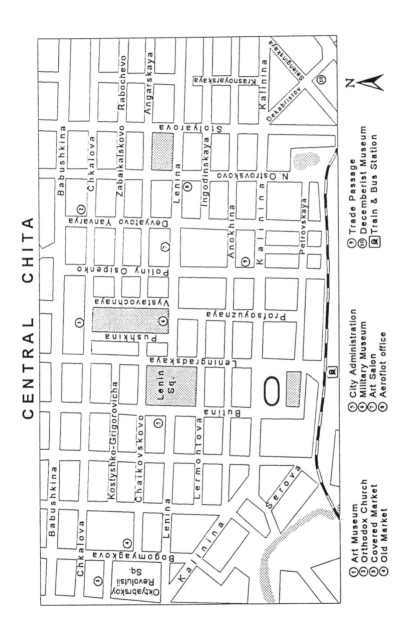

Along Chaikovskovo are the Oblast Administration and the infamous high school No. 4, which now specializes in the Chinese language, and once was visited by Mao Tse Tung. The Hotel Zabaikalye takes up half the Leningradskaya side, while across the street on Leningradskaya is the railway administration.

Walk along Lenina: While in Lenin Square, face the huge pink stone Lenin and turn to your right, walking towards the Zabaikalye Hotel. This will take you onto Lenina Street, the main shopping boulevard. About one block down on your left is a gateway to a small **park**, just behind the officer's club, with tanks from World War II on display and a small monument to Afghan vets. Back on Lenina, continue past the officer's club to the **military museum** at 88 Lenina, which covers the history of the Soviet Army in the Zabaikal region, and includes a candid section on political repression in Chita during the Stalin years. The first floor has a small shop with pins, old coins, and other small memorabilia.

At Lenina 84 at the corner of Osipenko is a frilly peach-colored building, with white angel faces gazing down. This was known as the Shumov palace, built by the Shumov family, brothers who commanded a great fortune due to their success in gold mining. They moved in the highest circles, and in keeping with their exalted status they

A collective farmer, soldier, and worker grace the top of the military museum

ordered the construction of a palace, complete with winter garden and art gallery. Unfortunately, just as construction was nearing completion in 1914, the outbreak of World War I disrupted their plans. During the ensuing years of war and revolution the art treasures "disappeared" as the palace was occupied by various military and government administrations. In 1918, it was here that the delegates to the first Zabaikal meeting of Soviets heard the details of the October Revolution. In the early 20's the building was renamed the "Palace of

Labor." Nowadays, the former palace houses the offices of the Security Ministry, but there are plans to transfer the Kraevecheski (Local History) Museum to this building.

Continuing along Lenina at No. 56 there is an **art salon**, which is your best bet for souvenir shopping (forget the places called "*souveniri*" and "*podarki*" (gifts), which now, more often than not, have refrigerators and electronics).

On the right-hand side of Lenina at No. 65 is the **Argun restaurant**, with a huge sign. A smaller cafe nearby on Ostrovskovo just past the Aeroflot office is *Tsyplyata Tabaka* (roast chicken), with wooden doors and a pleasant interior. Across the street on the left side of Lenina is another park, **"Square of the Decemberists"** (*ploschad Dekabristov*). The **Pushkin Library** is situated toward the back of the park. This library has a literary museum, a foreign book section (bring your passport for ID), and an exhibit on the Decemberists.

From Decemberist Square continue along Lenina straight to Barguzinskaya Street (one block past Stolyarova) and turn right. This will take you to an older part of the city. Turn right on Anokhina street to find the old **Muslim Mosque** at No. 3, built in 1904-06 by the architect Ponomarev. At the present time it simply stands abandoned, although there are rumors of plans to do "something" with it.

Former Muslim mosque on Anokhina

Back on Barguzinskaya, continue one block, then follow the diagonal Selenginskaya street, which leads to Ulitsa Dekabristov. Turn left and you will come to the **Decemberists Museum** (*Muzei Dekabristov*), the former Mikhailo-Archangelskaya church.

Heading back along Selenginskaya, turn left onto Kalinina. A stop in the **Zhemchuzhina restaurant** at No. 2 will refresh you, although there are many more cafes along the way.

Walk along Kalinina: Kalinina street used to be the main boulevard of Old Chita, often called the "Nevski Prospekt" of Chita (after the main boulevard in St. Petersburg). A prestigious address in those days, merchants vied for opportunities to build their shops and complexes in this street. As a result, many buildings from the turn of the century remain to this day.

Coming from the Decemberist Museum you can head straight down Kalinina to the corner of Osipenko, where there are three buildings of note. At No. 56 there is a fancy building which used to be the **Torgovi (trade) Passage**. Built in a unique style with a tower over the curved corner main entrance, the facade was covered in Dutch tile, produced at the local ceramics factory at the turn of the century. The construction of this complex was funded by the merchant Ignatev, a millionaire who had a hand in many construction projects in Chita. The complex itself was owned by Mr. Vtorov, and had a millenary shop and delicatessen, and was conveniently located right near the "Grand Hotel." The Vtorov family lasted through the revolution, transforming their complex into the "Comradship of Vtorov and Sons," and still advertising "always the latest styles of the season!" Now called Torgovi Dom Druzhba ("Friendship House of Trade"), it is completely modern inside, with strange stained glass and reliefs of "happy workers," but little of the high-class imported goods of yesteryear.

Across the street the **Kino Zabaikalets** at No. 69 looks Spanish, with a crenilated roof and carved wood doors depicting fairy tale characters. The inside is also worth looking at.

Back on the right-hand side at No. 58 were city administration offices, which have now been transformed into a bookstore, with a small selection of jewelry and art. At the next corner (Profsoyuznaya), No. 68 Kalinina was the Hotel "Select" and Cafe "Moderne," the first 4-story stone building in the city. Built in 1914 by the merchant Samsonovich, he, too, found his plans disrupted by the war and ensuing revolution. He was forced to flee, leaving his building behind. After his departure the hotel continued to operate, and among its guests the infamous White Guard leader Ataman Semyonov set up his headquarters here. The building now houses departments of the Oblast Administration and the representative office of the President of the Russian Federation.

Across the street at No. 80-86 is the **Dauria Hotel**, named after one of the rivers which flows through the Zabaikal region.

Built in 1907, it was one of the first brick buildings in Chita. At that time it belonged to the merchant Ignatev, and was a whole complex with a hotel and restaurant occupying the top 2 floors, various shops on the ground floor, including a wine store, delicatessen, Viennese coffee shop, and a beer hall in the basement. At the present time the Hotel Dauria still operates, but despite the fact that there is a sign for the restaurant, you will rarely catch it open.

At the next corner (Leningradskaya) you can turn right, back to Lenin Square, or continue straight ahead along Kalinina. About halfway down the block is a new **monument** to "victims of political repression in the 30's and 40's."

Walk along Anokhina: If you enjoy architecture from the turn of the century, then you will want to stroll along Anokhina. This is a quiet residential street, once at the very edge of the early town. On the corner of Leningradskaya and Anokhina is a pink building (No. 74), which has been a government bank since the early days of Chita. The next corner is Profsoyuznaya. Where once was the city park on the outskirts of the town there is now a small **park** dedicated to Anokhin, "secretary of the Dalbyuro TsK RKP" (Central Committee of the Russian Communist Party). One block down on the corner of Osipenko the pink and orange building at No. 56 was built in 1890 by the famous architect Ponomarev. The building was commissioned by a local merchant and cattle-rancher, Mr. Zazovski. He chose the location specifically because it was right across from what was then the trade center of town (now Anokhina square). Because of its desirable location, it was easy for him to find merchants who wanted to rent space from him. Among the shops in this building were a wine merchant, a butcher shop, a bank, an insurance company, and many more. Nowadays students can be seen coming and going to the Agricultural Institute located there.

Across the street at No. 53 was home of the merchant Ignatev, whom we've already met as the owner of the Dauria Hotel complex and the patron of the Torgovi Passage. Despite his millions he was not given to ostentatious shows of wealth, although he did have a wooden sidewalk (a luxury in those days). The house also had a beautiful work of stained glass in the bay window above the front door, which caught the sun at dawn. Right next door he built another building, which he rented out to a Chinese bank. Nowadays this is still a savings bank.

At the next corner, Devyatovo Yanvarya, is a brick building which was owned by Vasily Khlynovski, one of the leading citizens of Chita at the turn of the century and mayor of Chita from 1899-1904. Both a wealthy merchant and a town activist, he was the treasurer of the volunteer fire brigade, was the first to lay wooden sidewalks and cobblestones, and began negotiations for providing Chita with electric street lights. His building had many international firms: a Russian-Chinese bank, a St. Petersburg insurance company, and a restaurant called "Japan," among others. Nowadays the main occupant in the building is the Oblast book publishing house.

Further along Anokhina, at the very start of the street is No. 3, the former Muslim Mosque (see Walk along Lenina).

Walk along Gorkovo: If you are in the mood for a quiet stroll through nature, head for Babushkina and Gorkovo (about 3 blocks north of Lenin Square) and look for the T-34 tank. The **Tank Komsomolets** stands at the beginning of Gorkovo, which is a lane completely covered by arching trees. When these trees are in bloom, you can stroll along in the heart of the city and breath in the aroma of springtime. This path travels uphill about 4 long blocks, taking you to Novobulvarnaya. Here you can either turn right, and after a couple of blocks of housing projects you will come to **ZaBVO stadium,** which is also a pleasant park for strolling, or turn left until you come to Zhuravleva. If you turn right here, you will head into the hills toward the **city cemetery**. Russian cemeteries do not have rolling lawns of green grass, but rather are seemingly packed with benches and small tables by each grave so that the family can come and share special occasions with their loved ones. Worth a look.

PRACTICAL INFORMATION

Code for calling Chita from outside the city: **30222.**
Information when calling from inside the city: **09.**
Information from outside the city: **302-99-09111.**
Committee for International Affairs and Foreign Economic Relations *(Komitet po mezhdunarodnim delam i vneshneekonomicheskim svyazam)* Chita is one of the few cities whose administration is actually gearing up for tourism. New

books have been published on the history of Chita, and a small guide-book in English for tourists is in the works. The Committee for International Relations is interested in creating and strengthening ties between Chita and other countries. The last line of their proposed guidebook states: "Dear foreign tourists, if you have any difficulties, the city administration can assist you" at: Butina 39, room 16. Tel: 6-38-82.

Main office of Central Bank of Russia, Commercial Bank "Zabaikalski" Anokhina 74. Tel: 3-37-42, 6-87-02.

Weather Bureau Forecasts in Russian. Tel: 6-77-79, recording of tomorrow's forecast: 6-42-55.

Main Post Office For mail service only. Butina 37. Open Mon-Fri 8-20, Sat, Sun 8-18. Tel: 3-41-43.

Business Center Has *zheton* telephones (*avtomati,* where you can dial yourself), or you can order a call through the operator. You can also send a fax. Chaikovskovo 24. Tel: 6-84-93.

Post Office No. 4 (at Train Station) Has a *peregovorni punkt* where you can order long distance or international calls through the operator, pay the cashier, and wait for your call to come through. Open round the clock. Tel: 3-51-40.

HOTELS

Hotel of the Oblast Administration (Oblispolkom) Right in the center of town but on a quiet side street, this hotel was previously open only to Party members. It is now open to anyone with a *zayavka* (application) filled out by a government organ. The administration is polite and helpful, the rooms are clean and spacious. Moderate. Unadvertised, it is right next to the Dauria Hotel on Profsoyuznaya. Tel: 6-23-97.

Krasni Drakon Motel (Red Dragon Motel) A Chinese/Russian joint venture. The rooms are small but clean, and most of the staff are polite and helpful. There is a small private sauna, which you can order in advance, and a dimly lit restaurant. Also has a gas station (hence the title "Motel"). Come by car, or bus No. 14. Ask the bus driver to tell you when to get out, since the bus stop is beyond the motel. Moderate. Ulitsa Magistralnaya (on the road to the airport). Tel: 1-19-73 (motel), 1-42-88 (restaurant).

Hotel Tourist A large hotel farther from the center. Moderate. Babushkina 42. Tel: 6-52-70.

Hotel Ingoda A large State-run hotel located right across the street from the Drama Theater. Has a restaurant on the ground floor. Inexpensive. Profsoyuznaya 23. Tel: 3-32-22.

Hotel Zabaikalye This is the main state-run hotel, and the place you are most likely to be put up. If you have any choice in the matter, avoid this hotel. The state employees are uninterested in your welfare, and the atmosphere is dismal. Inexpensive. Leningradskaya 27. Tel: 6-45-20.

Hotel Dauria Rude, hostile Soviet service. Seedy characters in the hall knock on your door or call late at night. Cafe never seems to work. Small souvenir kiosk and exchange office in lobby. Inexpensive. Profsoyuznaya 17. Tel: 6-23-65, 6-23-88.

Hotel Taiga Dormitory-style hotel with shared "conveniences." Perfect for the budget-conscious backpacker. Cheap. Lenina 75. Tel: 3-90-48.

FOOD

Chita seems to be big on fixed-price meals with set menus. This offers you limited choice, but does tend to speed up service.

Restaurant Krasni Drakon At the Krasni Drakon Motel. Dimly lit and with loud music, they offer a wide selection of appetizers and entrees. The catch is that despite the fact that the restaurant is open until 10 pm, the kitchen closes at 8, so you must make a reservation during the day. (Some of the staff speak English). Expensive. Ulitsa Magistralnaya. Open 12-22. Tel: 1-42-88.

Restaurant Moran Supposedly a Korean restaurant, they tend to be out of the one Korean dish they offer, although the standard Russian fare is decent. The restaurant is huge, with a loud band. After 6 pm there is a cover charge, so to get your money's worth you should dance up a storm with the rest of the crowd. There is a small bar near the entrance. Moderate. Bogomyakova 23. Tel: 3-92-41.

Cafe Tsyplyata Tabaka Small and quiet, serving a set menu of roast chicken. Nicely set tables, good atmosphere. Polite service, inexpensive. Ostrovskovo 20. Open 11-21 (15-17). Tel: 3-97-39.

Cafe Odessa This small cafe is set back from the street, hidden in an apartment building. Each table is in its own small alcove, offering dining in privacy. The set menu provides quick service, plus the waitresses are attentive. Moderate. Lenina 120. Open 10-22.

Ingoda Cafe Walk through the grimy entrance hall to the brightly painted restaurant. Large paintings of local scenery and pink curtains fail to enliven this cafe. The Ingoda has a fixed menu for lunch and dinner, which makes for fast service. Moderate prices. Profsoyuznaya 23.

Cafe Skazka Quiet and clean, offering ice cream and shakes. Kalinina 64. Open 9-21.

Stolovaya (Cafeteria) in the Pedagogical Institute This *stolovaya* is mainly for students of the institute, and as students 'round the world tend to be poor, the prices are very cheap. Large selection of quick-to-pick-up items (pizza, cakes, sodas), although since there is only one person behind the counter, the line moves slowly. Get there by noon, before it fills up. Cheap. Butina 129. Open 11-14.

Restaurant Argun A clean interior with flowers and wall decorations. Set menu. Moderate. Lenina 65. Open 12-23 (17-18). Tel: 2-46-58, 3-90-22.

Cafe Tsinsya This cafe is dirt cheap but dirty. The draw is that the service is immediate. Despite the fact that it is run by Chinese, the main dish offered is Russian *pelmeni*. However, there are also fried peanuts and Chinese cold noodles (don't expect sesame sauce!). You have to pay a small deposit for your forks and glasses. Cheap. Kalinina 62. Open 11-20 (15-16).

Restaurant Zabaikalye The only reason for mentioning this restaurant is to warn you away from it. The food is unremarkable, the staff is more surly than usual, and the hours are unreliable. In the words of the administrator at 8 pm, "I don't care what the sign says, we're closed!" Supposedly open till 11 pm. Leningradskaya 36. Tel: 3-74-33, 6-12-41.

Cafe Zhemchuzhina Kalinina 2. Open 12-23 (16-17).

Restaurant Tourist Babushkina 42. Tel: 6-59-09, cafe/bar 6-59-84.

SHOPPING

Art Salon (*Zabaikalski Khudozhestvenni Salon*) This art salon offers jewelry, lacquer boxes, and paintings by local artists. A favorite scene is of the woods in springtime, with *bagulniki* (purple rhododendrons) in bloom under the pines. If you are lucky enough to visit during *bagulniki* season, you can take home a reminder of your travels. If you came in another season, these paintings might just encourage you to return! Lenina 56. Open 10-19 (14-15). Tel: 6-16-19.

Dom Knigi   State bookstore.   If you read Russian, this is the place to go.   The Chita city government has recently issued two new books on the history of the city.   One, called *Vsya Chita* (All Chita) is a reissue of a 1923 city guide.   The other, simply <u>Chita</u>, has historical notes and pictures of buildings and people who influenced the early life of the city.   There is also a small book of the memoirs of Princess Volkonskaya, wife of one of the Decemberists.   Right next door (through a separate entrance) is another department with paintings and crafts by local artists, and a small selection of jewelry.   Kalinina 58. Open 9-18 (14-15), closed Sun. Tel: 2-30-23.

Bukinist   Although "Bukinist" usually has antique books, the oldest item around here is the building itself, which has elegant, ornate wrought iron and an interesting brick facade. Devyatovo Yanvarya 35. Tel: 6-62-11.

Military Univermag   Being such a military city, the military department store is clean and well-stocked.   Check for the Stalin watches.   The military section has an interesting photo display of Soviet medals on the wall.   The store also has household goods and electronics. Kalinina 123.   Open 10-19 (14-15), closed Sun. Tel: 6-42-14.

Voennaya Kniga (Military Bookstore)   No military books, but presumably a selection of what the military likes to read. (Western detective novels seem popular).   Lenina 111.   Open from 10-19 (14-15), closed Sun. Tel: 3-53-79.

TsUM (Central Department Store)   2 floors of fabrics, dresses, household goods, and the occasional Chita city pin or other small souvenirs. Corner of Lenina and Vystavochnaya.

Filatleia   Blocks of stamps, plus newspapers, magazines and stationary supplies. Chkalova 135. Tel: 3-08-16.

Rubin   Small jewelry store with a selection of gold, silver and precious stones. Zhuravleva 16. Tel: 3-39-48.

MARKETS

Covered Market   For your food needs.   Babushkina 157. Tel: 2-18-88.

Old Market (*Stary Rynok*) Chinese flea market and Chinese-made goods. On corner of Bogomyakova and Chaikovskovo, right near the philharmonic.

MUSEUMS

Kraevecheski Museum At the present time the museum building at Babushkina 113 is under reconstruction, and it has been proposed that in any case the entire collection will be relocated to Lenina 84, but when this will happen and when the museum will reopen is uncertain. You can address questions to 3-55-30.

Art Museum (*Khudozhestvenni Muzei*) A modern building with three floors. Unfortunately, economic constraints have led the museum to lease out the ground floor to an electronics shop, and part of the second floor to a furniture dealer, but the remaining space is occupied by interesting art, with paintings by local artists, native crafts of indigenous ethnic groups, and recently they had items on loan from the Aginski Datsan (Buddhist temple). A small "salon" on the ground floor has wood carvings, jewelry, and old coins for sale. Chkalova 120. Open from 10-18, closed Mon and Tue. Tel: 3-85-36 (museum), 3-85-36 (salon).

Decemberists Museum (*Muzei Dekabristov*) The Decemberist Museum is housed in the former Mikhailo-Archangelskaya Church. Built in 1771, it is the only building in Chita remaining from the 18th century. The Decemberists Paulina Gebel and Ivan Annenkov were married here and their lives were immortalized in Alexander Dumas' novel "The Fencing Master." Dekabristov 3b. Take bus No. 17 along Kalinina to last stop. Open Tue-Sun 10-18. Tel: 3-48-03.

Decemberists Museum

Military Museum Traces the history of the military in the Zabaikal region, from the Cossack troops who founded the first fort to Afghanistan. There are exhibits on the revolution, a large World War II section including a diorama, and a section on political repression under Stalin. On the ground floor there is a small shop which sells old coins, bills, and military pins. Lenina 86. Open 10-18 Wed-Fri, 10-17 Sat, Sun, closed Mon and Tue. Tel: 2-41-32.

Lenin Museum As of the summer of '94 this museum still exists, tucked away in the Pedagogical Institute. Chkalova 140. Tel: 6-89-22.

ENTERTAINMENT

Drama Theater Offers a full range of performances, from classics to modern authors. Profsoyuznaya 26. Tel: 3-39-75.

Puppet Theater (*Teatr Kukol*) Performances start at 10 am. Ticket booth open 9-15. Verkholenskaya 2. Tel: 3-58-69.

Philharmonic On the edge of town, near October Revolution square. Due to re-open in 1995. Bogomyakova 23. Tel: 2-42-56, 2-46-94.

Movie Theater *Udokan* Lenina 79, Tel: 3-09-69.

Movie Theater *Zabaikalets* Kalinina 69, Tel: 3-62-53.

Casino 777 Has a bar, restaurant and casino. Bar open 24 hours, every day. Restaurant and casino open 22-6, closed Mon. Stolyarova 44. Tel: 3-12-30.

Public Banya No. 3 Separate halls for men and women, 1 hour sessions. Chaikovskovo 28. Open from 9-21. Tel: 3-17-22.

Hang gliding Club (*Deltaplanni Klub*) This active club meets regularly to hang glide through the hills and over the lakes around Chita. They give lessons which last 1 to 2 weeks, and can offer "rides" in two-seaters. Hang gliders for sale and for rent. Kalinina 107. Tel: 6-04-68, fax: 6-84-93 (write: attention Deltaplanni Klub).

Neptune Swimming Pool Offers monthly membership with classes for children during the day, 45-minute open sessions for adults from 18:30-20, Mon-Sat. Mezhdurechiye, near Locomotive Stadium. Take trolley Nos. 2 or 3 to "stadium" stop. Tel: 6-34-25.

Locomotiv Stadium Chita's soccer team "Locomotiv" plays here, check signboards in town for schedule. Mezhdurechiye. Trolley Nos. 2 or 3 to "stadium" stop. Tel: 2-30-28.

ZaBVO Stadium Well-maintained sports stadium for military teams. Novobulvarnaya 1. Trolley No. 2 runs from outside the Stadium along Novobulvarnaya to Butina, then to the train station. Tel: 99-25-12.

Trud Stadium Leningradskaya 1, across from train station. Tel: 2-31-81.

OTHER SIGHTS

Tank "Komsomolets Zabaikalya" Chita was an industrial powerhouse during World War II, manufacturing tanks and other military hardware and shipping it to the front in great quantities. This is a T-34 tank, considered to be one of the best of World War II, which contributed greatly to the Soviet victory over Germany. This tank is a monument to the Komsomolets Zabaikal tank column sent from Chita to the front. Babushkina and Gorkovo.

Memorial Complex Large entertainment park and memorial complex in honor of "military and labor glory of Zabaikalye" during World War II. Visit the eternal flame, flanked by statues and military hardware from the war. There is also a ferris wheel and a children's railroad (run by children, it works during summer holidays) which travels around the park, or out along the river toward dacha territory. Closed Monday. Bus Nos. 4, 6, 14, 17, 18, 19 from the train station all run along Lenina and past the complex, but the best stop is before you even see the entrance archway to the park. So as not to get carried across the river and have to hike back, ask the bus driver to let you off at *park pobedy*.

Fire Station Built in 1903 by Ponomarev, this two-story building with a bell tower used to be the small town jail. Currently used as a fire station, there are plans to turn it into a museum of the history of the Zabaikal militia. Chkalova 116 (corner of Osipenko).

PLACES OF WORSHIP

Around the turn of the century there were more than 20 places of worship in Chita, including a synagogue, mosque and

Buddhist Datsan (temple). Most didn't last through the 20's and 30's, but you can still see the synagogue building (at Ingodinskaya and Stolyarova) and the mosque (at No. 3 Anokhina). The only active church at the present time is the **Russian Orthodox**. Originally Roman Catholic, it was built in 1851 to "Anna, Peter and Paul." Chkalova 94 (corner of Devyatovo Yanvarya).

OTHER

Center of Eastern Medicine   Offers acupuncture and "vacuum massage" (a form of "cupping"). Lenina 109. Tel: (registration) 6-65-20.

TRANSPORTATION

Airport About 30 minutes from downtown Chita. Take the No. 4 express bus from the train station or from in front of the Zabaikalye Hotel. Runs frequently.

The International Hall is the pretty, small classical building to the left. Between international flights there is often no one in the hall except for one guard, who may well tell you to go to the "regular" (main) hall (called the "*obschi zal*").   Be forewarned, at the present time "international" passengers (that means all foreigners) are ONLY allowed to register in the international hall. Plus, the international hall is a much more comfortable place to sit than the regular hall. If there is no one around, knock on the door or ring the bell by the small door off to the right. This is not a place to be shy. If necessary, go to the dispatcher in the main hall, and they can inform the international staff that a foreign passenger has arrived for a flight, and the hall will then be opened to you. It is well heated, there are comfortable couches, and a small buffet.

If you have the time (and, as any hard-core traveler in Russia knows, your flight is likely to be delayed by weather, fuel shortages, or any number of reasons), take a turn around the main hall. There are many kiosks, book shops, and a small cafe. There is also a post office on the second floor, where you can make long distance calls. If you order a call through the lady at the desk, you will probably wait about one hour for the call to come through. You can also buy small tokens (*zhetoni*) at the counter to use in the automatic phones. Each token lasts about

30 seconds, depending on where you are calling. These tokens are particularly useful if your flight is repeatedly delayed and you are expecting someone to meet you. Also keep in mind that the desk closes occasionally for accounting, so if you plan to make a few calls, be sure to lay in a supply of tokens. Airport Information 4-29-24.

Aeroflot City Office The main office for buying plane tickets. Only one window serves foreigners, so look for the carefully hidden sign, or ask at the information desk (*spravochni bureau*). Lenina 55. Tel: 3-43-81 (info).

Train and Bus Stations The transportation center of the city is the Chita II train station (*vokzal*), at the start of Butina Street. (Chita I train station is in the suburbs). At the *vokzal* you can catch long distance trains to Moscow, Vladivostok, or Peking, or suburban trains to nearby towns and villages. The bus station (*avtovokzal*) is to the left as you face the station square. Schedules inside list destinations and departure times. If you are planning a bus trip, check the schedule the day before, since some buses run only twice daily: early morning and late evening.

Bureau for ordering train tickets Tel: 3-21-87, 97-51-87.

Train Station Information Tel: 3-21-19, 97-51-19.

Bus station *(Avtovokzal)* Dispatcher 3-68-97.

To order a **taxi** call 3-04-07. Taxis also wait by the *vokzal*.

AROUND CHITA

Chita is situated in a scenic area which pleased even the critical Anton Chekhov. In the summer of 1890, during his travels around Siberia, he stopped off in Chita. Although he wasn't overly impressed with the city, he did enjoy the countryside. In <u>From Siberia</u> he wrote, "Zabaikalye is wonderful... a mixture of Switzerland, the Don, and Finland." It is definitely recommended to get out into the countryside while you are in the area. For those with minimal free time, a taxi can speedily take you anywhere you want to go, for a price. For the intrepid traveler with more time and a limited budget, check out the train and bus stations. Local transportation is extremely inexpensive.

There are also many mineral springs in the area, widely touted at having curative properties for all sorts of ailments from skin diseases, to arthritis, to neurological problems.

Chitakurort Agency A *kurort* is a kind of health spa or curative center, and this agency can arrange a stay at any of the nearby spas—Darasun, Shivanda, Yamarovka, or Urguchan. You can stay for just one week, or for a full treatment of 24 days. Treatments consist of "taking the waters" and enjoying the clean air, as well as various "curative procedures." The spas are located from 20 to 200 km from Chita, and different locations are recommended for various ailments. Some take children. Consult with the representative for the spa which fits your ills. Angarskaya 15. Tel: 3-23-79, 3-19-24.

Titov Hills Located just outside the city, the Titov hills offer a fine view of the surrounding area and Chita itself. There is also a monument to those who were shot in the uprising of 1905.

Lake Kenon Located just outside the city, Lake Kenon has a convenient beach. Unfortunately, each year industry encroaches on the lake—there is a factory on one side, and some people discourage actually swimming, but the beaches are still full of sunbathers. Take bus Nos. 17 or 18 and ask for the *plyazh*.

Atamanovka A nice half-day trip out of the city is to Atamanovka, a small town 18 km from Chita. The bus leaves the Chita bus station frequently (check schedule inside), and drives through the countryside, passing dachas, fields and pine forest (late May - early June is *bagulniki* season, the most colorful, with purple bushes under the pines). As you approach Atamanovka you'll see more houses again, but stay on the bus to the very last stop, which is by a stream leading to the river. Cross the bridge, turn left, and head to the river. You'll find locals sunbathing, swimming and fishing in this scenic spot. If you want a picnic, bring your lunch along, as the village store is poorly stocked. The bus heads back to the city again in about 20 minutes, or just hang around for a couple of hours till the next bus comes.

Nikishikha River If you're looking for a shady spot, along the way to Atamanovka the road crosses the river Nikishikha, a favorite stop among the locals for cookouts. The river is highest in the spring, fed by the melting snows of the Daurski mountain range, but can fall quite low in the summer, when there is little rain. The bus stop in either direction is just past the river, but is not an obligatory stop, so ask the driver in advance to let you off there.

Lizhnaya Baza (ski base)   Offers cross-country skis for rent, and offers some good trails in winter.   Kaidalovskaya 37. Tel: 3-56-73.

About 50 kilometers from Chita is **Lake Arakhlei**. A nice place to swim, sunbathe, or just unwind from the city. Buses run twice daily from the bus station, make sure you confirm when the last bus returns. About 1/2 way to the lake at the top of the Yablonnovo hills you will pass a Buddhist prayer spot, noticeable by the strips of cloth tied to the trees. Prayers are written on these cloths and then tied to trees, preferably on hills to be closer to God, in the hope that the breeze and fortune will turn their way.

The small town of **Krasnokamensk** in the southeast of the region is of little note except for the legend that Genghis Khan and his great treasures are buried here.

The **Aginski Autonomous Okrug** is an enclave of ethnic Buryats inside Chita. Aginskoe, the capital of the district, is noted for its Datsan where students learn about Buddhism and Tibetan medicine. There is also a mountain in the area that is considered to be one of the 7 holiest Buddhist places in the world.

REPUBLIC OF BURYATIYA

Ust Barguzin

Turka

Lake Baikal

Uda R.

Arshan

Selenga R.

Ulan-Ude

Kyakhta

- - - - - RR

CHAPTER 6

THE REPUBLIC OF BURYATIYA

Land of epic heroes and legends, Buryatiya once formed part of the greater Mongolian Empire that controlled much of the known world. Today, although Buryatiya is part of the Russian Federation, you will find a culture very distinct from other regions of Eastern Siberia and the Russian Far East. After a long period of neglect, ties are being strengthened once again with Mongolia and a revival of Buryat culture and traditions is also making its presence felt throughout the region. Unfortunately, as the culture has flourished, the economy is seeing hard times. Long a military industrial production region, Buryatiya is seeing slow conversion, with the result that unemployment is high. However, in June of 1994, Buryatiya chose its first democratically elected president, who is promising to lead the republic back to economic stability and better times.

The Buryats are a minority in their own republic, representing about 24% of the population. The republic is unique in that it is one of the few places in the former Soviet Union where the Russians and the local populace bear no ill will toward each other. You will not hear discussions of the "Buryat question" or see demonstrations demanding that Russians leave Buryatiya. For better or worse, Buryatiya has chosen to stay within the Russian Federation and work together with the Russians to create a better future.

RELIGION

Buryatiya (including the Buryat enclave near Chita) differs from the rest of the Far East in that it is the center of Buddhism in Russia. Specifically it is the *Gelugpa* (School of Virtue) which is practiced, a part of the Northern Mahayana branch of Buddhism. The Northern Mahayana branch is based in Tibet and recognizes the Dalai Lama as its cultural and spiritual head. A lama is a spiritual teacher and the word lama means "yellow," which is the color of the priests' caps.

Buddhism was introduced to Buryatiya when it was part of the Great Mongol Empire. In 1576, Buddhism in its Mahayana form was declared the state religion, and became a strong political power within the empire. Even as Buryatiya drew closer to Russia and the star of the Mongolian Empire waned, Buddhism continued to be a force. In 1712 its position was strengthened further in Buryatiya by the arrival of 150 Tibetan and Mongolian lamas fleeing from fighting in Mongolia. In 1741, by which time Buryatiya was considered a part of the Russian Empire, Tsarina Elizabeth officially recognized Buddhism in Russia. By the turn of the century there were said to be 47 datsans (Buddhist temples) functioning in Buryatiya, with the main one Hambinsky Datsan in Gusinozersk.

During the 1930's Buddhism was discouraged, as were many religions. Lamas were imprisoned, their followers persecuted, and all the datsans were either destroyed or put to non-religious purposes. It was only in 1972 that a new datsan was constructed in Ivolginsk, which today is the center for Buddhism in Buryatiya and the CIS.

In the last few years Buddhism has experienced a revival in Buryatiya and other parts of Russia. New datsans are being constructed, and older ones are being restored. Schools for the study of Tibetan medicine and Tibetan language have also opened. The 14th Dalai Lama, Tyenzin Gyatsu, visited Buryatiya in 1991 to mark the 250th anniversary of Buddhism in Russia, and visited again in 1993. Traditional Buryat Buddhist holidays are also being celebrated more openly and a general revival of Buddhist culture, repressed in the 1930's and 70's, is being experienced throughout Buryatiya.

THE BURYATS

The Buryats are a Mongol-speaking people located in Buryatiya, the Ust-Ordynski Autonomous District (in Irkustkaya Oblast) and the Aginski Autonomous District (in Chitinskaya Oblast). A nomadic herding people before the arrival of Soviet power, the Buryats put up some of the stiffest resistance to early Russian explorers and settlers. Mass emigrations to Mongolia took place during World War I and during the collectivization of the 30's. Connected to Mongolia by ethnic ties and with Tibet by religion, Buryat culture was repressed in the 30's as being nationalistic and anti-Soviet. In 1931, classical Mongolian script was replaced by the Latin alphabet, which was itself replaced by the Cyrillic alphabet in 1939. In the mid 1970's teaching in the Buryat language was prohibited and its use in radio and television broadcasts curtailed. Today, however, Buryatiya is enjoying a renaissance of cultural identity. Buryats now participate in Pan-Mongolian competitions and are expanding cultural and religious ties with their neighbors in Mongolia, Tibet and China.

HISTORY

The Buryats are first mentioned in 13th century Mongol manuscripts listing the different "forest peoples" that were subjugated by the Mongol armies. For the next 4 1/2 centuries, Buryatiya formed part of the greater Mongolian Empire, sending troops and participating in campaigns that reached to Western Europe.

In the second half of the 17th century, Russian Cossacks and settlers began expanding eastward. As early as 1643 an attempt was made to build settlements in the Transbaikal region, but was defeated by the local Mongol forces in the area. Five years later Ivan Galkin, "the Russian Pissaro," was more successful and founded the settlement of Barguzinsk with his 60 men. The outpost became a fortress from which fur tribute was collected and subsequent military expeditions were sent. The garrison consisted of 70 men, who were changed every two years. Their first and only goal was to collect and store as much fur tribute from the local population as possible. From time to time military expeditions were launched in order to "widen the tax base" from which this tribute was collected.

In 1665, Selenginsk (now Novoselenginsk) was founded on the Selenga River as a military outpost, to be used as a base for future expansion. The location was ideal from a military standpoint, as it was protected on two sides by rivers and on the third side by hills. The settlers needed this protection, for they were constantly threatened and attacked by local Mongolian leaders who resented the Russian intrusion. However, the flow of settlers could not be stopped, and the next year, 1666, Udinsk, modern Ulan-Ude, was founded.

All of these settlements succeeded in surviving and growing, albeit slowly. By 1700 Udinsk could claim only 300 male inhabitants. By the mid 18th century the regional population swelled as the mass exile of the Old Believers began. These religious traditionalists refused to go along with church reforms which would change certain church rituals and bring Russian Orthodoxy more into conformity with Greek Orthodoxy. Rather than go along with practices which they considered heretical, many Old Believers, as they came to be called, were executed or exiled. Exact numbers are hard to find, but it is safe to say that around 25,000 Old Believers came to the Transbaikal region from 1756-1780. These exiles differed from others in that they came and settled in family groups, forming tight-knit communities throughout Buryatiya and the Irkutsk region. By 1811 a regular exile system had been set in place, and the silver mines of Nerchinsk and the Kara gold mines, well-known for their harsh labor regimes and brutal conditions, were well-stocked with laborers.

After the failed uprising in St. Petersburg, 14 Decemberists were exiled to Buryatiya. These Decemberists were nobles and officers, members of the Russian intelligentsia. During their exile, most actively worked in the societies they lived in, publishing newspapers, studying the local flora and fauna, writing ethnographic books on the local tribes in the area, and so on. Due to their work with the people and their ideas of overthrowing the Tsar, Soviet history has made the Decemberists into heroic figures, with monuments and plaques honoring their activities placed throughout the oblast.

In 1900, a series of Tsarist land "reforms" created a wave of discontent among the Buryats and a national liberation movement was born. This movement had three main goals: 1) to halt the seizure of land by the government for redistribution among the non-Buryats, 2) to develop and strengthen Buryat culture, religion and language, 3) to replace the newly installed administrative organs. During the revolution of 1905, a general congress of the Transbaikal Buryats was held to discuss the question of independence and land reform. During World War I, many Buryats were mobilized by the government into Cossack formations to be sent to the front, which caused protests and a mass emigration to Mongolia. This emigration reached such levels as to be commented on by the Russian Minister of Foreign Affairs, but nothing was done to slow or limit the mobilization. On the contrary, in 1916 the Tsar issued a decree allowing for the mobilization of the general population in the rear to provide the needed work force for the war effort.

After the February Revolution in 1917, the national movement was embodied in the Buryat National Committee, or BurNatsKom. The BurNatsKom, although it supported the Provisional Government, also announced its readiness to cooperate with the Soviet government if the sovereignty of Buryat national institutions were left intact, a decision which immediately brought protests from the local Bolsheviks. In the Transbaikal elections of 1917, the BurNatsKom came in 2nd place with 14.7% of the vote, while the Bolsheviks ran third with 9.7%. The winner of the elections by a large margin were the Esers, strong nationalists, with 58.7% of the vote.

Nevertheless, in December of 1917 and January of 1918, some local soviets declared their loyalty to their larger worker soviets and were followed by several railroad stations and Cossack units. On February 5th, the Verkhne-Udinsk Soviet declared itself the head of the western Transbaikal region. In March, the 2nd Baikal Workers' Congress declared that the only recognized authority was the Soviets. At this congress the Buryats and representatives of BurNatsKom were noticeably absent. With the armed uprising of the Czechoslovak legion in 1918, Soviet power in Buryatiya and the Transbaikal region fell. A unit of American troops was stationed in Verkhne-Udinsk until the establishment of the buffer Far Eastern Republic in 1920. In 1922, the Far Eastern Republic was united with Soviet Russia, and the following year the two Buryat autonomous regions in the Chitinskaya and Irkutsk regions were united with the Buryat Autonomous Republic within Soviet Russia.

Under Soviet rule, life in Buryatiya underwent great changes. Collectivization and anti-religion programs were pursued with great fervor, but with varying results. In 1923 in the Buryat Republic there were 44 datsans, 211 Orthodox temples, 81 Old Believers prayer houses, 7 synagogues, 6 mosques as well as 5 Baptist and one Catholic church. By the beginning of World War II, not one was left standing.[1] The 30's were a tragic time for Buryatiya. As the unpopular Soviet policies increased in number and severity, dissent grew to rebellion. In 1930 and 1931, Buryatiya was the scene of several armed uprisings. These were crushed, and with the famine, arrests and police terror of the following two years, active resistance disappeared. In 1937 and 1938, another wave of repression resulted in 6836 arrests, with a third of that number being shot. More than 1800 lamas were arrested, as well as thousands of "wreckers, terrorists, counter-revolutionaries, spies and enemies of the people."

After World War II, Japanese prisoners of war were sent to Buryatiya, numbering 18,000 by the end of 1945. Used as a labor force, the prisoners built several structures around Ulan-Ude, including the Opera and Ballet Theater, several apartment buildings and an aircraft factory. Living and working conditions were appalling, with the result that death rates in some camps reached 150 per month in 1946. In 1947 and 1948 the remaining prisoners were repatriated to Japan.

After the war, Buryatiya continued to develop as the transport and industrial center of the Transbaikal region. In 1986, the BAM began operation at Severobaikalsk, increasing access to the northern regions of Buryatiya, the Amurskaya Oblast and Khabarovski Krai. In 1994, the first presidential elections were held.

After the fall of Communism, Buryatiya got a new flag, tied to its cultural roots. The blue, along with the images of the sun and the moon represent the sky; the color white, purity; and the yellow represents Buddhism and/or land. The 3 flames in the middle of the flag represent the past, present and the future.

ULAN-UDE

Administrative and cultural capital of the Republic of Buryatiya, Ulan-Ude is located at the junction of the Selenga and Uda rivers. Founded in 1666, the town of Udinsk, as it was then called, was built as a fortress, in an an attempt to stop

---

[1] History of Buryatiya in Questions and Answers, Volume Three. Republic of Buryatiya Ministy of Education, Ulan-Ude 1992.

Mongol forays into Russian territory. By the turn of the century Udinsk was known as a trading center and travel crossroads, as well as a strong military outpost. Renamed Verkhne (Upper)-Udinsk, the town grew, but remained little more than an outpost.

As other settlements on the frontier, Verkhne-Udinsk was also a place of exile. Members of secret societies, democratic reform groups and other organizations "dangerous" to the state were sent here, away from the politics and large population centers of European Russia. In the late 1820's some of the famous Decemberists were sent to Verkhne-Udinsk, including Alexander Muravyov. However, little remains in Ulan-Ude to mark their presence.

PRACTICAL INFORMATION

Moscow time +5 hours.

Code for calling Ulan-Ude from outside the city: **30122.**

Information when calling from inside the city: **09.**

Information from outside the city: **301-99-09-111**.

Central Post Office Located just off Soviet Square, on Sukhe-Batora St. Send telexes, faxes, packages and make photocopies. Open 8-19 Mon-Fri, 9-18 Sat, closed Sun.

MosBusinessBank (in Hotel Geser) Open 8-16 (12-13) Mon-Fri.

Weather Forecast Tel: 416-66, 418-66.

Language Although all speak Russian in Buryatiya, a few words in Buryat are greatly appreciated. "Hello" in Buryat is "*Sain baina.*" "Thank you" in Buryat is "*Yekhe khain daa.*"

Mongolian Consulate If you have an invitation from a Mongolian organization or individual, then this is the place to process your visa. If not, Intourist can get you a tourist visa. Current price for an entry/exit visa is $65. Next-day service. Yerbanova 12 (located in the Hotel Baikal on the second floor).

WALKING AROUND TOWN

A nice area for walking is along the Selenga River. To get there, walk out of Soviet Square (*Ploschad Sovietov*) along Yerbanova Street past the **Buryat Theater** with its fountain out front. This will take you to Smolina, where you turn left and enter a more residential area of wooden houses. When you

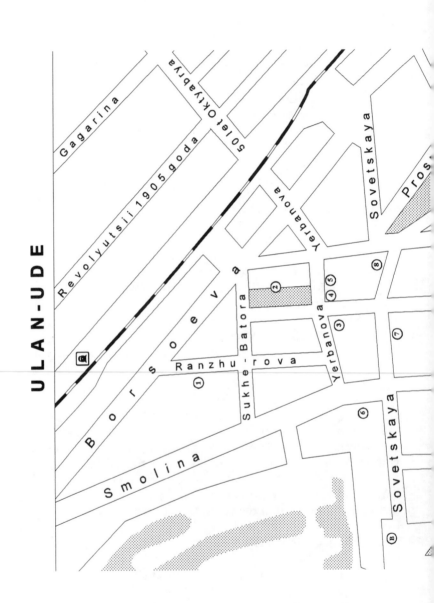

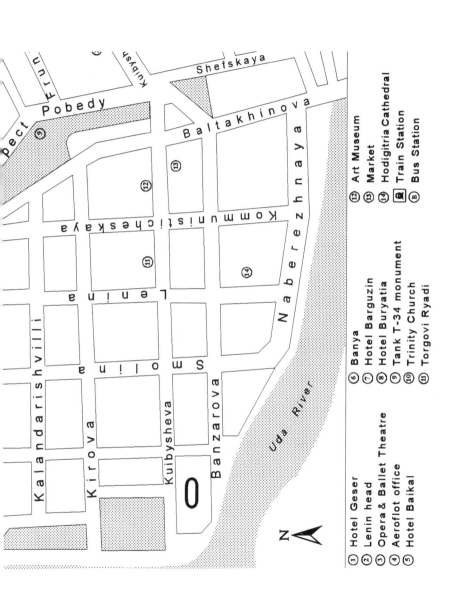

① Hotel Geser
② Lenin head
③ Opera & Ballet Theatre
④ Aeroflot office
⑤ Hotel Baikal
⑥ Banya
⑦ Hotel Barguzin
⑧ Hotel Buryatia
⑨ Tank T-34 monument
⑩ Trinity Church
⑪ Torgovi Ryadi
⑫ Art Museum
⑬ Market
⑭ Hodigitria Cathedral
Ⓡ Train Station
Ⓑ Bus Station

come to Sovietskaya St., turn right and head toward the bus station, a seedy run-down place. Just beyond the bus station you will see steps up, which lead to a sort of concrete promenade along the river. "Promenade" sounds a bit posher than what you will actually find—a cracked concrete retaining wall with a sidewalk on top. However, you get a nice view along the river from here, with sandbars and islands, depending on the season and the height of the water. Turn left (your only choice) and head along the river. There is a park on your left, and the river on your right. If the weather is nice, families or small groups of students gather in the evening on the steps leading down to the river, and you can be serenaded by Russian folk songs. Other times your walk will be interrupted only by the birds which swoop overhead.

The promenade curves around the edge of the city, following where the river Uda meets the Selenga. After a 20 minute walk, you will see the spires of a cathedral. This is the **Hodigitria Cathedral**, and the start of Lenina St. The Cathedral was built in 1745, and at the present time seems to be under reconstruction. However, take a turn around the grounds, as there is a children's playground out back with interesting wood carvings of storybook characters.

If you are tired after your walk along the river, you can catch a bus from here back to Soviet Square. If you feel like shopping, just keep heading straight along Lenina. On weekends Lenina is closed to traffic, which makes it a perfect time to walk around the city center. At the corner of Kuibysheva you will see the *Torgovie Ryadi*, Trade Rows, built in 1865 and still housing many stores and cafes. The best shop is right on the corner, a **Buryat Crafts Store** where you can find paintings and pastels of Lake Baikal and the surrounding

Hodigitria Cathedral

countryside done by local artists (and less expensive than at Intourist!), fur hats, wood carvings, jewelry and more. A bit farther along Lenina you will come to **Revolution Square** (*Ploschad Revolutsii*). The monument (in Buryat and Russian) is to those who participated in the Revolution and it used to stand in Soviet Square before the "Big Head" came along and displaced it. Just off the square is the **Children's Department Store** (*Dyetski Univermag*), which might offer a few small souvenirs. Beyond the square are some more small shops, few of note except for the **Art Salon** at Lenina 33, filled with more offerings of local artists.

HOTELS

Hotel Geser (formerly Oktyabrskaya, the Communist Party hotel) Named after the legendary epic Buryat hero, the Geser is probably the best hotel in town. Clean, quiet, with remarkably friendly and helpful service, it is also centrally located, about 2 blocks from the main square. The buffet works round the clock and there are two stores selling souvenirs on the first floor. The Geser has a good restaurant as well as a sauna and a Russian billiards room. Satellite telephone communications available. The Intourist office on the first floor can arrange trips around Buryatiya and to Mongolia. Ul. Ranzhurova 11. Moderate. Restaurant open 12-15, 16-22. Tel: 281-51.

Hotel Buryatiya A modern clean hotel in the downtown area, the Buryatiya features a barbershop, currency exchange office, international phone communications and an Intourist office. Rooms have a view of the city (in one direction the river and Hodigitria Cathedral in the distance, in the other direction the famous Biggest Head of Lenin), and come with refrigerators and televisions. If you're strapped for cash ask for a room with neither. Conference rooms on the 12th floor can be reserved for luncheons or business meetings. Helpful staff. Restaurant next door. Prices moderate. Located on the corner of Kommunisticheskaya and Sovietskaya. Tel: 218-35.

Hotel Baikal Situated on the main square overlooking Lenin's head, the Hotel Baikal is great on location, but needs improvement in the service sector. Mongolian consulate located on the second floor, restaurant on first floor. Inexpensive. Yerbanova 12. Tel: 237-18.

Hotel Barguzin   Low scale, no frills state-owned hotel. Located on a quiet side-street just off Lenina, the main shopping area.   Restaurant on second floor.   Very cheap.   Sovetskaya 28. Tel: 257-47, 281-03.

Hotel Odon   Located a short walk from the train station. Standard rooms, very cheap.   Ordinary restaurant adjoining hotel.   Gagarina 43.   Tel: 434-80.

FOOD

Traditional Buryat food reflects the history and culture of its ancestors.   Consequently, a lot of Buryat food is based on milk products and horse meat.   Dairy products are particularly important culturally—as the Russians greet guests with bread and salt, the Buryats greet guests with milk or dishes made with milk. It is an ancient custom that a guest should first be served some sort of milk product, and there are numerous recipes for milk-based dishes, ranging from *koumys* (fermented mare's milk, praised for its nutritive qualities and also used for ceremonial purposes), to *urme* (foam from boiled milk, either frozen or dried, depending on the season).   *Salamat*, favored for its high calories, is a dish with Central Asian antecedents.   In Buryatiya it is a mix of boiled sour cream and flour, slightly different from the version preferred by Yakuts, which is butter and flour.

Meat is also an essential ingredient in Buryat cooking. *Khirmasa*, a hearty soup, makes good use of sheep intestines. Beef, lamb, veal, deer, pony, wild goose, and boar all show up in recipe books, although city folk might have to make due with canned pony.   The more exotic meats are rather rare.

The food in Buryatiya that you find in restaurants, and that which you will be offered at someone's house, differ in that restaurant food has been highly influenced by Russia.   Certain Buryat dishes can be found, but for the most part restaurants serve up traditional Russian fare: soup, beef, whatever few vegetables are in season.   Lots of onions in winter, partly because they are hardy, partly because they are chock full of vitamins to stave off winter colds.   Meat, considered necessary protein to protect against the harsh climate, shows up in just about every course—appetizer, soup, main dish.

One native dish that you can find in restaurants and cafes is *pozi*, a type of large steamed meat dumpling.   It is pinched together at the top, and it is said that the finest chefs can put

100 delicate pinches around the crown. If you go so far as to count, you will most likely find fewer than that, however, the chef's break from tradition should not influence you. You should eat *pozi* in the traditional manner, which is to pick one up in your fingers, kiss the bottom edge, take a little bite and then sip out the juice. After that, chomp however you like.

Another popular dish is *omul*, the Baikal salmon, often eaten dried and salted, or in restaurants simply broiled. *Nerpa,* the famous fresh-water seal is also eaten.

Many Buryat traditions revolve around drinking, from simple tea to more potent offerings. Tea is drunk with milk and sometimes salt, a Tibetan specialty, and is usually served in small tea bowls, accompanied by a particular ritual. The person offering the tea holds out the bowl in their right hand, with the left hand supporting the right elbow. This supposedly came about in Central Asian history as a way of showing that you weren't concealing any weapons in your other hand. The person accepting the tea also shows their lack of weapons by accepting the bowl with both hands. When it comes to stronger drinks, there are even more rituals. Before drinking, Buryats dip the fourth finger of their right hand, supposedly the "cleanest" finger, into the drink and *kapayut,* that is, they shake drops in the four directions as an offering. Buryats are notoriously strong drinkers, even by Russian standards, so get ready for lots of toasts, and no shirking, drinking just a sip— you'll be expected to drink *do dnya* (to the bottom) each time, or you won't be showing the proper respect to your hosts. However, you needn't simply drink straight vodka each time. Ulan-Ude has its own bottling plant, Krystal, which produces all sorts of vodkas and *nastoyki. Nastoyki* are based on vodka or spirits, with various additions, such as ginseng, berries, or even reindeer antler. These additions add flavor and other valuable nutrients or qualities. *Pantocrinovaya* (antler) vodka is particularly valued for its strengthening properties, particularly for men.

Buryatiya Restaurant This restaurant and the hotel of the same name were 25 years in the building and apparently the management of the construction company is now running the restaurant. If you can ever get the staff to wait on you, the food is quite tasty. There is a choice of salads and the sweet & sour beef, although not particularly sweet or sour, is recommended. For a quick snack or drink, try the Express Bar Buryatiya on the

same floor.   Corner of Kommunisticheskaya and Sovietskaya.
Open from 11-23 Mon-Fri with a break from 17-18.

Geser Restaurant This restaurant combines polite, efficient
service with good food to make one of the better restaurants in
Ulan-Ude.   Try the *kharcho* soup for lunch or the *pozi* for
dinner.   Panels with paintings of Buryat legends hang on the
wall.   There is a cover charge in the evenings to listen to the
band and dance as you eat.   For similar food in humbler
surroundings, try the **buffet** down the hall, which is open around
the clock.   At the buffet you can also take a look at many of the
vodkas and *nastoyki* produced by the Krystal factory.
Ranzhurova 11.   The Geser is open from 12-15 and from 16-22.

Barguzin Restaurant One of the few state-run hotel
restaurants that is worth the time and the money.   Enter through
the cellar-like entrance hall, then go through the double-headed
eagle gate.   The restaurant on the second floor has all the
trappings of another state-run establishment, but fortunately this
is not the case.   The *de rigueur* loud band is actually quite good,
the service is attentive and the food is decent, too.   Vegetarians
can ask for just the vegetable side order (*garnir*) and not get
yelled at.   Moderate prices.   Sovietskaya 28.

Vokzal Restaurant Nicer than your standard railroad
station establishment, but still not a place to make a special trip
to.   As intended, this is a good place to buy food and drink for
your train trip.   Cold chicken seems to be the specialty.   To get
to the station, take buses 7, 10 or 36 from downtown.   Central
Railroad Station, Revolutsii 1905 Goda 51.

Baikal Restaurant Located next to the Hotel Baikal, this
restaurant has tasty, if unexciting dishes.   Service is cranky and
reluctant, so smile and be patient.   Moderate.   Yerbanova 8.
Tel: 223-40.

Cafe Okhotnik (The Hunter) Small, popular cafe with a
wooden interior decorated with hunting trophies.   The menu is
unexceptional, but service is quick and the food is cheap.
Mayakovskovo 3.

Cafe Bagulnik At night, turns into a casino and bar.
Trubacheeva 20.   Tel: 373-74.

Odon Gagarina 43.   Restaurant of the hotel of the same
name.

Cafe Lakomka Yerbanova 22.   Tel: 264-73.

Restaurant Myf (Myth) Mayakovskovo 17.

SHOPPING

Torgovie Ryadi (Trade Rows), Gostiny Dvorskie Built in the 19th century and reputed to be the first stone structures in Buryatiya, this pre-revolutionary building continues to serve its original purpose and houses many stores and cafes.

Buryat Crafts Store Great store with colorful paintings by local artists, wood carvings and horse hair wall hangings. Jewelry, engravings, and Buryat fur hats also on sale. In Torgovie Ryadi, corner of Kuibysheva and Lenina. Open Tue-Sat 10-18 (14-15).

BaikalTourist In addition to electronics, clothes, etc., this shop sells small Buddhas, crafts, and pins. Across from the Natural History Museum. Open from 9-21 (13-14).

Dyetski Univermag Large department store has good selection of toys, tea sets and other miscellaneous household goods. Ploschad Revolutsii. Open 10-19 (14-15) Mon-Sat.

Art Salon Wide selection of souvenirs including jewelry, paintings, birch bark boxes, wood carvings and more. Lenina 33. Open Mon-Sat 10-19 (14-15).

Intourist Sells paintings, wall hangings, maps, books about the region, even tapes of Buryat folk music. (see also Around Ulan-Ude). Offices in the Hotel Geser and Hotel Buryatiya.

Podarki (gifts) Tea sets, jewelry, embroidered napkins. Lenina 40. Open Mon-Sat 10-19 (14-15).

Yantar (Amber) Jewelry store. Pobeda 16. Tel: 2-42-25.

Dom Knigi (House of Books) On Lenina. Open 10-19 (14-15) Mon-Sat.

MARKET

At Kuibysheva and Baltazhinova Sts. Outside is a labyrinth of stalls selling clothing, shoes and miscellaneous goods. Inside you will find fruit, vegetables, bread and meat. Interesting to watch the ax-man delicately hack off your meat purchases by the kilogram.

MUSEUMS AND THEATERS

Natural History Museum Exhibits on wildlife of the Transbaikal region, with a special section devoted to Lake Baikal. Interesting exhibit showing all the items that can be made from birch trees and their importance to the early Russian settlers. Lenina 46. Open Wed-Sun 10-18. Tel: 280-49.

The Sampilova Art Museum   Modern building housing Russian and Buryat art. Each section is paid for separately, so if you want to see the whole museum, ask for all (*vsyeh*) tickets at the ticket booth. The Buryat engravings and hall of students' art are especially interesting. Kuibyshova 29. Open 11-19 Tue-Sun. Tel: 229-09.

Old Believer's Complex, Ethnographic Museum

Transbaikal Ethnographic Museum (Sri Chinoy Peace Monument)   This open air museum is located near the little village of Beryozovka about 20 minutes from downtown Ulan-Ude and can be reached by bus or taxi. Each section of the museum re-creates the lifestyles of a certain people of the Transbaikal region. Here one can see the conical structures of the Evenks, called *yarngas* made out of bark and fur. Further along are felt yurts of the early nomads, log cabins of the Cossack settlers and wooden houses of the Old Believers with elaborate wood decorations on the doors and windows. Most of the buildings are originals, brought here from the various areas of Buryatiya. The interiors also have been furnished with original clothes and furniture, giving the buildings an authentic lived-in look.

The museum also has a small zoo with camels, goats, caribou and yaks.

There is a much steeper entrance fee for foreigners than for Russians. A guided tour in English is offered at yet again an increase in price. Then again, understanding the exhibits greatly enhances your enjoyment. Call in advance to ensure an English speaking guide is available. To get there, on weekends take bus No. 35 from the main square to the last stop at the museum. On weekdays, take bus No. 8 until you see the hippodrome on your left (approximately 20 minutes), and get out at that stop. Keep walking in the direction the bus was going and take the first road on your left to reach the museum. About a 20 minute walk.

If you start early in the day, you can make this a half-day excursion, but to get the most out of your visit and not be rushed (or not have to worry about the frequency of buses), it's best to pack a lunch and plan for a picnic in the forest. The museum is near a couple of small villages, but the shops are poorly stocked and have capricious hours. Summer: 10-18 (*kassa* open till 17) Winter: 10-17:15 (*kassa* open till 16:15), closed last Tuesday of every month for cleaning. Tel: 357-54.

Opera and Ballet Theater Built by Japanese POW labor, this attractive building not only houses local operas and ballets, but is probably the only theater in the world to have a yurt on top of it. It is also reputed to be the best opera and theater company east of Novosibirsk. Great socialist paintings inside depicting happy Buryats glorifying Lenin. Yerbanova 6. Tel: 236-00.

Buryat Opera and Ballet Theater

Buryat Historical Museum   Currently undergoing major repairs, but is scheduled to re-open in mid-1995. Profsoyuznaya 29. Tel: 240-08.

Geological Museum Lenina 57. Open Tuesday and Friday from 10-16 (13-14).

Russian Drama Theater Tereshkovoi 1. Tel: 302-10.

Philharmonic Lenina 56. Tel: 218-93.

Puppet Theater (*Teatr Kukol*) Pushkina 3a. Tel: 222-92.

Namsaraev Drama Theater (Buryat Theater)   Upcoming performances are posted at the theater and around town. Come by just for a look at the monumental art above the entrance. Kuibysheva 38. Tel: 248-37.

BURYAT HOLIDAYS

June 1 is International Childrens' Day, which is celebrated in Ulan-Ude by a festival at the Opera House in which local childrens' choral and dance groups perform in traditional costume.

Sukharban (from *suxha* - arrow)   First Sunday in July (actually two days: Sat - trials, Sun - finals). Archery and riding competitions at the hippodrome. Biggest event of the year, and one of the few times the hippodrome sees any action. Highly recommended.

Tsagaalgan is a Buddhist holiday celebrated on the eve of the lunar New Year. The ceremonies last for 16 days as the twelve miracles of Buddha are celebrated. Buddhists from around Buryatiya gather at the Datsan to pray together for peace and well-being.

In mid summer a two-day festival is held, dedicated to the Buddha of the Future, the **Maidari**. During the ceremony, a statue of the Maidari is brought out of the temple and placed on a decorated chariot, led by a green plaster horse, covered in ribbons. The chariot makes a tour of the grounds of the Datsan, with prayers being read and drums and cymbals sounding. Money is thrown by the faithful to the foot of the statue for good luck.

OTHER SIGHTS AND ENTERTAINMENT

Hippodrome   near village of Verkhni Beryozovka. This huge stadium for horse races sees little action throughout the year, but in July, during the holdiay of Sukharban, there are horse races and competitions in the national sports of archery and wrestling. When the Hippodrome is open, the Cafe Sukharban serves drinks and snack food.

The HEAD! No description of Ulan-Ude would be complete without mention of the huge head of Lenin which stands in Soviet Square. This head was sculpted for a Canadian exposition in 1972 but afterwards no one wanted to buy it, so Ulan-Ude proudly took the head and placed it in the main square, relocating the obelisk which used to stand there. Some say this Lenin has a slight slant to his eyes, as if he were becoming Buryat. Any way you look at it, in the land of Lenin statues, great and small, Ulan-Ude has the largest head of them all.

Public Banya #1 Good clean fun, and cheap, too! Smolina 57. Tel: 2-50-94.

City Park Small walkways thread their way through the trees, leading to the church in the middle of the park. There is a World War II monument hidden near the entrance, dedicated to those who died during the war.

Stadium Spartak Kuibysheva 1. Tel: 2-62-76.

Lizhnaya Baza Trud ("Labor" ski base) Posyolok (village) Verkhni Beryozovka. Tel: 4-36-94.

T-34 Tank on Ulitsa Pobeda. One of the most effective tanks in the World War II, this particular T-34 is one of those that entered Berlin with the victorious Soviet troops in 1945.

PLACES OF WORSHIP

Trinity Church Constructed in 1798, the church used to be surrounded by the city cemetery until it was plowed under and renamed, ironically enough, *Park Kultury* (Culture Park) for use as the city park. Simple, with pretty green cupolas.

Russian Orthodox Church on Proisvodstvennaya 6. Farther from the center of town, this church is pink, and much more lavishly decorated, with a green-gold iconostasis. It remained open during the Soviet era.

Ivolginski Datsan (Buddhist temple) Forty minutes southwest of Ulan-Ude is the Ivolginski Datsan. The religious and cultural center for Buddhists in Buryatiya and the CIS, the Ivolginski Datsan was visited by the Dalai Lama in 1991 and 1993.

The Datsan complex is comprised of the houses of the lamas and students, a guest house for official visitors, a cafeteria, banya, and of course the datsans (temples) themselves. The proper way to approach the

At Ivolginski Datsan

main temple is to enter the gates and circle the complex

clockwise. When you enter the gates, immediately turn left. In this way you are following the path of the sun. No smoking or drinking is allowed on the grounds and hats should be removed. As you walk around the complex you will come to prayer drums of various sizes. The drums have prayers painted on them in Tibetan and you should spin them as you walk past, sending your prayers up to heaven. You will also see that people leave coins next to the drums as offerings. Behind the back wall you can see trees and bushes with small strips of cloth tied to them. Prayers are written on these cloths, which are then tied to the branches in the hope that the wind will turn fortune your way.

As you come around the third side of the complex you will approach one of the two temples where services take place. Outsiders are welcome to enter the temples and even participate in the services as long as they are respectful. Remember, never turn your back to the altar at the front of the temple. The main temple is flanked by tigers. The interior is beautifully painted in striking colors. The main throne is reserved for the Dalai Lama himself—the priests sit around the center on cushions. There is a small booth where you can buy religious articles.

Main temple, Ivolginski Datsan

If you are hungry, there is a cafeteria at the far right corner from the entrance, which offers tasty *pozi* and tea at reasonable prices. Open 9-16.

The Datsan is open daily from 9-17. Buses Nos. 104 and 130 leave Ulan-Ude twice daily for the Datsan, the most frugal option, or you can take a taxi (ask the driver to wait). Intourist can also arrange a half-day excursion.

TRANSPORTATION

The **Airport** is only about 20 minutes from the center of town. There is a small international section, but foreigners can also go through the regular hall. Information: 321-10, Intourist: 375-64. Bus Nos. 10 and 34 head to the airport from Soviet Square.

City Aeroflot Office Yerbanova 14 (near Hotel Baikal). Open Mon-Sat from 9-19 (13-14), 9-18 Sun. For information call: 222-48, for reservations: 266-00.

Bus Station (*Avtovokzal*) Small and on a neglected side street. Sovietskaya 1. Information: 221-85.

Train Station (*Vokzal*) Revolutsii 1905. Information: 4-31-37. Take Bus Nos. 10 or 36 from Soviet Square. Local trains to Lake Baikal and long distance trains to Mongolia, Moscow and Vladivostok.

Soviet Square (*ploschad Sovietov*) is the center of town. Most local buses make a stop here (in front of the Hotel Baikal) and the square is also one of the better places to catch a taxi. If you wish to order a **taxi**, call 225-01.

AROUND ULAN-UDE

Intourist Ulan-Ude is almost unique in that the Intourist offices are helpful, friendly and offer interesting tours for reasonable prices. Intourist offers hiking and camping tours in Buryatiya, including week-long trips to Lake Baikal. They can also arrange visas and trips to Mongolia. If you want to travel alone, visas can be prepared in one day and there are direct flights to Ulan Bator 3 times per week. If you want to join a tour group, Intourist can arrange accommodations, sightseeing, and even horseback riding trips through the Mongolian steppes!

Intourist has two offices: one at Hotel Geser, Ul. Ranzhurova 11. Tel: 292-67, 269-54; the other is as Hotel Buryatiya, on the corner of Kommunisticheskaya and Sovietskaya. Tel: 627-89.

If you are only in Ulan-Ude for a short while and don't have time to take a longer trip to some of the more distant parts of Buryatiya, don't despair. There are plenty of beautiful spots that can be reached in a day or weekend trip from Ulan-Ude. The local trains (*prigorodnaya*) leaving from the train station are a good way to get out of the city for the day. The line Ulan-Ude-Mysovaya goes west to Lake Baikal, the east line goes to Novosilinsk. The best way to go is to buy a ticket to the end station and get a window seat. You will roll past many small towns in scenic places where you can get off and enjoy the beautiful countryside. Bring a lunch, as many of the towns are too small to have more than one store, let alone a cafe or restaurant. Also, be sure to check the schedule for returning trains at the train station when you leave AND when you get off, otherwise you could be left stranded. Below are a few places that might be of interest.

Gusino Ozero   (Not to be confused with Gusinoozyorsk, which is an industrial town) Located on Lake Gusino, this small town can be reached by a 3 hour bus ride from Ulan-Ude. The town itself is not very interesting, with just a few old buildings dating back to the 18th century, but is a good starting point for those wanting to explore the Khamar-Dabaan mountain range or camp near the lake.

Baikalskaya   Located on Lake Baikal, this town is also on the border of the Baikalski preserve. Reached by train (5 hrs) or bus.

Petukhovka   Picturesque village on a bend of the Selenga River, with hills in background. 45 minutes by train on the line Ulan-Ude-Mysovaya.

Boyarsky   Whistle-stop 3 hrs from Ulan-Ude, right on the shore of Lake Baikal. Walk past houses down to the beach. Quintessential small Siberian village with wooden houses, no running water, but good scenery.

Tunka Valley (tunKA) is known for its picturesque scenery and is another "must" for the traveler in Buryatiya who wants to get away from it all and enjoy the great outdoors. The blue spruce that line the Kremlin walls were taken from this valley. Its mineral waters were appreciated even in the time of Genghis Khan, who decreed the whole valley off-limits to all, reserved for his personal use. Surprisingly, the road through the valley is well paved and is a pleasant drive. Located in the southwest corner of Buryatiya, in the Sayan mountain range, Tunka can be reached by long distance bus from Ulan-Ude. The extinct Potukhshii volcano and the Irkut River, known for its great fishing, add to the local scenery. Also located in the valley is the town of **Arshan.** Arshan is a health resort, built for and frequented by Leonid Brezhnev, and well-known throughout the former Soviet Union for its curative mineral waters and beautiful mountain vistas. A perfect base for further excursions, follow the river up from the town into the mountains for a several hour hike; note the Buddhist prayer ribbons tied to the bushes along the way. There are mountain lakes, waterfalls, pine forests and marble quarries as well as two extinct volcanoes to be explored nearby, and Arshan also borders the Badary Nature Preserve. Further along the road is the town of **Kyren,** where one can rent horses and spend the day riding through the countryside. Contact the national park office in town for details.

Kyakhta   Founded in 1728 and situated right across the border from Mongolia, Kyakhta (originally called Troiskosavsk) was an instant trade center and was part of the great Tea Route. Kyakhta grew to include a market hall, several churches and even a cathedral. Eventually, the town began to be compared with Suzdal, a city located on the golden ring outside Moscow and noted for its beautiful churches and buildings.

LAKE BAIKAL

Lake Baikal, the world's deepest lake, has long been known as one of Eastern Siberia's natural tourist attractions. Containing one-fifth of the planet's fresh water, if emptied it would take all the rivers in the world a whole year to refill it. The "eye of Siberia" is a fascinating biological environment where some three-quarters of the 1800 species of flora and fauna found there are endemic to the lake region. *Nerpa* (the world's only freshwater seals), the tasty *omul* fish and the transparent *golomyanka* fish are just a few of the more well-known, unique species to be found there.

Baikal has also served as a source of controversy, as grass roots movements protested the construction of a paper mill in the town of Baikalsk on the lake's southern shores. The mill would have dumped masses of untreated waste water into the lake, causing irreparable damage to the lake's delicate ecosystem, critics claimed. Although the mill was constructed as planned, the protests brought national and international attention to the area and resulted in the installation of a water purification system at the Baikalsk mill and plans were dropped to construct two additional mills. Today local and international organizations continue their efforts to clean up one of the world's natural treasures.

Most of the lake's tourism industry has centered around Irkutsk and the town of Listvyanka. Ferries shuttle tourists up and down the lake, and the historic Baikal Railroad Line, stretching from the Port of Baikal to Kultuk, is deserving of the praise it receives.

However, little mention is made of the Republic of Buryatiya, which encloses more than half of the lake's shores. The towns of Severobaikalsk and Baikalskoe sit on the northern shores of the lake, and parallel to the northeastern third of the shoreline runs the magnificent Barguzin mountain range. On the lake side of the range are the Barguzin Nature Reserve and Zabaikalski National Park, while on its eastern flank high rugged peaks fall sharply into the wide pastoral valley of the Barguzin River. The upper reaches of the Barguzin River and several of its tributaries are favorite rafting destinations, and the valley itself is a haven for photographers and bird-watchers.

A permit and modest fee are required for entrance into the park. This is accomplished at the park office on Balnichny Pereulok (alley) in Ust-Barguzin, tel: 92578 (no code, call must be ordered through operator).

The area around Lake Baikal is home to an abundance of wildlife, including bears, sables, elk and lynxes. The whole district is dotted with natural sights and "points of interest," such as hot springs, waterfalls, rock formations and sandy beaches, as well as beautiful vistas of Lake Baikal itself. Justifiably known as the Pearl of Siberia, Baikal is beautiful in any season and not to be missed.

Boat trips up and across Lake Baikal can be started from Ust-Barguzin, a port north of Ulan-Ude. Buses leave daily from the bus station in Ulan-Ude. In the Zabaikalski National Park are the **Barguzinski** and **Chivyrkuiski Gulfs,** known for their sandy beaches and warm water temperature, allowing pleasant swimming. Of particular beauty is the **Svatoi Nos** (Holy Nose) isthmus. Just off the isthmus are the **Ushkani Islands**, with the breeding grounds for *nerpa*, the famous Baikal freshwater seal. The **Barguzinski Nature Reserve** was Russia's first, created by a decree of Tsar Nicholas II in 1916 to protect the dwindling sable population. Boats reach the preserve at the Port of Davsha. Ask at the park office in **Ust-Barguzin** for details on renting kayaks for Lake Baikal or for organizing river trips down the River Barguzin. The only hotel in town is a two-story white stone building, near the *chistka odezhda* (laundromat) and *stolovoya* (cafeteria). Ust-Barguzin can be reached by bus from Ulan-Ude or by boat from Irkutsk.

Nizhne-Angarsk and **Severobaikalsk** are good starting places for those looking to explore the lesser frequented regions of northern Lake Baikal. **Baikalskoe**, just south of Severobaikalsk, is known for its ancient rock paintings, and nearby **Lake Slyudinskoe** and the cliffs of Cape Ludar are considered to be two of the prettiest areas in the region. Hard to reach, but worth the trouble, is the **Frolkhinski Republican Zakaznik** with the **Singing Sands of Turala,** hot springs, glacial Lake Frolikha and peaceful forests.

REPUBLIC OF SAKHA
(YAKUTIA)

Novosibirskie Islands

Verkhoyansk

Ust-Nera

Oimyakon

Lena River

Vilyuisk

Aldan R.

Chulapcha

Vilyui R.

Verkhne-
Vilyuisk

Yakutsk

Mirny

Lena R.

CHAPTER 7

THE REPUBLIC OF SAKHA (YAKUTIA)

For many people the name "Yakutia" conjures up images of frozen tundra and herds of reindeer, and not much else. Yakuts themselves will be quick to disabuse you of the notion that this is what Yakutia is "all about." "I have never seen a reindeer," many city dwellers will scornfully say, "they are in the north." In fact, one schoolteacher laughed over the fact that a few years ago a Yakut with an entrepreneurial spirit brought a live reindeer into town, and the locals lined up to have their pictures taken with it, just like "tourists."

The Republic of Sakha does indeed cover a huge territory: 3 million square kilometers—more than three times the size of Alaska, and though Yakutsk lies at a latitude which most Westerners would consider to be "north" (Yakutsk is on approximately the 62nd parallel, similar to Anchorage), the Lena River, which flows north past the city, still has about 800 miles to go before it reaches the sea. Half of Yakutia lies beyond the Arctic Circle.

Yakutia is sparsely populated, with the majority of the population concentrated in the mining cities of Mirny (diamonds), Aldan (gold), and Neryungri (coal), as well as the capital city of Yakutsk. Non-industrial cities have smaller, mostly native, populations, which depend more on agriculture and animal husbandry.

The present population of approximately 1,100,000 is comprised of about 33% native Yakuts, and the rest are Russians, Ukrainians, ethnic Germans, and other indigenous nationalities. Beginning in the 1920's there was a great influx of

non-natives to Yakutia to work the diamond and gold mines, and these "visitors" were joined by others who chose or were sent to increase the industrial power of Yakutia. Many stayed and adapted to conditions in the north. Under Stalin and the standard Soviet program of "Russification," native languages and customs were repressed, and Russians received the best jobs and advantages. Now that Yakutia is having a resurgence of nationalism, it is the Russians who find themselves in an awkward position. Many have lived in Yakutia for a couple of generations and consider it their home. Children of mixed marriages are particularly confused, since to Russians they appear to be Yakut, while they may speak only Russian at home and know nothing of native customs. The ethnic question in Yakutia, as in many other parts of the Former Soviet Union, is far from settled.

HISTORY

Yakutia was first investigated by the Cossack Pyotr Beketov. Leading a group of 30 Cossacks, he sailed down the Lena in search of new lands and natives from whom to collect *yasak*, or fur tribute. He founded a fort named Lensky on the banks of the river, but it was a poorly chosen location and in the spring the river threatened to undermine the fort, so he abandoned Lensky and in 1632 built a new fort a few miles further up the river in an area already inhabited by natives. He named this fort Yakutsk. Since the area was rich in furs as well as mammoth and walrus tusks, Yakutsk quickly became a major trade center and the capital of the Yakut District. Conveniently located at a bend in the river, many future expeditions for exploration set off from the town, and throughout the 1700's it was a supply center along the way from Irkutsk to Okhotsk and Kamchatka.

In the 19th century, Yakutia was considered a "prison without bars" due to its harsh climate. It was here that the Tsar sent his political prisoners, including some of the Decemberists, to live their lives in exile.

In 1922, Yakutsk was named the capital of the Yakut Autonomous Soviet Socialist Republic. Under the Soviets many Yakut herdsmen, like their counterparts in Buryatiya, slaughtered their own herds rather than go through the process of collectivization. During the Stalin years, political prisoners were sent to work the gold and diamond mines, where they died in the thousands due to exposure and malnutrition.

In 1990, Yakutia was renamed the Republic of Sakha. Traditionally controlled by Moscow, the Yakuts are now trying to have more of a say in, and retain more of the profits from, the sale of the Republic's gold and diamonds. In 1992, Sakha elected its first president, Mikhail Yefimovich Nikolaev, an ethnic Yakut. Currently, Yakutsk has sister city relationships with Fairbanks, Alaska, Guirin in China, Muroyama in Japan, and Darmstadt, Germany.

YAKUTIA'S INDIGENOUS POPULATIONS

The Evens, Evenks and Yukaghirs were some of the earliest inhabitants of the area which is now Yakutia. Predominantly reindeer herders, these paleosiberian tribes roamed the tundra following their herds. The Yukaghirs were once very numerous, and their territory stretched from the Lena to the Anadyr River, but by the time the Russians arrived, intertribal warfare had greatly reduced their numbers, and they lived in a comparatively small area between the Yakuts along the Lena and the Tungus along the coast. By the late 1800's there were only about 1,600 Yukaghirs left, and nowadays there are few representatives of this once-powerful race.

In the Even language, "*Even*" means "the people who live here." They lived in the northeast of Siberia from the Sea of Okhotsk to the Lena River, in close contact with the Evenks and the Yukaghirs. The other local tribes called the Evens by different names depending on their location. Those who lived near the Sea of Okhotsk were called "*Lamuti*," which in Even means "those who live by the sea," and Evens who migrated to Kamchatka were called "*Orochi*," which means "Deer People."

Yakuts

There are many theories as to the origin of the Yakuts. According to early foreign researchers, the Yakuts considered themselves descended from the Krasnoyar Tatars. One legend has it that a Tatar by the name of Omogoi-Bai split from the rest, with 150 followers, and headed east. When they reached the steppes, they met the Buryats. They heard that the Buryats planned to destroy them, but they had arrived while the moon was on the wane, a time during which the Buryats took no important action, so Omogoi built rafts for all his people, their possessions and animals, and sailed down the Lena, settling where Yakutsk now stands. After a while a Tatar named Ellei came and fell in love with one of the daughters of Omogoi. They had 12 sons, and from these sons the 12 clans of the Yakuts are descended.[1]

Another theory is that the Yakuts are descended from the Huns, but that when they settled in the north it was not so cold, and they have gradually adapted as the climate changed. Despite the various theories of specific origin, it is clear that the Yakuts came from Asiatic stock, somewhere in the south. Their language is Turkic, they have words for animals which don't inhabit the north (for example lion and snake), and these words are similar to the Turkish or Mongolian words for such animals.[2]

Since the first settlement in Yakutsk, Yakuts have spread out along the rivers Viliui, Amga and Aldan, which flow into the Lena. Natives from one village or area can easily identify the home district of another by the differences between facial characteristics, as well as by dialect and speech patterns. Originally, the Yakuts called themselves "Sakha." Supposedly, when the first Russian explorers came to the area they asked a group of Evenks the name of the other natives in the area. The Evenks, having no "s" in their language, told the Russians

---

[1]N. Schukin, Travel to Yakutsk, 1844 in Uraangkhai-Sakhaler: ocherki pogrevnei istorii. G.V. Ksonofontov. Natsionalnoye Izdatelstvo Respubliki Sakha (Yakutia), 1992.
[2]Uraangkhai-Sakhaler: ocherki pogrevnei istorii Yakutov. G.V. Ksonofontov. Natsionalnoye Izdatelstvo Respubliki Sakha (Yakutia) 1992. P. 81

"Yakha," hence the origin of the name "Yakut." Nowadays, with the resurgence of nationalism, Yakuts are once again calling themselves "Sakha," and their land "The Republic of Sakha."

CLOTHING

If you plan to visit Yakutia in the winter, you'd best be of hardy stock. The average winter temperature is -40C, while temperatures can get down to -60C and below in January and February. Due to its climate, Yakutsk is about 20C colder than other places in Russia at the same latitude, and Verkhoyansk and Oimyakon vie for the dubious honor of being known as the coldest place on earth. When the thermometer dips below -40C, a thick fog falls over most cities, brought about by car exhausts and human exhalation. This puts a frosty fuzz on the bare winter branches, and makes driving a hazard. The temperature also causes your breath to freeze on your hair, cheeks and eyelashes. In fact, if the temperature dips below -58C, when you exhale you can hear a little "tinkle" as your breath freezes. This is known as the "whisper of stars." Yakuts have adapted to these conditions by wearing lots of fur, keeping bundled up, and having well-heated houses, at least in the cities. There is also a system of three doors (two antechambers) to most public buildings and stores for keeping the cold air out and the warm air in. All the same, in some areas it is still chilly indoors. Yakutia is one place where the Russian tradition of taking one's shoes off at the door is not observed as rigorously as elsewhere, since the reindeer boots worn by all Yakuts are as comfortable indoors as out, and warmer than slippers.

Unty, as these boots are called, are made of reindeer leg fur. Decorated with beading or with alternating patterns of fur, these boots are not only remarkably warm, but light and comfortable. You can wear these boots with only one pair of socks; much more comfortable than layer upon layer of wool, which you would need under regular boots. Furthermore, rubber becomes brittle at temperatures below -60C, so Sorels, which in other climes keep you toasty warm, can lose their effectiveness. If you purchase a pair of *unty*, keep in mind that the soles are of thick felt, designed for walking on snow and not for rugged city sidewalks.

Winter habitation fog puts a frosty fuzz on all the branches

Fur hats in Yakutia are also bigger and warmer than in other parts of the Far East. For ladies, rounded fluffy hats with hanging "earflaps" to cover delicate ears and cheeks are not only fashionable, but necessary as protection from the elements. Some hats for girls have triangular beaded decorations on top, harking back to native outfits from the 1800's. For men, hats are more conservative, but temperatures are such that there is no shame in walking around with "flaps down."

Noon sun in Yakutsk in January

Regarding other winter clothing, most Yakuts have fur coats or *shubas*, since walking around in anything but fur through the coldest winter months is risking illness, not to mention frostbite.

There is relief from the cold in the summer, when temperatures rise. The average summer temperature is 13C (55F), but can reach as high as 37C (100F), an amazing swing of 100 degrees from winter to summer. There is an abundance of mosquitos, but other forms of "dreaded" insect life such as ticks are not to be found.

EVENTS

The great festival of the year occurs on June 20th and lasts the two days of the solstice. Called *isikh*, the festival celebrates the White Nights, and is held in most towns and cities (but not in Yakutsk). It begins with ceremonies giving thanks to the "powers that be," and ends with everyone meeting the sun by joining in the traditional dance, called *ohonkhai* or *osoukhai*, which is danced in a huge circle. The leader sings of whatever inspires him/her, and the crowd repeats the song. Other events at the *isikh* include theatrical spectacles, a singing contest, competitions in the national sports of wrestling and archery, a prize for best hand-made national costume, and horseraces on the famous Yakut pony.

The Yakut pony is famous mostly for its ability to survive the harsh Yakut winter. These ponies, still owned by the state, are left free to roam the taiga through the winter. They know how to dig through the snow to find food (as opposed to cattle, who must be housed and fed through the winter). The ponies are short, stocky and thickly furred. In Yakut epic literature and art, ponies are always depicted with blazing eyes, head held high, mane proudly streaming, one hoof raised to strongly stamp the ground. Yakuts are justifiably proud of their ponies, who have adapted so well to the bitter conditions of their environment.

FOOD

Ironically, one Yakut delicacy is, in fact, pony. Pony can be prepared in various ways, most often simply frozen raw, sliced very thinly, and eaten while still frozen. Raw frozen pony liver is also a treat. Called *tongber*, it is chopped into small pieces so it can be picked up in the fingers, dipped in salt, and eaten. Another delicacy for the adventurous is *khatta*, sauteed pony intestines. Reindeer and moose are also eaten, and occasionally appear in the markets. Other national dishes are *karas*, a small freshwater fish, fried whole (watch out for tiny bones!), and *salamat*, a mixture of melted butter and flour, considered especially nutritious for new mothers. *Stroganina*, a white fish frozen and thinly sliced, is eaten throughout the north. Ice cream is made by beating cream, sometimes adding *brusniki* or other berries, dropping it in dollops onto a plate, and putting it outside briefly until it freezes. Many of these items can be kept through the summer in a *buloos*, or outdoor underground storage area.

In Yakutsk and all large cities there is indoor plumbing and running water. However, in most smaller cities and villages the people prefer to gather river or lake ice to use as water. When the lake or river begins freezing, the men go out and bring home huge chunks of ice, which lie in the backyard to be cut up and melted when desired throughout the winter. In summer the ice is put into a ground storage container for later use. This ice water is preferred over other water, since it is considered to be more pure, free of chemicals, radiation and dirt.

If you are thirsty, non-alcoholic drinks are made by soaking berries in water to make a *napitok*. The choice of stronger drinks includes Russian vodka, a local Yakut vodka, and *koumys*, made from fermented mare's milk. When consumed for ceremonial purposes, it is served in a *charon*, a vase-shaped container of wood, with 3 legs in the shape of horses hooves. *Koumys* is definitely an acquired taste.

In general, Yakuts seem to drink less than Russians, or at least are not as insistent about it. Ladies can get away with sipping champagne, and men do not necessarily drink *do dnya* (to the bottom) each time they toast with vodka, as is the custom in the rest of Russia. However, it is still expected as common courtesy to drink with your host. *Che!* (Bottoms up!)

TRADITIONS

A major aspect of Yakut life is surviving the winter. As many Yakuts are hunters who must tramp through the woods for months at a time, often far from their original bases, one tradition is that hunters' huts are always ready for guests:

unlocked, supplied with food and wood for the stove. Any hunter who comes upon another's hut is welcome to spend the night. Of course, common courtesy requires that the guest will replenish the wood and food, so the hut will be ready for the next guest, or the original owner.

Another tradition is that if you see the cranes dance, you will be happy all your life. Unfortunately, these cranes are in the Red Book, the Russian version of the Endangered Species List, so the opportunity to see the cranes dance nowadays is slim. (However, many items of native jewelry have cranes dancing on them, so you can ensure your good luck by pruchasing a pretty pendant or earrings.)

Before contact with the Russians, the Yakuts had no written language and thus had a strong oral tradition. *Olonkhos*, folk epics, were related during the long winter nights by *olonkhosuts* or story-tellers. The greatest *olonkho* is Nyurgun Bootur, the Swift. A tremendous epic, it is composed of nine "songs" and took a week to narrate. It describes the deeds of Nyurgun Bootur in the struggle of the Children of the Sun (from whom the Yakuts consider themselves descended), against the cyclopses and flesh-eaters of the Lower World. Since the introduction of a Yakut alphabet, it has been written down and also translated into various languages. There is a particularly beautiful Russian edition with striking color plates. The epic has also been published in French, but only recently has the first "song" been translated into English, to be published in 1995.

NATIVE CRAFTS

Yakut artists are famous for their skill in carving mammoth bone. Carvings can be found in most art shops, and can be as simple as a small pendant, or as complex as a dramatic nature scene of a wolf attacking a reindeer. Keep in mind that importing certain kinds of ivory into the United States is illegal, and though the shopkeeper may calm you by insisting that the carving is of ancient mammoth and not endangered walrus tusk, you may have complications at U.S. customs. If you are interested in ivory, before your trip you should check with the U.S. Fish and Wildlife Service, Department of the Interior, Washington, DC 20240 and ask for their pamphlet "Fish and Wildlife."

Another traditional native craft you can find are round boxes made out of birch bark. These boxes are sewn together with horsehair, and are designed for a variety of purposes, from holding milk products (they are sewn so tightly that they are waterproof), to gathering berries, to storing cheese. You, of course, might choose to keep your milk in the refrigerator and put earrings or other small objects in your box. In any case they are prettily decorated, and less expensive than ivory.

These tether posts have become a symbol of Yakut hospitality. Note building on stilts in background

As Yakuts have been hunters and trappers from time immemorial, fur is another item of native industry. There are no "animal rights activists" protesting against hunting in this region where fur is so necessary to survival. In fact there are some fur farms, but many animals are indeed trapped by hunters. Among the popular furs for hats, collars, and coats are arctic fox (*pisets*), blue fox (*chernoburka*), and of course mink (*nurka*). The muskrat, which is not native to Yakutia but was introduced from Canada in the 60's, has also become a popular choice.

Reindeer and pony hides are also used for decoration, sometimes being made into wall-hangings of geometric shapes, or depicting scenes from nature. Pony saddle-bags, decorated with embroidery, also make unique wall-hangings.

Yakutia, which once sent the fruits of its labors to Moscow, receiving only a token payment in return, now has more control over the gold, silver, and diamonds which it extracts. Therefore attractive items can be found in the stores, at prices lower than elsewhere. Lovely native designs for pendants and earrings often include cranes or reindeer. Chromdiopsid, a green crystal, is called the "Siberian emerald," and in all of Russia it is found only in Yakutia.

YAKUTSK

Yakutsk is the capital city of Yakutia, situated on the banks of the Lena River. Built on permafrost, a layer of frozen soil hundreds of meters deep which never melts, constructors have learned to build on stilts so the heat from the buildings doesn't melt the layers below and cause the buildings to sink into the tundra. You can still see some early houses, built right onto the ground, which are now settling and sagging.

In the winter Yakutsk is shrouded in "habitation fog," brought about when the air is so cold that hot air from houses, people and cars cannot rise. Cars drive slowly, drivers peering into the mist to avoid accidents. In summer Yakutsk is hot and dusty, little shade to be found on the streets, since trees never grow very tall in the harsh climate. Take care where you walk, as the sidewalks have buckled under the extremes of temperature.

Some addresses are difficult to find, since entire blocks of buildings have the same number. An address with a / usually means that the building is set back from the main street.

HIGHLIGHTS TOUR

Considering that walking around Yakutsk is not a good idea in winter (even locals will advise you to not spend more time outdoors than necessary), and in summer is a hot and dusty proposition, a highlights tour is suggested instead of a walking tour, which will enable you to get the most out of a day in Yakutsk without freezing or frying!

An ideal starting point is **Lenin Square**. This square has a fountain in summer, and is considered the heart of the city. Lenin himself is pointing in the direction you should head, which is down Kirova street. About 1 1/2 blocks down the street on your left, carefully hidden behind a tall fence, is the **Museum of the Music and Folklore of Yakutia**. This very small museum will give you a good look at the native cultures which flourished in the area before the arrival of the Russians. Not just Yakut

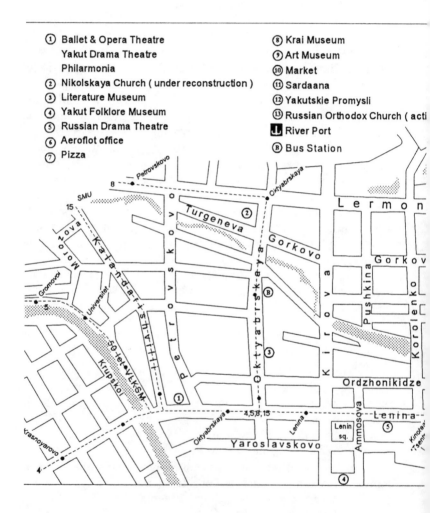

① Ballet & Opera Theatre
   Yakut Drama Theatre
   Philarmonia
② Nikolskaya Church (under reconstruction)
③ Literature Museum
④ Yakut Folklore Museum
⑤ Russian Drama Theatre
⑥ Aeroflot office
⑦ Pizza

⑧ Krai Museum
⑨ Art Museum
⑩ Market
⑪ Sardaana
⑫ Yakutskie Promysli
⑬ Russian Orthodox Church (acti
🚢 River Port
Ⓑ Bus Station

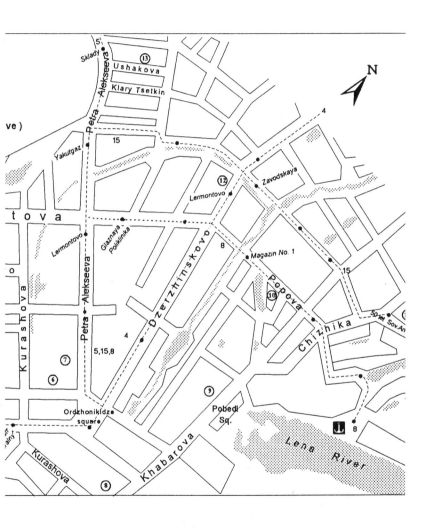

folklore, but also Even and Evenk traditions and artifacts are described. The museum is greatly enhanced by the knowledge and enthusiasm of the guide, who has been known to suddenly break into song, imitating the *olonkhosuti* (singers of the traditional native epic, the *olonkho*). She can bring past traditions to life, and also tell you how they are continued today. A must-see museum.

Leaving the museum, return to Lenin Square. Turn left, and you will see the bus stop. Get on a No. 15 bus, and take it to the last stop (called "Aviagruppa"). Ahead of you, on the opposite side of the road, you will see a white building with a carved wooden facade. This is the **Sardaana Fur Factory**. Approaching it, there are two entrances. The one to the right is the factory outlet shop. This is your best bet for souvenirs, as the prices here are much lower than at other souvenir stores. You can find fur hats, *unty*, wall hangings, even an entire mounted moose head! The service is polite and helpful, and you will certainly find some unique items here.

Leaving Sardaana, head back to the bus stop (but stay on the same side of the road—the bus turns around here). Getting back on a No. 15, look out the right hand window. If it is not foggy, you will see the onion domes and crosses of the **Orthodox Church** in the distance. Get out at the stop called "Yakutgas" on Petra Alekseeva St. (about 5 stops from Sardaana). The neighborhood here consists mostly of wooden houses, with a few industrial complexes thrown in for good measure. Cross the

Active Russian Orthodox church on Ushakova

street, and, staying on the right side of Petra Alekseeva St., go
about 4 blocks up to Ushakova St. Turn right on Ushakova, and
you will see the church halfway down the block. It is a fine
example of traditional wood construction (*zodchestvo*). It is also
the only active Russian Orthodox Church in Yakutsk (until the
Nikolski Cathedral is remodeled and reconsecrated). Take a
look at the lovely wood and gold interior.

Retracing your steps to Petra Alekseeva, cross the street
and head for the bus stop to the right (heading back to town).
Here you can catch bus No. 5, which will take you all the way
back to the center of town, along Prospekt Lenina. Stay on
three stops past Lenin Square, and get off at the "Universitet"
stop. Many students will get off with you, as this is the main
stop for the **Yakutsk State University**. There are many buildings
to the University—at the present time the main building is
painted in an eye-catching pattern of pink and blue. The main
building (*glavni korpus*), with gray columns in front, has a
mammoth skeleton on display on the second floor. If you don't
have time to get to the Kraevecheski Museum, stop by here for a
look. If you don't feel like stopping into the University, walk
back the way the bus came, along the edge of **Warm Lake
(*Ozero Tyoploe*)**. In the summer the banks are grassy and
wildflowers grow, offering a pretty view. In winter the lake, not
living up to its name, freezes solid and you can walk on it
instead of beside it. Walking along the lake, you will come once
again to Prospekt Lenina, where you turn left. The large white
and wood building set back from the street on the left is the
Government Ballet and Opera Theater, which has performances
year round. To the right of the theater, the white building with
green domed roof used to be the Museum of Western European
Art, but is now waiting to be remodeled.

From here you can hop on a bus back along Lenina. You
will pass one other building of note, the **Pushkin Library** at
Lenina 40. A brick building built in 1911, the library is
currently sinking and under reconstruction, but is still open
(entrance around the back). Once again in Lenin Square, you
might want to drop in to **Dom Torgovli (House of Trade)** at the
far left corner of the square. Here, on the ground floor to the
left of the entrance, is another small native crafts shop, ***Kudai
Bakhisy***, where you can check to see if you have missed any
nifty souvenirs. To the right is a lovely stained glass depiction of
the cranes dancing, symbol of happiness.

Some early buildings are sinking into the ground

PRACTICAL INFORMATION

Moscow time + 6 hours.
Code for calling Yakutsk from outside the city: **41122.**
Information when calling from inside the city: **09.**
Information from outside the city: **411-99-09111.**
Main Post Office Ulitsa Dzerzhinskovo 4. Open 8-20, Sat 9-18, Sun 10-18. Tel: 2-38-43.
Intercity telephone station At this central location you can order intercity and international calls. Fill out a slip with the number you are calling, and how long you want to talk. Pay for the call in advance, then sit and wait until your call is announced. A smoky crowded place, but with a nice touch in that the doors to the phone cabins are carved wood and there are faded photos of native scenes above the doors. Ulitsa Lenina, next to Lena Hotel.

HOTELS

Ontario Hotel Built by Canadians and now run as a Canadian/Russian joint venture, this small hotel is reminiscent of a cabin in the woods. About 20 minutes from downtown Yakutsk, it has a bar, restaurant, satellite phone and fax. Credit cards accepted (no Amex). Expensive. Ulitsa Viliuiskaya, 6 km. Tel: 6-50-58, 2-20-46, Fax: (095) 230-2919.
Hotel Sterkh (Crane) Centrally located, this hotel is slightly nicer than its neighbor, the Lena. The rooms are clean,

with small amenities and a water heater for making tea in your room. Moderate. On the corner of Lenina and Ordzhonikidze Square, enter through Lena Restaurant and go upstairs to reception on the second floor. Tel: 4-27-01.

Hotel Lena Large rooms with decent bathrooms. There are luxury suites on the 2nd floor. The hotel has a tour office, gift shop, hairdresser, late night bar. Moderate. Prospekt Lenina 8. Tel: 4-48-90.

Hotel Yakutsk Inexpensive. Ulitsa Lomonosova 48. Tel: 5-07-00.

Hotel Shakhtyor (Miner) Although generally reserved for mining bigwigs, you can stay here if it is not fully booked. A very small hotel with a few two-room suites. Pleasant rooms. Inexpensive. Alekseeva 7/2. Tel: 4-00-09.

FOOD

It must be said about Yakutsk that eating out is not a simple prospect. If you want to venture farther afield than merely your hotel restaurant, the choices are slim. If you ask a local what they do for lunch, Yakutsk is so small that many people will tell you they simply dash home during their break. A few new cafes have opened, good for a quick lunch, but with a cover charge in the evenings. Many official buildings have *stolovayas* (cafeterias), ostensibly for workers in the building or of a particular organization, but actually anyone can drop in. Stolovayas are not particularly appealing, but usually have inexpensive, filling food.

In winter, meat is the local dish of choice. Don't be surprised to find that your appetizer has meat in it, your soup has meat in it, and your main dish is meat. Locals will insist that you need the protein to keep you warm. There is also the fact that the growing season is extremely short, even in greenhouses, and that vegetables besides onions, potatoes and other winter staples are scarce. In summer, fruits and vegetables are both grown locally and imported from warmer areas, but their prices are exorbitant, double or triple the price in other parts of Russia. In fact, if you are visiting friends, buy some fresh fruits before hopping on the plane. They will make a very nice gift, since they are either scarce, or prohibitively expensive.

Lena Hotel Restaurant A charming place with carved wood interior and deep red tablecloths. Accustomed to serving tourists, the service is polite and not too slow. However, even if the waitress comes over and recites the few choices, ask to see a menu. Keep in mind that vegetables are hard to come by in Yakutia and check the prices before ordering. A tiny salad of cucumber and tomato (a standard throughout Russia) counts as two vegetables, mind you, and can set you back $4. Other than vegetables, prices are reasonable. Lenina 8. Tel: 4-46-48.

Pizza This is as close as you'll come to "real" pizza, with a tomato base and "stuff" on top. Best of all, the service is quick—just walk up to the counter and order. For seating there are only a few large booths, which probably means you'll end up sitting with strangers, but in summer you can sit outside under the red and white umbrellas. Reasonable prices, courteous service. Petra Alekseeva 15. Open 9-21 (14-15) every day.

Visit Cafe Supposedly open 24 hours, good luck catching them open between breaks, inventory, cleaning, etc. However, if you can actually get in, there is a decent selection of appetizers and hot dishes. Very small, with reasonable prices. Gruff service. Corner of Kurashova and Ordzhonikidze. Tel: 2-21-03, 4-30-86.

Yakutsk Hotel Restaurant Ulitsa Lomonosova 48. Open 12-24. Cover charge in the evenings for music and dancing. Tel: 5-16-54.

Cafe Fantasia Quiet atmosphere, decent food. Covercharge after 6 pm. Prospekt Lenina, just off Lenin square. Open 12-24 (16-18:30).

Cafe Minuta A stand-up cafe with minimal selection. Right on Ordzhonikidze square, behind the Lena Hotel. Open 10-20 (15-16).

Bar Vils A dim place with loud music and a serious-looking guard. Steep cover charge after 16:00. Corner of Chiryaeva and Ordzhonikidze Square (behind main post office). Open from 10-12, 16-23.

Stolovaya Kholbos Very small, very crowded, very cheap. Kholbos is a manufacturer of sodas, among other things, and this stolovaya is located in their office building. Krupskoi 21, on first floor, left of entrance. Open Mon-Fri 13-14:40 (open to general public after 13:40).

Stolovaya Yakstroi Lenina 17, on first floor, left of entrance and down the hall. Open Mon-Fri 12-14.

Tuimaada Food Store If you are on a budget or have exhausted the restaurant selection, this food store is the best stocked in the city.   Lenina 37.   Open 8-21 every day.   Tel: 2-41-61.

MARKETS

Covered Market (Food)   In the summer, fruits and vegetables are sold at the outdoor stands, meat and dairy products inside.   In winter, of course, the whole operation moves indoors. Ulitsa Fyodora Popova 13/2.

At the present time there is also an impromptu summer fruit and vegetable market at Ordzhonikidze Square, on the open building site.

Veschevoi **(Flea Market)**   Also called the *Arbat* after the famous pedestrian mall in Moscow, the Veschevoi has clothing and household goods, mostly imported from China and Korea. Weekends at Komsomol Square.

SHOPPING

Sardaana   This store is the outlet for the fur and leather factory, and is the best place to start looking for souvenirs. There is a selection of fur hats, boots, and coats, as well as wall hangings of leather and fur depicting native scenes and designs. There is intricate silver jewelry and carved mammoth bone.   The prices here are lower than at all other souvenir stores in Yakutsk, so start your shopping here.   Take bus No. 15 to last stop (Aviagruppa): the wood facade of the factory will be ahead of you on the left side of the road.   50 Let Sovietskoi Armii.   Open Mon-Sat 10-18 (14-15).

Dom Torgovli   Centrally located on Lenin Square, this is the main department store, with a broad selection of household goods, fabrics, etc.   To the left of the front door is a separate shop, *Kudai Bakhisy*, with native crafts, fur wall hangings and jewelry, wood table sets, mounted antlers and stuffed squirrels. On the third floor of Dom Torgovli itself is a jewelry department, with gold, silver and precious stones.   Ulitsa Ammosova 6.   Open 10-19.   Tel: 2-36-82.

Yakutskiye Promysly   This store specializes in native crafts: fur boots and hats, wall hangings, birch-bark boxes, and more. A wider selection than at Sardaana, but the prices are higher. You can also buy uncut furs of black or silver fox, sable, even whole reindeer hides.   Dzerzhinskovo 31/1.   Take bus No. 1, 4,

14, 16 to "Lermontova" stop on Dzerzhinskovo. Open 10-18 (14-15). Tel: 3-80-04.

Manchari (Store No. 1) A small department store. There is a small souvenir section to the left of the front door, and in winter a wide selection of fur hats and boots. Bus Nos. 6 or 8 to "Magazine No. 1." Ulitsa F. Popova 15. Open Mon-Fri 10-19 (14-15), Sat 10-18. Tel: 4-24-61.

Zoloto A wide selection of gold and silver jewelry, many pendants and earrings bearing native designs of reindeer and cranes. Chromdiopsid ("Siberian emerald") and garnet rings. Lenina 11. Open Mon-Fri 10-18 (14-15), Sat 10-17.

Atlases This shop is only open a few hours each day, but if you can catch it open you can find maps of Yakutsk and the surrounding area, including routes for camping and boating trips. Lenina 18, corner of Korolenko 2. Open Mon-Fri 11-14.

Bukinist Ulitsa Yaroslavskovo 20. Tel: 2-95-73.

MUSEUMS

Museum of the Music and Folklore of Yakutia It is hard to see the address and museum sign, since they are behind a tall fence, but this small museum is worth looking into. Pay a bit extra to have a guided tour-the energetic guide will greatly enrich your visit with fascinating tidbits, like with the fact that the short sleeves on the bridal outfit symbolize that the bride's "wings" are now clipped. The museum has several rooms, one with a model of a typical Yakut dwelling, another with an Evenk summer yurt, one with musical instruments including the *bubin* (drum) and several types of *kyrymp* (stringed instrument). All the mannequins are actual portraits of famous people. Ulitsa Kirova 10. Open 10-17, closed Mon and the last day of the month. Tel: 2-82-39.

Kraevecheski (Natural History) Museum This museum covers the history of the region, both of man and of the flora and fauna. The natural history section begins with a mammoth skeleton, and includes stuffed birds and animals from small foxes to large moose. The history of man section includes shaman outfits and information about early native tribes, as well as about the early Russian explorers. A model of the tower of a Russian fort stands in the courtyard, near the skeleton of a huge whale. Moderate entrance fee, more expensive for foreigners. Tours available in Russian or English (extra charge). Fee for taking your picture with the mammoth. The museum is a little hard to find since it is not right on Lenina, but if you follow the right side of Lenina past Ordzhonikidze square, eventually to your right you will spy the fort tower in front of the museum. Prospekt Lenina 5/2. Open April-October 11-18, October-April 10-17 (closed Mon and Tue). Tel: 2-37-53.

Archaeological and Ethnographic Museum This museum is run by the University, and has artifacts from archaeological digs which the University is participating in. In the summer all the curators and professors are conducting digs, so call to find out if the museum is open. Ulitsa P. Morozova. Bus No. 5 to "Universitet" or 2 or 15 to "SMU." Tel: 5-27-55.

Literature Museum A yurt stands before this museum, which is just 1 1/2 blocks from Lenina. The main museum contains a collection of antique and modern books on Yakutia and the Yakut language by foreign authors, and books by Yakut authors. There is a small section on authors repressed by Stalin for their work. The museum is a bit dry, especially if you don't speak Russian, but the hall has a very lovely mural, and there are occasionally cultural evenings which are interesting no matter what language you speak. You can sip *koumys* while enjoying native poetry, or some other such event. Small entrance fee to museum (including yurt), special events more expensive. Ulitsa Oktyabrskaya 12. Take bus No. 6 or 8 to "Biblioteka." Open Tue 11-16, Wed-Sun 11-18, (*kassa* closes one hour before museum), closed Mon. Tel: 2-42-64.

Gabysheva Art Museum Ulitsa Khabarova 27. Open 10-18. Tel: 4-35-36.

Art Gallery *Urgel* This gallery represents the Artist's Union of Sakha, and has an interesting selection of works by local artists. Lermontova 35/1.

Permafrost Institute *(Institut Merzlotovedeniya)* You never knew permafrost was so interesting. You'll have to make an appointment for a tour; the director speaks English. Tour includes an underground room where you can look at the permafrost. Out front is a fountain of a baby mammoth (many mammoths have been found in Yakutia, well preserved by the permafrost). Open 8-17:15 (12:30-13:30). Call 5-38-31 for appointment and directions.

ENTERTAINMENT

Government Ballet and Opera Theater   Prospekt Lenina 46/1. Tel: 3-53-37.

Yakut Drama Theater   At present sharing space with the Ballet and Opera Theater, but a new theater is scheduled to be built on Ordzhonikidze Square, across from Aeroflot, where right now there is a fruit and vegetable market. Prospekt Lenina 46/1. Tel: 4-17-49.

Russian Drama Theater   Pr. Lenina 23. Tel: 2-32-53.

Yakut Republican Philharmonic   Ulitsa Kalandarishvili 2. Tel: 5-08-44.

Musical Salon "Charoite"   This building used to be the Holy Trinity Cathedral. Nowadays it serves various purposes. Enter through the pretty carved wooden facade. In the summer there is a disco, a hangout for students on vacation. In winter there are concerts of Yakut music and culture. The sign outside lists the upcoming events. Open Wed-Sun 19-24. *Kassa* open 14-21. Cover charge. Kalandarishvili 2. Reservations Tel: 6-31-18.

Swimming pool "Samorodok"   Ulitsa Ordzhonikidze 28. Tel: 4-41-47.

Hippodrome   Horseraces (*skachki*) occur in June, related to the *isikh* festival. Aside from that, the hippodrome rarely sees activity, although sometimes special events are held here. Prihippodromnaya Shosse. Bus No. 5 to "Ippodrom."

CHURCHES

Nikolski Cathedral
Built in 1852, this Russian Orthodox Church was taken over for the Communist Archives, but has recently been "reclaimed" by the Church and is now undergoing restoration. There is a small kiosk in front of the church which sells religious

Nikolski Cathedral

articles and can give you information on how the restoration is progressing and when the church will be reconsecrated. You can see the church from Prospekt Lenina, up Oktyabrskaya St., past the bus station. Ulitsa Turgeneva.

Russian Orthodox   This small wood church is a beautiful example of traditional wood carving and construction (*zodchestvo*). The interior has beautiful gold-framed icons. Take bus No. 15 to "Yakutgas" or 5 to "sklady." Ulitsa Ushakova 5.

OTHER SIGHTS

Victory Square (*Ploschad Pobedy*)   This used to be a huge open space with a tank as the center attraction, and plaques to war heroes. It is currently undergoing construction—supposedly a new church is going to be built here. Despite the wooden construction fence around it you can still see the statue of Manchari, which towers over the square. Manchari was a Yakut "Robin Hood" who lived from 1805-1870.

Manchari was a local "Robin Hood"

Victory Square is also the approach to the **city beach**, a relatively unattractive place, crisscrossed by water pipes and with industry down river.

Komsomolskaya Square has a *barakholka* or flea market on weekends, and the nearby **Park of Culture and Rest** has a small amusement park.

Ordzhonikidze Square is not much of a square. It is really just a large traffic circle, central spot for catching most local buses.

TRANSPORTATION

The following are the names of the stops in central Yakutsk made by local buses mentioned in the text. All bus stops are marked on the map with a dot, but in order to avoid crowding, only significant stops are named on the map.

Bus No. 15
SMU (on Kalandarshvili)
Oiunskovo
Dramteatr
Oktyabrskaya (on Lenina)
Lenina
Kinoteatr "Tsentralny"
Ordzhonikidze Sq.
Dom Pensii (on P. Alekseeva)
Lermontova
Yakutgaz

Kinoteatr "Mir" (on Kalvitsa)
Zavodskaya
YaGATP No. 1
Rabochi Gorodok
Aviagruppa(50 Let Sov. Armii)

Bus No. 8
Petrovskovo (on Lermontova)
Oktyabrskaya
Avtovokzal (on Oktyabrskaya)
Biblioteka
Lenina (on Lenina)
Kinoteatr "Tsentralny"
Ordzhonikidze Sq.
Dom Pensii (on P. Alekseeva)
Lermontova
Glaznaya Polyklinika
    (on Lermontova)
Transagentstvo
Magazin No. 1 (on F. Popova)
DOSAF
Electroseti (on Energetikov)
Rechnoi Port

Bus No. 4
Krasnoyarova
Kinoteatr "Lena" (on Lenina)
Oktyabrskaya
Lenina
Kinoteatr "Tsentralny"
Ordzhonikidze Sq.
ShkolaNo.9(onDzerzhinskovo)
Lermontovo
Khlebozavod
...to airport

Bus No. 5
Gromovoi (50 Let VLSKM)
Universitet
MedFak
Oktyabrskaya (on Lenina)
Lenina
Kinoteatr "Tsentralny"
Ordzhonikidze Sq.
Dom Pensii (on P. Alekseeva)
Lermontova
Yakutgaz
Sklady

Taxis can be ordered by calling 2-07-32 or 2-23-41. The farther in advance you order, the more likely you are of getting a cab, especially for early morning flights.

Bus Station Long distance buses travel up and down the left side of the Lena to towns such as Tyektyur and Vladimirovka. In the winter, service is increased, since buses can cross the Lena River. City buses Nos. 6 and 8 go to the bus station. Oktyabrskaya 24/1.

Local buses crisscross the city, but be forewarned that 7-8 pm is "dinner hour" for the drivers, and after 8 service is reduced.

River Port The place to catch ferries to *dachas* and other villages. Take bus No. 8 to last stop. Information: 2-13-50.

Aeroflot City Office A large hectic place, the international booth is to the far left. Ordzhonikidze 8, just off the square. Open Mon-Fri 8-19 (13-14), 9-17 Sat, Sun.

Airport About 30 minutes from the heart of town. There is a small international section to the far right of the main hall. If you are traveling in winter, it is wise to confirm whether your flight is leaving on time. All flights are canceled if the temperature dips below -56C, since at such temperatures rubber becomes brittle and there is the risk that the plane's tires will shatter on impact. Bus No. 4 travels along Lenina, through Ordzhonikidze Square and to the airport. Information: 2-24-60, 9-54-62.

Sputnik Youth Tourism This travel agency can arrange boat cruises on the river Lena, hunting or fishing trips, visits to reindeer farms in the north, and other special events. Prospekt Lenina 30. Tel: 2-77-15.

AROUND YAKUTSK

RIVER TRIPS
There are two ways of taking trips along the river. The LenaRechFlot is an organization which offers tourist cruises of a few days to two weeks. The Rechvokzal is the local passenger terminal for ferries to outlying villages. Neither service can tell you about the other one.

LenaRechFlot The ships are Austrian-built and carry over a hundred passengers. Tours start from Yakutsk, and travel up and down river to such towns as Pokrovsk, Zhigansk, Tiksi. Stops are made at various "green" spots, small villages, and archaeological sites. Entertainment includes various cultural events, perhaps a lecture on the native cultures of Yakutia, meeting local inhabitants of villages, and various parties on board. Both long and short trips stop at the Lena Pillars. The LenaRechFlot office is helpful and can show you brochures and itineraries in English. Dzerzhinskovo 2. Tel: 2-72-62.

Rechvokzal (River Port)   Ferries and "Rocketa" hydrofoil travel up and down the river, taking locals to their summer *dachas* and to other villages. The *vokzal* is usually a place of chaos, as the ticket window doesn't open up until close to the time there is a ferry leaving, by which time the line is quite long. Precise information is rarely given, and locals scramble around asking each other where a certain ferry leaves from. Follow the crowd—they eventually all head to one of the waiting boats. Take bus No. 8 to the last stop.

Lena Pillars   About 140 kilometers from Yakutsk are the Lena Pillars, an area of stark cliffs and striking geological formations. Most cruises stop here, or you can make a special trip by ferry. Well worth a trip to see these unique and beautiful geological formations.

Druzhba (Friendship) Outdoor Museum,   near village of Sotintsi. This outdoor museum is not particularly convenient to get to, but provides a nice day in the country (weather permitting), and a glimpse into the past of Yakutia, both Russian and Native. Established on the spot where the original founder of Yakutsk established his first settlement, one of the outstanding buildings is a reconstruction of the 17th century fort and church (the actual original church was dismantled and relocated to the outdoor museum near Irkutsk). You can climb the small bell tower and scout the landscape for invaders, or sit in the lovely church. There is also a *balagan*, a native yakut winter dwelling (windows used to be filled with ice in the winter, to let in light, or with a fine horsehair net in summer, to keep out mosquitos), and a yurt, the summer home. At the present time a reconstruction of an early merchant's house is being built.

On the hill beyond the river there is a fire tower, which offers a great view of the entire area. Walking along the top of the ridge there are reconstructions of native burial sites, from early Yakut to later Russian Orthodox. The hill is covered in pine trees and, in the spring, delicate wildflowers, an ideal place for a picnic.

At the present time, the entrance fee is pay-what-you-wish (the equivalent of about $2.50 was the "suggested" fee), and all proceeds go to improving the museum. Your entrance includes a guided tour (in Russian), which, even if you don't speak Russian, greatly improves your understanding and enjoyment of the buildings, since without a guide the doors are locked and you can only peer inside the various buildings.

How to get there: A hydrofoil leaves the River Port at 11:00, arriving at the port of Sotintsi in about 50 minutes. The ride is not particularly exciting since the hydrofoil is enclosed—most people simply fall asleep. The boat makes one brief stop at a place where only people with backpacks and tents get out, then continues to Sotintsi. If you have people meeting you in a jeep, you are lucky. Otherwise you can crowd onto the one bus going to town and ask to be let off at the turn-off to the museum. If you don't want to cram into the bus, start hiking. Near the ferry station there is a sign pointing (when we were there) in the wrong direction, away from a path through the woods to the museum. No matter which direction the sign is pointing, this shortcut is not recommended. Although you might get to see a *sardaana* (an endangered species of tiger lily) in the woods, in the spring you risk sinking into the mud, or being eaten alive by mosquitos. Best bet—stick to the road. It's

Reconstruction of Beketov's original fort at Druzhba outdoor museum

about a half-hour walk. By the time you get to the fork in the road which goes to Sotintsi, you can see the fort of the museum off to your left. If you walk, you are likely to arrive during lunchtime, and you won't be able to find a guide. Have your picnic in the woods, but don't dally, because you want to catch the very first tour after lunch, so you can head back to the port in time for the next (and last!) boat, which is around 16:00. Don't miss this boat, because if you do, you'll have to camp out till the next boat, the next day!

VERKHNI-VILIUISK

This small town is a 1 1/2 hour flight from Yakutsk. Its main industries are mining tin, oil, and diamonds It is also a place which managed to preserve Yakut traditions despite Soviet rule. The *isikh* ceremony continued here when it had been suppressed elsewhere. Many people come here for the festival from other towns and cities.

Hotel Almaz This hotel belongs to the diamond factory, but anyone with a "reason" to come to Verkhni-Viliuisk can probably stay here, since the only other hotel in town is not up to "international" standards. It used to be a private home, but was bought by Japanese investors in the factory, and refurbished into a charming guesthouse. 3 small bedrooms open onto a common living room. The housekeeper will make tea for you. There is even indoor plumbing, which works year round, unless the pipes freeze. Warm and cozy, this hotel is recommended. Reasonable prices. 50 Let YaASSR 41. Tel: 2-11-55.

CHURAPCHA

The claim to fame of this agricultural village is that Dmitri Petrovich Korkin lived and worked here. Korkin is revered for having trained 3 Olympic wrestlers during his career. There is a museum dedicated to him, giving a detailed look at his life and work, and containing personal items, like his sweat suit and electric razor.

There is also a sport school here, where the traditional sports of wrestling and archery are practiced. In keeping with the current revival in native culture, they have also opened a building devoted to native crafts and traditions, where girls learn to cook native dishes, to sew traditional birchbark boxes and native clothing, embroidery, etc, and boys learn about hunting, tracking, living outdoors, building houses, etc. The schoolrooms are charmingly made into traditional "summer" and "winter" houses, and Yakut history, culture and language are also taught.

Churapcha can be reached by bus during the winter, when there is an "ice bridge" across the river Lena. In the summer a ferry crosses the river.

MAGADANSKAYA OBLAST

CHAPTER 8

MAGADANSKAYA OBLAST

A land of harsh climate and breath-taking beauty, Magadanskaya Oblast is 8 time zones away from Moscow. With 1/3 of the territory lying in the Arctic Circle and winter lasting from 5 1/2 to 7 1/2 months a year, Magadanskaya Oblast in winter is not for the weak or frail. Temperatures in January can be as low as -60C with an average temperature of -17C around the capital. Summers are short and cool, with temperatures averaging 12 Celsius. Snow stays on the ground until June and starts falling again as early as September.

The area is considered the "hard currency shop" of Russia, providing great quantities of valuable raw materials that are usually sold abroad. Gold (70% of the gold in Russia is mined here), silver, tungsten, tin, lumber and coal are what brought the settlers, and are still the big money-makers for Russia, although little benefit is gained by the region itself, since Moscow still controls the profits. Fishing is also big business; Magadanskaya Oblast is surrounded by the Bering and East Siberian seas as well as the seas of Okhotsk and Chukotka, giving it more coastline than any other region in the former Soviet Union. Agriculture is limited due to the short growing season, although reindeer farming is a big business in Chukotka.

The northern half of the oblast is the Autonomous Region of Chukotka, with its capital in Anadyr. Chukotka owes most of its inhabitants (excluding the indigenous peoples) to mining, mostly precious minerals, particularly gold. In the Soviet days, miners received triple pay for working in this bitterly harsh region, but now federal salaries come months late, if at all, and the population continues to thin.

Today, Alaska Airlines flies through Magadan, giving a needed boost to the local economy by bringing businessmen and tourists from the United States. Neglected by Moscow, both Chukotka and Magadan are striving to strengthen their international ties.

HISTORY

Although Magadanskaya Oblast officially received separate status as an Oblast as recently as 1953, Russia's contacts with Magadan and Chukotka go back to the 17th Century.

In 1648 the explorer Dezhnev headed an expedition that went from the head of the Kolyma River to the Pacific Ocean, inadvertently discovering and passing through the Bering Strait years before it received the name of its "discoverer," Vitus Bering. After much hardship and adventure he found his goal, the mouth of the river Anadyr. Another Cossack explorer, Mikhail Stadukhin, had also set out to look for the mouth of the Anadyr River at the same time. Stakukhin's trip took him by land and he also found the Anadyr, but to his disappointment and annoyance found Dezhnev had beaten him to the punch. The efforts of these two explorers and their expeditions opened the area of modern day Magadanskaya Oblast to Russian settlers and traders. These traders came to seek their fortunes by exporting furs and walrus tusks, both abundant in the region. Due to the extreme harshness of the climate, settlements grew slowly and painfully. Some American and Japanese companies traded in the area, mostly buying fish.

It wasn't until the beginning of the 20th century that individuals began actively seeking gold in the area. As organized efforts were interrupted by the October Revolution and the ensuing civil war, it was only in the late 20's that geological expeditions traveled throughout the area and confirmed what many had guessed before—that Chukotka had rich deposits of gold, oil and tin for the taking. The only problem was how to get at it.

This problem was solved very quickly. In 1931 the NKVD (predecessors of the KGB) set up an organization called DalStroy, a section of the Far Eastern Construction Trust. DalStroy was to oversee the development and mining of the area using labor camps. Magadan itself was constructed to serve as a base for the mining camps in the Kolyma basin. The labor was provided by political prisoners and criminals supplied in great numbers by Stalin's police state. Millions of convicts were shipped to the desolate area that was the Magadan territory to construct the port of Nagaev, the city of Magadan, and to work the mines. Under the harshest conditions, roads were built, buildings constructed, and countless tons of ore were shipped to western Russia, all at the expense of the prisoners. DalStroy controlled over 160 camps in the area, including the infamous Kolyma gold mining camps. As extensive and brutal as Stalin's system of labor camps were, the Kolyma camps were considered the worst, the place of no return. Although exact figures will never be known, prison camp deaths are estimated to have been from 12 to 20 million, of which the Kolyma camps were responsible for 2.5 to 4 million.

After Stalin's death in 1953, the infamous DalStroy was abolished and large numbers of prisoners were granted amnesty. The camp system continued to operate but would never again reach the scale of butchery of the Stalin years. With the breakup of the Soviet Union, Magadan has tried to obtain more control over the export of its resources, although with meager success. Alaska Airlines flights now stop in Magadan and the capital has sister city ties with both Anchorage and Soldatno, a small Russian community in Alaska.

MAGADAN'S INDIGENOUS PEOPLES

The **Chukchi** are one of the northern tribes that fought the Russians every step of the way in the latter's colonization of the North. After the conquest, they refused to convert to Russian Orthodoxy, retaining their belief in Shamanism. The Chukchi were also effective traders. To make a transaction, the Chukchi would not deal directly with the Russian traders, but hung furs off the ends of their lances and expected the Russians to replace them with something of equal value. In this way, transactions were conducted on a more honest level, for if the native felt he was being cheated, the consequences were swift and lethal. The Chukchi, like the Koryaks in Kamchatka, are divided into nomadic and sedentary groups. The nomadic groups roamed the tundra with reindeer herds, living in large tents in the summer and subterranean dwellings in the winter.

The **Evens**, who live around the Sea of Okhotsk and the area around the river Lena, spread to the northern Kamchatka peninsula in the mid 1800's. Like other northern tribes, the Evens are a nomadic people who practice reindeer herding. However, in contrast to the shamanism practiced by the majority of the local indigenous groups, the Evens practice a form of animism and totemism.

MAGADAN

Founded as a port and base of operations to support the Kolyma mining camp activities, Magadan is considered one of the Soviet Union's "miracle" cities, seemingly springing up overnight. With convicts in the millions being used as laborers, Magadan and Nagaev port were indeed quickly built in the early 30's, and in 1939 Magadan received the status of "city." Today, Magadan (population 165,000) is a pleasant city, built on gently rolling hills overlooking Nagaev Bay, and is considered the cultural and economic center of the northeast provinces of Russia.

WALKING AROUND TOWN

Magadan is small, and a stroll to most of the main sights will give you a feel for the city. A good place to start a tour, whether you are staying there or not, is the **Magadan Hotel**, since it is centrally located. Exiting the hotel and turning left will bring you to Prospekt Lenina, one of the main streets of the city. City natives proudly claim that it's the longest street in the world because it doesn't end within the city boundaries, but simply continues into the Kolymskaya Trassa, the vital transportation artery of the entire oblast that travels 1168 km and connects Magadan with Yakutsk. Many of the buildings along the central part of Lenina are from the 30's and 40's, but quite a few house very modern shops. Walk up the hill one block, and on your left you will pass **Znania bookstore**, a good place to stop if you want to pick up maps of the city or the surrounding area. Depending on the season, maps are available describing cross-country ski routes, canoe trips, hiking trails, etc. A bit farther along, on the corner of Pushkinskaya Street, is

MAGADAN

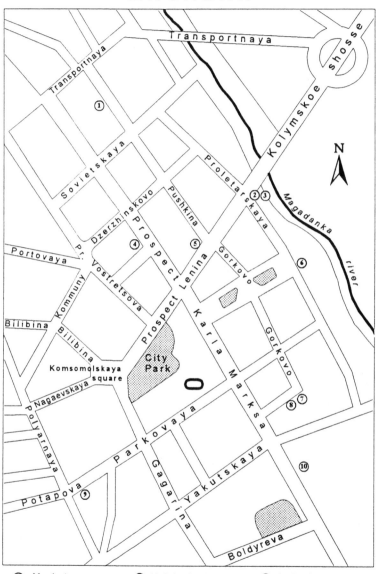

① Market
② Bus station
③ Aeroflot office
④ Drama Theatre
⑤ Kolektsionir
⑥ Lenin Sq.
⑦ Souvenirs
⑧ Chinese restaurant
⑨ Orthodox Church
⑩ Krai Museum
⬮ Spartak Sport Complex

Kolektsionir, a small privately owned shop with lots of art and other "collectibles." The owner is helpful and friendly. Cross back to the left-hand side of Lenina, and Pushkinskaya turns into Gorkovo St. There are many shops along Gorkovo, the most interesting being **Almaz**, the jewelry store, and, at the very end of the street, **Souvenirs**. If you are facing Souvenirs, you should turn right and go up past the Chinese restaurant to Prospekt Karla Marksa. Make another left and head down the hill. On Karla Marksa, between Yakutskaya and Boldyreva, is the **Kraevecheski Museum**. This is the natural history and ethnographic museum. The permanent halls give you a look into the history of the area, the native populations, and mineral resources. There are also changing exhibits. Recently, there was an exhibition on the Kolyma Prison Camps, reputed to be among the worst prison camps in Russia, but formerly so secret that they didn't "officially" exist.

After the museum you can head back toward Yakutskaya St. Across Karla Marksa on the corner you will see a huge squat building. This is the **Seventh Day Adventist Church**. A couple of years ago a very small contingent of Seventh Day Adventists came to Magadan from Alaska and took up residence. The Church was recently completed, and, although an eyesore from the outside, it is pretty on the inside.

If you'd like to look at more classical architecture, turn left on Yakutskaya and go up the hill. On Gagarina St. turn right, and left again onto Parkovaya. At the top of the hill is the **Russian Orthodox Church**. Built in 1991, its blue domes have recently been repainted, the walls newly white-washed. A sign inside lists the hours of services, and you are welcome to visit, as long as you do not interrupt a mass.

If you are still feeling energetic after your hike around Magadan's hills, you can head straight down Parkovaya to the **Sports Complex**. There is a swimming pool, ice skating rink, basketball court, etc. But if you'd rather continue strolling, then after you leave the church turn left on Gagarina and follow it to Komsomolskaya Square. Here you have the choice of stopping into **Dyetski Mir** (Children's World) toy store, turning left onto Nagaevskaya and heading to the city beach, or turning right, back onto Lenina. If you walk down Lenina, you will have the **city park** on your right. Go in the gates and stroll around—you'll find a nice oasis from the city, with statues, old men playing chess, and children's playgrounds. One playground even has statues of mink running in a circle, not the type of animals one expects to see statues of, but a hit with the small children.

The city park paths lead you back to Lenina, where you can end your tour with a stop in one of the cafes to be found on Lenina, Portovaya and Karla Marksa.

PRACTICAL INFORMATION

Moscow time +8 hours.

Code for calling Magadan from outside the city: **41322.**

Information when calling from inside Magadan: **09.**

Information from outside Magadan: **41322-2-09-99.**

Business Center Has fax machine, xerox, and typing service. Located in Business Center Hotel, which can also arrange for car hire and interpreter services. Proletarskaya 84v. Tel: 5-82-23 (business center) or 5-89-44 (hotel admin).

Main Post Office Proletarskaya 10.

Peregovorni Punkt (telephone and telegraph office) Proletarskaya 11. Tel: 2-82-31.

UPS Courier Service Lenina 1. Tel: 2-16-45.

Magadan Tourist Proletarskaya 14 or Karla Marksa 33.

HOTELS

Business Center Hotel This hotel is equipped to cater to the needs of an international traveler—the staff is helpful and the hotel offers many services including conference facilities and a business center with fax machine, xerox· and typing services. They can also arrange for interpreters, tours of the city and surrounding areas, a trip to a *gulag*, rental of a bus or car with driver, and further travel through their ticketing office. There is a restaurant "U Maxa" (At Max's) on the second floor, and a bar on the third. There is also the Fine Arts Gallery "Ligato" where you can find paintings of the surrounding countryside, jewelry, and fine native carvings of bone and ivory. This hotel used to be the local Intourist Hotel (but try not to hold that against them—they've come a long way). Moderate prices. Proletarskaya 84v. Tel: 5-81-57, 5-89-44.

Hotel Okean A newish hotel, opened in the past couple of years. The restaurant and bar tend to be quite busy, filled with mafia-types, "working girls," and mining people. Inexpensive. Portovaya 36/10 (bus #6 to Morgorodok stop). Tel: 3-57-09.

Hotel Magadan Your standard large Soviet hotel, with indifferent service, seedy characters in the halls, and loud music in the restaurant. The hotel you are most likely to stay at unless you specify otherwise. Moderate. Proletarskaya 8. Tel: 2-10-14.

Airport Hotel If your plane gets delayed by bad weather you might have to put up here rather than heading all the way back to town. Right across the street from the airport, in the town of Sokol. Inexpensive. Tel: 9-33-84.

FOOD

Restaurant U Maxa (At Max's) in Business Ctr. Hotel, Proletarskaya 84v. Usually serves only guests of the hotel, unless you make a reservation. Open 8-23. Tel: 5-82-55.

Green Crocodile Cafe corner of Pushkinskaya and Dzerzhinskovo (inside "Dom Kulturi Mettalurgov"). Pretty carved wood interior, and tasty food including delicious blini, with quick and polite service. Even has a stuffed baby crocodile. Pushkinskaya 6. Open 13-23. Tel: 2-42-62.

Tunkhua (Chinese Restaurant) on Gorkovo, just up from Souvenirs. Open 12-16, 18-23 everyday.

Cafe Russki Dvor Easy to recognize by its pretty carved wood door. Good pelmeni. Lenina 22. Open Tue-Sun 12-22 (15-17).

Primorski Open for lunch from 12-15, dinner from 20-23. Bar open from 20-1 am. Kommuny 14. Tel: 2-72-09.

Dzyalbu (means "meeting place" in Chukchi). Despite the exotic name, the cuisine is Russian. Friendly service. You can rent out the whole place for evening parties. Lyuksa 2. Open 11:30-16. Tel: 5-29-81.

Okean Restaurant In Hotel Okean. Portovaya 36/10. Tel: 3-10-63.

Magadan Hotel Restaurant Open 8-10, 12-23 (15:30-18) everyday.

Pelikan Cocktail Bar Portovaya 2. Open 10-22 (14-15).

Skazka Cafe Karla Marksa 32. Open 11-21 (16-17). Tel: 2-24-68.

Cafe Parus Bar, Cafe Dieta Portovaya 3. Open Mon-Sat 11:30-15, 17-19:30.

Ariran Korean Cafe (has dragons outside) Portovaya 2. Open 12-16 (closed Sun, Mon).

SHOPPING

Chukchi and Eskimo ivory carvings are known throughout Russia and abroad. Usually depicting scenes of native life and/or animals of the Far North, the carvings make a great souvenir to bring back memories of Magadan. Quality varies, but the works of masters such as Tukkai or Teyutina are amazing in their detail and workmanship. For the more expensive works, ask the shop for a *spravka*, a written receipt of cost and origin, which will allow you to take your buy out of the country.

Souvenirs The government souvenir store, with your standard choices of *matryoshkas* and lacquer boxes, plus many crafts made by the local native population. There is a factory in town which turns out lovely carvings from mammoth bones, walrus tusks, and moose antler. Again, keep in mind that U.S. customs restricts certain kinds of ivory imports. If you are interested in ivory carvings, it is best to check with the U.S. customs office for a booklet on restrictions before you travel. This shop also has fur wall hangings and bone and wood jewelry. Gorkovo 19. Open Mon-Fri 11-19 (14-15), Sat 11-16. Tel: 2-20-80.

Kolektsionir A private store with an interesting collection of ivory carvings, wall hangings with scenes made of fur, paintings by local artists, old coins, paper money, military uniforms. Helpful service. Lenina 14. Open Mon-Fri 10-19 (14-15), Sat 10-18.

Almaz Government jewelry store, with a large selection of gold, amber, and precious stones. Gorkovo 7. Open Mon-Fri 10-18 (14-15). Tel: 2-55-19.

Ligato Fine Arts Gallery Has a selection of art, jewelry, and native crafts. In Business Center Hotel, Proletarskaya 84v. Tel: 5-85-48.

Melodia Music store. Kommuny 2 (corner of Portovaya and Kommuny). Open Mon-Fri 10-19 (14-15), Sat 10-18.

Znania (Knowledge) Book Store Has oblast and city maps as well as hiking, boating and ski routes. Lenina 11. Open Mon-Fri 11-19 (14-15), Sat 10-16. Tel: 2-23-06.

Knigi (Bookstore) Corner of Portovaya and Dzerzhinskovo. Open Mon-Fri 11-19 (14-15), Sat 10-16.

Voskhod (Department Store) Lenina 17. Open Mon-Fri 10-19 (14-15), Sat 10-17.

MARKET

The main outdoor market is at Pushkina 19A, between Sovietskaya and Transportnaya.

ENTERTAINMENT

Geological Museum Make arrangements with Director Yuri Andreevich Kolyasnikov 3-00-38, or Deputy Alla Alexandrovna Vishnevski 3-09-34. Portovaya 16.

Kraevecheski Museum (Natural History and Ethnographic Museum) Karla Marksa 55. Open Wed-Sun 11-18. Tel: 5-35-28, 5-50-41, 5-21-08.

Gorky Music and Drama Theater Evening performances start at 19:00; Sat, Sun at 18:00; matinees at 11:00. Box office 13-19:30 (16-17). Karla Marksa 30. Tel: 2-22-09.

Philharmonic Lenina 22. Tel: 2-29-10, 2-90-64.

Gornyak Movie Theater Lenina 19 (just up the hill from Voskhod). Tel: 2-85-34.

Oktyabr Movie Theater Transportnaya 8. Tel: 2-94-09.

Puppet Theater Parkovaya 20. Tel: 2-80-16.

Imperial Night Club Proletarskaya, next to Hotel Magadan. Open 18-2. Tel: 2-12-57.

Ice Skating Located on Parkovaya at Spartak Sport Complex. Open Tue-Fri 17-21, Sat-Sun 10-21. Karate, boxing, basketball and other sports also available.

Swimming Pool The swimming pool is mostly monopolized by children's classes, but there are 45 minute sessions for adults Tue, Thu, Fri, Sat at 19:45. Parkovaya 18. Tel: 2-46-42.

Skiing at Snezhnaya Dolina, 23 kilometers north of Magadan proper. The favorite recreation spot among city residents and dwellers of adjacent villages. Due to its unique micro-climate, Snezhnaya Dolina has long been an excellent skiing area where snow stays till June (you can then see people skiing in bathing suits and bikinis!). It also hosts a great number of cross-country skiing competitions 6 months a year. Great cross-country ski routes through Bolshoi and Maly (Big and Small) mountain passes. City bus No. 5 connects downtown Magadan and this resort, about a 45 minute trip. Ski rentals available, although not the best quality brands. In summer the area is home to a pioneer camp for children. Tel: 4-41-89.

PLACES OF WORSHIP

Russian Orthodox Church, corner of Parkovaya and Polyarnaya. Has daily services, check sign inside for times.

Seventh Day Adventists, corner of Karla Marksa and Yakutskaya (you can't miss it). Read sign outside for hours of services.

TRANSPORTATION

The Magadan airport is about one hour from the city, near a town called Sokol. There is an international section, at present used only for the international flights to/from Alaska. It is also the **Alaska Airlines** and **Magadan Air Concern** office. **Kolyma Air**, which has flights to such places as Yakutsk, Okhotsk, and a host of small towns all over Magadanskaya Oblast and Chukotka, has a small desk in the main section of the airport. There are many cafes at the airport, however the only one which can be recommended is the **Maxim**, on the second floor of the main terminal.

Magadan Air, actually an affiliate of Aeroflot, is so far the only airline where the stewardesses do a little demonstration of how to put on life jackets, which are stored in small suitcases on the rack over the seats. Actually, most Russians on the flight were not happy to see the demonstration, as they took it as a dire warning, rather than a reassurance.

Aeroflot City Office A large and predictably gruff office. Naberezhnaya Magadanki 7 (across from Magadan Hotel). Open 9-20 (14-15). Information 2-88-91.

Kolyma Air at the airport in the town of Sokol. Information 2-88-91.

Alaska Airlines at airport, town of Sokol. Tel: 9-32-32.

Magadan Air Concern Central agency office (near Business Center Hotel) accepts credit cards. Some agents speak English. Open 9-18. Proletarskaya 88B. General Information: 5-89-14, Charters reservations: 2-10-03 (phone/fax).

Bus Station (*Avtovokzal*) For long distance buses. A bus goes to the airport about every half hour. The airport bus is simply labeled "airport." Prospekt Lenina 1 (across from Magadan Hotel). Tel: 2-16-02, 2-18-87.

Rybny Port (Fish Port)   The place to charter boats to the surrounding islands for fishing, swimming or just plain sightseeing.   Approach any small or medium-sized boat and make the owner an offer.   To get to the port, take bus #1 to the last stop.

OUTSIDE OF MAGADAN

If you have the time, Magadanskaya Oblast has many beautiful areas to explore.   The mountains offer breath-taking views and there are hot springs for you to soak your cares away. Bitterly cold in the winter, the northern tundra blooms in the summer and is quite beautiful.   The valleys were carved by glaciers, and many are still in the process of being created, making the region a wonderland for geologists and nature lovers alike.   Magadanskaya Oblast is really the land of 1000 lakes, including thermal lakes.

Road to Ola (35 km east of Magadan).   This hour-long drive follows the coast of the Sea of Okhotsk and passes through pretty mountain passes.   Great views of the ocean and the Far Eastern taiga.   Ola, an agricultural village, has a small museum, but the main idea is not to BE there, but to GET there and enjoy the views along the way, or get off the bus enroute and enjoy a day out in nature. (Make sure you know when the last bus returns to Magadan, or you'll be spending more time in nature than you planned).   Further along is the **Olysky Zakaznik (natural reserve)**, which can be reached by bus from Magadan. Beautiful scenery and geological formations as well as the chance to see bears, moose and salmon (in season) make it worth a trip.

Yagodnoye   This small town 542 km NW of Magadan is the jumping off point for hikes to **Jack London Lake**.   The town itself was named after the hills which surround it, which are rich not only in gold, but in berries (*yagodi*).   An industrial town due to its mining activities, Yagodnoye lies in an area which still includes untouched taiga.   Along the route to Jack London Lake are smaller lakes with such scenic names as Dream Lake, Gray Seagull, Invisible Lake, Dancing Khariusov (fish), etc.

In December 1993, an accident destroyed the town heating system, which immediately froze up at -50C.   All children, women and the elderly were evacuated, and looting occurred.   It is questionable whether the town will survive at all.

Talaya Health Resort   286 km north of Magadan, the Talaya Resort hot springs are known for their healing properties. A neurological sanatorium was opened here in 1940, but the hot springs were used long before that by the natives of the area. The resort is near scenic lakes which teem with fish, and in the fall the area is rich in berries and mushrooms.

If you really want to see a part of Magadan's Stalinist legacy, go see a **Gulag**. Not yet an open tourist attraction, "Official" groups can contact Galina Mikhailovna at the Pushkin Library for help in organizing trips by helicopter. Third floor Pushkin Library, International Section. Yakutskaya 35. Tel: 2-26-56.

Another way to escape Magadan is by water. If you head down to the **Fish Port** (*Rybny Port*), you might find someone with a boat, willing to take you to one of the nearby islands (*po ostrovam*). To get to the port take bus No. 1 to the last stop.

Tourism Agency "Talan" One of the most experienced tour groups of the Far North, Talan organizes scientific and environmental tours. Bear watching, salmon runs, hiking to volcanoes and through nature preserves, Talan does it all. Contact Valery Zapedny, Prospekt Karla Marksa 24. Tel: 2-29-65 or 5-30-82.

Omolon   A Chukchi and Yukaghir village, Omolon lies about 100 miles south of the Arctic Circle and is the base for nomad deer herders. As the herds are constantly roving around the huge territory, it is doubtful that you will see masses of reindeer, but if you have the money, this is the place to rent a helicopter and visit them, wherever they may be. Helicopters can be chartered at the airport. The airstrip was built in 1942 for the lend lease program and some of the original buildings are still standing. A trip down the Omolon River is a great excursion into the wilderness where one can travel for a thousand kilometers without seeing another human being, only bear and moose. Winning top awards for native language tongue twisters, **Ozero Elgigytgyn** is a glacial lake in a 10 km diameter crater with clean, clear water and local legends of a "Loch Ness" monster. Elgigytgyn can be reached by helicopter from Omolon.

Kolymskaya Trassa   Once one of the most dreaded regions in all of the Soviet Union, the Kolyma highway connects Magadan with the Kolyma gold mines and continues on to Yakutsk. During the height of the Stalinist terror, there was said to be a prison camp every 20 kilometers along the highway. Today, it serves as a monument to man's assault on nature. On both sides of the highway the forest has been clear cut, while the Kolyma River is brown and its banks eroding from the constant gold washing and processing that takes place.

ANADYR

Built as Novo-Mariinsk in 1889 and renamed in 1920, Anadyr is a small town with a population of 15,000, mostly Russians and Ukrainians. As the city is built on permafrost, most of the buildings are built on stilts to keep them from sinking into the ground. The large sea port operates only from July-September, as do all ports in Chukotka. Scarce resources (fuel, food, equipment) are delivered to the region in bulk during navigation season to support locals through the winter. With rising internal transportation costs, Chukotka has recently discovered it to be cheaper to purchase its supplies from the United States.

The local population lives by hunting (moose, elk, reindeer) and fishing. For the adventurous, try the local dish of boiled moose lips and moose ears! Local restaurants serve deer meat.

Anadyr is probably the least picturesque town in Russia. Gray unpainted buildings, all pretty much alike, a few fairly dirty streets (mostly unpaved), open to the strong winds—this is a brief portrait of Anadyr. One of the places to see is the **Kraevecheski Museum.** Located across the street from the Chukotka Hotel, the museum displays beautiful carvings from walrus tusk, mammoth bone and reindeer bone, native clothes made of skins, and other Chukchi folk art. A second museum is a memorial to labor camp prisoners who worked the mines in Chukotka. Exhibits include letters from the prisoners, as well as photos and some of the tools used in the mines.

The best time to visit is in summer and early fall—the tundra is beautiful and salmon fishing is popular.

The **airport** is located across the bay from the city, so depending on the season you will take various means of transport to town. In summer (July-Sept) there is a ferry across the bay. In winter an ice road (about 40 minutes by car) leads to town and in spring and fall/early winter (May-Jun and Oct-

Dec) take a helicopter (about 10 minutes). On the outskirts of city there is a **Chukchi village**, which often has festivals.

PRACTICAL INFORMATION

Moscow time +9 hours.
Code for calling Anadyr from outside the city: **41361.**
Information for Anadyr must be ordered through the operator.
Intourist Hotel Only nine double rooms in this small hotel. No restaurant, but the kitchen can prepare food for your party if you order in advance. Best idea is to book a room way in advance, as during the fall (Sept, Oct) they fill up quickly with foreign hunters. Inexpensive. Ulitsa Energetikov. Tel: 4-66-01.
Hotel Chukotka This hotel has a cafe. Very cheap. Tel: 4-27-94.

PROVIDENIYA

Located on a bay surrounded by sharp mountains, Provideniya (population 5000) is known for being at the edge of the world, and for having great hunting. Daily flights connect the town with Anadyr, but the flight is highly dependent on the weather conditions. The airstrip is not paved and the landings are a little hair-raising, but the approach is gorgeous. Airport officials may try to extract a fine from visitors who do not have approval to fly into the "restricted" area of Provideniya. Actually, visitors no longer need to have the city mentioned in their visas, but be prepared. Small twin prop planes also make regular flights connecting Provideniya to Alaska. As you might guess, tourist accommodations are limited. According to one visitor, there is only one restaurant in town that served "potatoes, boiled eggs, bread and Fanta, and that was it." On the other hand, the locals can pick up Alaskan TV channels.
Bering Air Offering tours of the Russian Far North, Bering Air flies from Nome, Alaska to Provideniya. Tel in Provideniya: 23302. Tel in Nome: 907-443-5620.

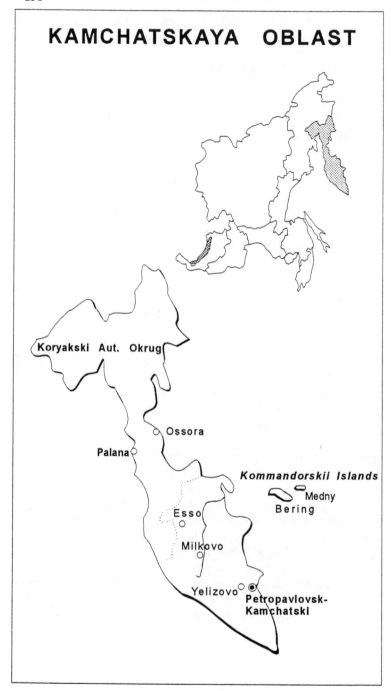

KAMCHATSKAYA OBLAST

CHAPTER 9

KAMCHATKA
"EHTO STRANNOE MESTO..."

Long a place shrouded in secrecy, Kamchatka was until recently known to Westerners only as a closed military region or as a name on the Risk game board. With the fall of the Communist Party in the Soviet Union in 1990, the Kamchatka Peninsula was opened to the outside world. A land still being born (the peninsula has 160 volcanoes, 29 of them active), Kamchatka is a place of breathtaking beauty and unique wildlife, mixing a striking scenery of mountains, tundra, forests and rugged coastline to create a wonderland for the adventurous traveler. The volcanoes not only contribute to the area's great scenery, but are also responsible for the numerous thermal pools found in the area. Here one can ski down snow covered mountain slopes to bathe in volcanic hot springs, go river rafting and rock climbing, see salmon spawning, watch geysers erupt and photograph sea lions in their natural environment. Fishing, hunting and photo safaris are also popular tourist activities. The weather is wet and cool, and although snow stays on the ground until May, the winters are not harsh. There is a saying in Kamchatka which loosely translates as, "In the winter it's not too cold, but in the summer it's not very warm!"

Kamchatka is also known for the amazing diversity and abundance of its wildlife. Sable, ermine, Siberian bighorn (or snow) sheep, the Kamchatka brown bear, crab and, of course, salmon are all found in large quantities, although some species have become endangered due to over-fishing and hunting. In the northern half of the peninsula, reindeer herds are kept by the Koryaks, one of the indigenous peoples of the area.

They say that Kamchatka's industries can be divided into two categories: fishing and those that support fishing. Seafood is plentiful, with crab, salmon and caviar being the main exports. During the spawning season, smoked salmon and red caviar can be found in every market and store.

A land unique not only in its scenery and wildlife, Kamchatka differs from the rest of Russia in its people and attitudes. Locals will tell you "Kamchatka, *ehto strannoe mesto*" (It's a strange place). Perhaps due to its distance from Moscow (11,000 km) or to the effect of living under the shadow of active volcanoes (volcanoes have erupted here as recently as 1994), one finds in Kamchatka a sense of the frontier and an independent spirit, fierce even by Far Eastern standards.

HISTORY

The existence of the Kamchatka Peninsula was known to Russia as far back as the 17th century. Famous Russian explorers such as Ivan Kamchatoy, Simon Dezhnev and the Cossack Ivan Rubetz all made exploratory trips to the area in the middle of the 17th century and spoke of an area rich in fish and fur. By the turn of the century interest in Kamchatka had increased and in 1697 Vladimir Atlasov, head of the Anadyr settlement, headed a group of 65 Cossacks and 60 Yukaghir natives to fully explore the peninsula. Dividing his command in two, Atlasov sent the groups down the east and west coasts of the peninsula, bringing the lands under Russian control by force or by consent.

After this first successful expedition, Cossack settlements of Verkhne (upper) and Nizhne (lower) Kamchatski were founded in 1704-1706. These Cossacks came to settle the land and collect fur tribute from the local tribes. These settlements, far from any supervision and government power, ruled the tribes with a heavy hand, extracting as much fur as possible while passing the minimum on to the government coffers. Excesses were such that the North West Administration in Yakutsk sent Atlasov with the authority (and the cannons) to restore government order, but it was too late. The local Cossacks had too much power in their own hands and in 1711 Atlasov was killed. From this time on, Kamchatka became a self-regulating region, with minimal interference from Yakutsk. By 1713 there were approximately 500 Cossacks living in the area. The cruelty and excesses of these Cossacks were widely known and first brought dissent, then open revolt from the local inhabitants. Uprisings were common, the largest being in 1731 when the settlement of Nizhne Kamchatski was razed and its inhabitants massacred. The remaining Cossacks regrouped and, reinforced with firearms and cannons, were able to put down the rebellion. It is telling that at the beginning of the 18th century the local native population was estimated at 20,000 but by the 1750's only 8,000 were counted.

Eager to colonize northwestern America which the French, Spanish and English had not yet claimed, in 1725 Peter the Great commissioned the famous captain Vitus Bering to lead an expedition to Kamchatka to explore the East Siberian lands and their relation to the American continent. For the next two years Bering sailed up and down the East Russian coastline, but due to bad weather was not able to find how or if the two continents of Asia and America were linked.

Returning to St. Petersburg, Bering asked the current ruler, the Tsarina Anna, that a second, more extensive expedition be organized and in 1732 this was granted. The scope of this second expedition was much more ambitious than the first. In addition to charting the Siberian Arctic coastline and solving the Asia-America question, Bering was to initiate the development of Eastern Siberia and locate and map the American coastline. This expedition came to be known as the Great Northern Expedition.

Bering left St. Petersburg in 1733, but it wasn't until 7 years later that he was equipped and ready to leave from Okhotsk. Bering built his ships there and set sail. In the autumn of 1740, the ships St. Peter and St. Paul sailed into Avachinskaya Bay, where Bering founded the town of Petropavlovsk, near an existing Itelmen settlement.

The founding of Petropavlovsk-Kamchatski began the "opening" of Kamchatka in earnest, helped by the fact that the government began to use the area as a place of exile.

Trying to encourage settlers, the Russian government established a program similar to the Homestead Act in the early days of the United States, whereby all those who came to Kamchatka were given the land they settled upon, as well as seeds and supplies. Although it was a long way to come for free land, some did come, and along the peninsula Russian peasants settled, trying for a new life.

Vitus Bering

Vitus Bering, a Danish explorer, served for most of his life in the Russian Navy and is responsible for exploring Kamchatka and the strait between Asia and America that now bears his name.

The first expedition of Bering was ordered by Peter the Great in 1725, just before he died. Peter told Bering to go to Kamchatka, and find out how the Siberian mainland was (or was not) connected to the American continent. Bering and his group traveled overland and by river from St. Petersburg to Okhotsk, a miserable small settlement on the Okhotsk Sea, across from Kamchatka. The arduous journey took Bering through forests, swamps and ice fields and by the time they reached Okhotsk the group's situation was desperate. Food had been rationed to the barest minimum, and they were forced to build a boat with the materials at hand, as the heavy boat-building materials had been left behind when their ship became ice-bound. No sturdy trees could grow in this windy northern area, and the nails had been abandoned during the journey, so they made a makeshift boat tied together with leather strips. Miraculously, this got them across the Sea of Okhotsk to Kamchatka, and from there the expedition traveled by dogsled over mountains to Nizhnekamchatsk on the Pacific coast. Here they set about constructing a new ship and frantically trying to stay alive under the harsh conditions, subsisting on fish, roots and berries.

In the summer of 1728 they were finally able to begin exploration. Bering sailed north along the coast of Kamchatka and rounded the Chukchi Peninsula, unwittingly passing through what is now known as the Bering Strait. As they continued north and the coast they were following turned northwest, Bering felt that he had established that America was not connected to Russia, and since winter was coming on, turned the ship around and returned to Kamchatka.

In the summer of 1729 Bering set out again, this time eastward. Again, he did not sight the coast of America, and, his task seemingly accomplished, he headed for Okhotsk and subsequently to St. Petersburg, submitting his report in 1730.

In St. Petersburg interest in America and its relation to Siberia had not waned. Under the authority of Tsarina Anna, a second expedition was organized, called the Great Northern Expedition. This was a huge operation, which was to include a large party from the Academy of Sciences. The intention was not only to determine *once and for all the Asia-America connection, but also to map the Arctic coast and conduct geological and other scientific research throughout the north of Siberia. Bering, as head of this expedition, was also to map the American coastline until he reached a settlement of another European power.*

The expedition took two years to arrange, and ultimately included over 3000 people. Bering left St. Petersburg at the head of this expedition in 1733.

Once the project got underway, it became a logistical nightmare, full of political infighting and personality conflicts. It took years for the main body of the expedition to get to Okhotsk and build ships. In 1740 Bering sailed around the coast of Kamchatka and into the natural harbor of Avachinskaya Bay, founding Petropavlovsk, named in honor of his two ships the St. Peter and St. Paul. In late spring, Bering set sail seeking America. Despite hardships, bad weather, and being separated from the St. Paul, in July of 1741 he finally sighted land, which proved to be Kayak Island off the Alaska coast.

Physically exhausted and wary of bad weather, Bering turned the St. Peter back towards Kamchatka. Strong headwinds, storms, miscalculations, and mass cases of scurvy among the crew slowed their return. With most of the crew dying and Bering himself sick from scurvy, on November 4 the ship sighted land, one of the Kommandorski Islands. Bering decided to spend the winter on the uninhabited island to recuperate and prepare for the spring, but died a month later on December 8, 1741 on the island which was later to bear his name. By the next summer the crew was able to build a boat and return to the mainland.

Despite its tragic end, the Great Northern Expedition achieved great results. The city of Petropavlovsk was founded, the Siberian and Arctic coasts were mapped, and the Kommandorski Islands discovered, not to mention the fact that Bering's expedition was the first to explore that now famous body of water, the Bering Strait.

As in the early European settlements in America, the new settlers brought diseases with them to the new world, to which the natives had no defenses. In 1799 more than 1700 Kamchadals died of disease. By 1812 the native population had been so reduced that there were only 3200 natives counted in the whole peninsula, while the Russian population had increased to 2500.

In 1854 Kamchatka was caught in the middle of the Crimean War. England and France, fighting against Russia on the Crimean Peninsula, decided to use their forces in the Far East to occupy Kamchatka and the port of Petropavlovsk. The port was lightly defended; a total of 988 sailors and volunteers with 68 guns would have to defend against 6 ships holding 206 guns and 2540 English and French marines and sailors. Nevertheless, with extreme heroism and bravery the Russian defenders survived the bombardment and repulsed the landing, capturing the colors of the British Marine Regiment of Gibraltar, a copy of which can be seen in the local museum (the original hangs in the Hermitage in St. Petersburg).

Despite the heroic defense, after the Anglo-French forces withdrew, Petropavlovsk was abandoned as a strategic liability. The next year when a second enemy force came to attack the port, they found it deserted. Frustrated, the ships bombarded the city and withdrew.

The next 50 years were lean ones for Kamchatka. The military naval port was moved to Ust-Amur and in 1867 Alaska was sold to the United States, making Petropavlovsk obsolete as a transit point for traders and explorers on their way to the new territories. In 1860 the Primorski (Maritime) Region was established and Kamchatka was placed under its jurisdiction. In 1875 the Kuril Islands were ceded to Japan in return for Russian sovereignty over Sakhalin. The Russian population of Kamchatka stayed around 2500 until the turn of the century, while the native population increased to 5000.

The Russo-Japanese War of 1904-05 also affected Kamchatka. Poorly defended and cut off from Moscow, the garrison only received news of the outbreak of war 3 months after the fact. Fortunately, the Japanese did not make a serious effort to take the peninsula. A small landing of 150 men was repulsed by the Russians and a few Japanese trading ships were confiscated or burned.

In August of 1905, two Japanese cruisers entered Avachinskaya Bay and shelled Petropavlovsk, and the town was abandoned as indefensible. As a result of the Portsmouth Treaty ending the war, Russia ceded fishing rights on the Okhotsk, Japan and Bering Seas to Japan .

At this time the Russian government decided to strengthen its hold on Kamchatkta by actively promoting the development of the area. In 1909, Kamchatka was separated from the

Primorski Territory and granted its own Oblast administrative status. Numerous scientific expeditions were organized, and in 1912 Kamchatka was opened to all "free settlers." The economy at that time consisted almost entirely of fishing, fur and goods trading. So heavy was the hunting of sables that in 1912 the government banned hunting of them for 3 years to allow the population to increase. By this time the human population (including natives) reached 10,800.

During the Civil War, neither the Whites nor the Reds had regular troops present, although partisan skirmishes continued until 1924. However, it wasn't until 1927 that the last Japanese left the peninsula and Kamchatka became entirely Soviet. The town of Yelizovo is named in honor of the leader of the partisans.

During World War II, Kamchatka saw little action except as a base to launch the "liberation of the Kuriles" in late 1945. After the war, Kamchatka developed as a military region. Military towns with such imaginative names as "Petropavlovsk-50" and "Petropavlovsk-53," as well as submarine and border unit bases stretched throughout its length. Due to its strategic importance, Kamchatka was closed to Russians until 1989 and to foreigners until 1990. Today the peninsula is looking to the future: prospects for tourism and conversion of its massive fishing industry to a free market footing seem promising.

Nomadic reindeer herders

KAMCHATKA'S INDIGENOUS PEOPLES

Itelmen   Currently numbering around 1500, the Itelmen, or Kamchadals as they are called by the Russians, are one of the original inhabitants of Kamchatka, belonging to the Chukotsk-Koryak language group.   In the past, the Itelmen lifestyle revolved around fishing, and they traded with their Koryak neighbors for deer skins and other supplies.   The Itelmen practiced animism, with bears playing an especially important role (the rituals of the Itelmen Bear Cult are well known among ethnographers).   Culturally, ritual dances and music play an important role in Itelmen life, as was noted by the first Russian explorers who came in contact with the tribe.   Today the Itelmen are trying to revive their culture and history, and every year there is a colorful festival with performances of native dances, songs and rituals.

The **Koryaks** inhabit the northern half of Kamchatka, called the Koryak Autonomous Okrug, with its capital in Palana. Koryaks are divided into two groups; the Nymlan, or sedentary Koryaks, and the Chavchuvens, or nomadic Koryaks.   The Nymlyan have settled along the east and west coasts of the peninsula and have a lifestyle centered around fishing and hunting.   The early Russian explorers remarked on the developed hunting and fishing implements of these people as well as their well-constructed dog sleds.

The nomadic reindeer-herding Koryaks call themselves the Chavchuvens, or "deer people."   The males of the tribe, as soon as they come of age, move with their herds around the tundra from pasture to pasture, returning to their families for a brief time only in the fall, before starting off again.   After the revolution the herders were organized into collectives, but not without great resistance.   Today the Koryaks number around 7200.

PETROPAVLOVSK-KAMCHATSKI

INTRODUCTION

Petropavlovsk-Kamchatski (pop. 273,000) grew up around the Avachinskaya Bay, with the Avacha and Koryakski volcanoes brooding over the town.   Due to the topography of the region,

Avachinskaya Bay

the city itself is long and thin, snaking around the bay and between the mountains. There are essentially two main areas in Petropavlovsk: one centered around Avachinskaya Bay and Lenin Square, the other a bus ride away near Komsomolskaya Square. Lenin Square is the administrative and cultural center of the city. The city and oblast administration offices are located on the square, and the drama theater, philharmonic, and various museums are nearby. However, most of the main hotels are located near 50 Let Oktyabrya Street. This is a more residential neighborhood, dominated by large standard Russian housing projects. Here you can find the central department store, as well as numerous smaller food and commercial stores. This area is more spread out and less scenic than around Lenin Square, and it takes various buses and lots of question-asking to find the places you are looking for. In general, Petropavlovsk is looking to tourism for its future, but hasn't quite got the idea yet of how to make things easy for the visitor.

WALKING AROUND TOWN

A good place to start is from **Lenin Square**, where there is a good view of the harbor and mountains in the distance. Built in 1978, the square used to witness May Day and military parades, but is pretty quiet lately.

Facing up Leninskaya Street, on your left is a white building which houses the Regional Kamchatski Administration. On your right is the city **Drama Theater**. Next to the Drama Theater is the **Philharmonic** concert hall which also serves as a voting center and holds church services and other functions

PETROPAVLOVSK - KAMCHATSKI

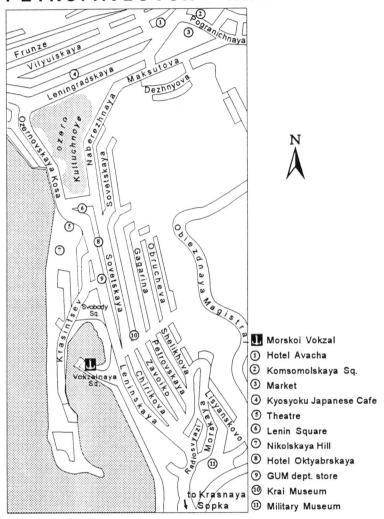

N
↑

🚇 Morskoi Vokzal
① Hotel Avacha
② Komsomolskaya Sq.
③ Market
④ Kyosyoku Japanese Cafe
⑤ Theatre
⑥ Lenin Square
⑦ Nikolskaya Hill
⑧ Hotel Oktyabrskaya
⑨ GUM dept. store
⑩ Krai Museum
⑪ Military Museum

requiring large spaces. Although theater tickets can be bought at the theater, for some reason concert tickets for the Philharmonic are sold at a booth by the Post Office.

Facing the Philharmonic on the left hand side of Leninskaya is the **Kamchatka movie theater**. Even if you are not in the mood to see a movie, take a look inside, if only to see the strange electronic signboard announcing when the next showing is. Church services are held here on Sunday.

Leaving the theater and continuing up Leninskaya, on your right you will see a path leading up to a small **chapel** flanked by crosses. This was the first monument erected to the defenders of Petropavlovsk in 1854. Facing the chapel, the Russian defenders are buried under the right cross (their cause being righteous), the fallen English and French attackers under the left one. For many years on August 24 (the date of the invasion), a church procession would start from this monument and wind its way up to Nikolskaya hill.

Continuing up Leninskaya you cannot miss the **Holkam** store, a large western style supermarket with a cafe on the upper floor. Further up the street on the left at #54 is **GUM**, the state department store. Next to GUM is a large building built in a classical style. Previously housing the local Communist Party, the building now holds local justice departments and arbitration courts, but of more interest is the humble gray **obelisk** in front. One of the few foreign memorials in the Russian Far East, this obelisk was brought to Petropavlovsk-Kamchatski from England in 1913 and marks the grave of Captain Charles Clerke. Clerke assumed command of the expedition of the famous Captain Cook after Cook was killed in Hawaii. Across the street is the **monument** to the "liberators" of the Kuril Islands. Although the islands are part of Sakhalinskaya Oblast, the attack was launched from the much closer land mass of Kamchatka. Four thousand soldiers died in an all-out assault to recapture these strategically located islands from the Japanese in the last days of the war (the islands were liberated from the 20-28th of August, 1945).

Back on the right-hand side of Leninskaya, take a right onto Krasintsev street and follow it until you come to some large green cement gates. Follow this path up **Nikolskaya Hill**, where in 1854 the English-French landing was repulsed. From this vantage point, one has a beautiful view of the city and bay and can easily see why this hill was the focal point of the city's defense. Nearby stands another **memorial** to those fallen in that defense of Petropavlovsk. Constructed in 1879 in St. Petersburg and shipped to Kamchatka to commemorate the 25th anniversary of victory, this monument was erected with great ceremony, including a church procession, military salute and parade. Facing away from the city and on the lower left side of the hill you can see the monument erected in honor of the **Third Battery**. This battery of 5 guns heroically dueled with 6 English ships during the assault. Copies of the cannons are placed along the embankment and the monument itself is also topped by a cannon. On a clear spring or summer day, these hills are the perfect place to have a picnic lunch and watch the ships go by. This area is also known as "lovers' rock" due to the number of couples found here, seeking a secluded spot.

PRACTICAL INFORMATION

Note: Petropavlovsk and Yelizovo are about one hour apart by car. The airport is located in Yelizovo, and many outdoor activities are more easily accessible from Yelizovo.

Moscow time +9 hours.
Code for calling Petropavlovsk from outside Kamchatka: **41522.**
Code for calling Petropavlovsk from Yelizovo: **8.**
Code for calling Yelizovo from Petropavlovsk: **8-321.**
Code for calling Yelizovo from outside Kamchatka: **41551.**
Petropavlovsk Info. when calling from the city: **09.**
Petropavlovsk Info. from outside the city: **41522-91909.**
Yelizovo Info: 627-31.
Weather forecasts in Russian: 594-81.
KamchatPromBank Sovietskaya 14. Tel: 222-14.
Address Bureau Tel: 222-77.
Main Post Office International phone calls can be ordered. Also fax, telex, e-mail on the second floor. Leninskaya 65. Open Mon-Fri 8-20, Sun 10-16.
Peregovorni Punkt (Telephone office) Leninskaya 56. Tel: 249-32.

HOTELS

Hotel Petropavlovsk Non-descript from the outside, the inside of this hotel has been remodeled and is quite comfortable, if a bit frilly. The hotel is conveniently located next to the Aerovokzal, with regular buses running to the airport. Rooms are carpeted and walls are newly papered with large floral designs. The showers actually have curtains, a fact not to be taken for granted in most Russian hotels. Satellite telephone on 3rd floor. Restaurant in basement, cafe on 2nd floor. Expensive. Karla Marksa 31. Tel: 503-74.

Oktyabrskaya A small and quiet hotel, formerly for Party members. The only hotel right in the center of town near the museums, theater, etc. Long distance calls can be direct-dialed from your room (cheaper than ordering a call), ask the administration what to dial. International calls can be made by satellite at the current hard currency rate (expensive). A small buffet in the basement operates from 8-10, 18-22, where you can have a bite for breakfast, or a quick dinner. Ask what the hot dishes are. Moderate. Sovietskaya 51. Tel: 246-84.

Hotel Russ Not conveniently located and offers no special services. Inexpensive. Zvyozdnaya 11/1. Tel: 755-15.

Hotel Avacha Named after the nearby volcano, this is a large hotel designed for tourists. Inexpensive. Leningradskaya 61 Tel: 273-31.

Hotel Geizer Down a side street on a cliff overlooking the city and bay. There is a restaurant, a cafe, and a tourist office. Groups are booked in here, so a reservation is suggested, not only because it might be full, but because if no groups are booked, the hotel is liable to close down completely. Cheap. Toporkova 10. Tel: 579-96.

FOOD

It must be said about Petropavlovsk-Kamchatski that it is difficult to find a good place to eat, not because there are no good restaurants, but because they are hidden and don't advertise. If you are in one of the main hotels, certainly you will gravitate toward the ease of simply going downstairs, but don't fall into a rut! A short bus or taxi ride and a few requests for directions will land you in some unique and worthwhile places. Since many places are so hard to get to, it is recommended that you call in advance.

Petropavlovsk Hotel Restaurant The striking geometric tiles when you get off the elevator at floor zero might make you think you have walked into Alice's shrinking nightmare, but turn to the right and you will find the restaurant. The interior is completely different from the hallway: frilly painted low-relief roses grace the walls, interspersed with life-sized photos of Kamchatka scenery. The food is tasty, but the service is slow, perhaps to ensure that you stick around for the music, which means that they can tack an extra charge (per person) to your bill. The Las Vegas-style lounge singer is pleasant, but the music is too loud for the small space. If you want to skip the music, make sure you are served before 8:30 pm. Open every day from 12-17, 19-24. Karla Marksa 31. Tel: 906-80.

Kazachi Shlyag (Cossack Road) This small restaurant (seven tables) is the headquarters of the Far Eastern Cossack Association, and although completely undistinguished and hard to find from the outside, inside they have replicated a Cossack *izba* (wooden cabin). The entire interior is of decorated wood, with spiral columns, candle sticks, an ornate Tsarist eagle, and an icon in the corner. Small menu, but the food is good, IF it ever gets to you. The service is so slow it brings tears to your eyes and if there is a party already booked before you, expect an hour wait even for your hors d'oeuvres and you won't be disappointed. However, if you have the time the food is good and the atmosphere is great. Expensive. Take bus No. 26 or 28 to Zvyozdnaya stop, head toward ugly apartment building on same side of street as bus stop, go under arch and turn right. Ask along the way. Open from 13-2. Kosmicheski Proezd 3, Blok B. Tel: 756-62, 796-91.

Geyser Hotel Restaurant Only open if the hotel is full of guests, so call in advance. There is also a small cafe on the first floor with a good view. Toporkova 10. Tel: 549-88.

Kyosyoku Japanese Cafe Small, nice restaurant serving a variety of Japanese and Russian specialties. Items on the menu include scallops, gohan (rice), noodles, and pizza with ferns. Open Mon-Fri 11-16. Leningradskaya 35. Tel: 370-71.

Pingvin Cafe European ice cream makes this non-descript cafe a tasty spot to stop into. Don't be deceived by the pictures of sundaes on the wall, so far all they have are cones. Inexpensive. Open 11-19 (14:30-15), Sun 11-18. Sovietskaya 38.

Khinushky Cafe On the second floor, past the grocery store. Tasty hot sandwiches. Probably the only place in the center of town where you can get a quick bite on a Sunday morning. Take a look at the sled dogs and volcano on the wrought iron grill at the top of the stairs. Open from 9-21. Sovietskaya 45.

Vernisage Business Club Tsiolkovskovo 25, 2nd floor. Tel: 747-87, 747-86.

Vulcan Restaurant Klyuchevskaya 32. Tel: 250-09.

Stolovaya No. 5   On Lenin Square, second floor of Administration building. Usually only for government workers, from 13:30-15 it is open to the general public. Not as cheap as a regular *stolovaya*, but better service than a run-of-the-mill cafeteria. In Oblast Administration building on Lenin Square. Tel: 222-41.

SHOPPING

Rubin (Ruby) Wide selection of gold and silver jewelry, as well as amber and other semi-precious stones. Sovietskaya 48. Tel: 256-51.

GUM This all-purpose store is filled with a wide selection of Russian and imported goods. Behind the central stairway is a beautiful pseudo-stained glass window of Kamchatka's volcanoes. On the third floor there is a separate souvenir section selling small paintings and crafts made by the local tribes. Open Mon-Sat 10-20. Leninskaya 54. Tel: 234-22.

Holkam Supermarket The top floor of this Dutch/Russian joint venture has clothes, perfumes, household goods, and other imported items, as well as a small stand-up cafe. Downstairs is the Western-style grocery store. Take a basket and roam the aisles.   You'll find foods imported from America, Holland, China and more. On Leninskaya St., two blocks up from Lenin Square, across from chapel-monument to those fallen during the invasion of 1854. Open Mon-Fri 9-20 (14-15), Sat 10-18.

Antikvar Follow the stairs down to a dungeon-like cellar where you will find books, icons, coins, and medals for sale. Open 11-17 Mon-Sat. Closed Sunday because that is the day when coin and medal collectors gather at the Oblastnoi Library at Karl Marx 33/1 to trade wares from 9-12. Leninskaya 32.

Knigi (Bookstore #1) Paintings, books, pet supplies. Open Mon-Thu 10-19 (14-15), Fri-Sat 10-18. Leninskaya 34.

Voentorg (Military Department Store) Look for the green signs outside. There are two Voentorg stores here side by side, one selling electronics and furniture, the other clothes, souvenirs and military items such as hats and patches. Open 11-19 (14-15). Maksutova 36a. Tel: 264-72, 264-42.

Exhibition Hall Paintings, jewelry, leather purses, fur hats, native crafts, ceramics. Open Wed-Fri 11-19 (14-15), Sat-Sun 11-15. Leninskaya 36.

Filateliya (Stamp Store) Labeled "Store #2," this small shop is located under the sign that says "*Krugozor,*" and sells inexpensive stamps along with a good selection of newspapers and magazines. Open Mon-Sat 8-20. Leningradskaya 74. Tel: 261-37.

Intim For better or worse, the owner is proud to have the only sex store in the Russian Far East, selling lingerie, magazines and sex aids.   Open from 10-20 every day. Leninskaya 46. Tel: 235-87.

Melodia Mostly Russian records and cassettes. Sadovaya 2. Tel: 480-98.

TsUM "Petropavlovsk" The central department store, with both imported and local goods. Prospect 50 Let Oktyabrya 15A. Tel: 317-15.

ENTERTAINMENT

Kraevecheski Museum   Said to be the only surviving building from before the revolution, the local museum is housed in the former governor's office. The museum has exhibits on the discovery and development of Kamchatka by the Russians, and the culture and lifestyles of the various indigenous peoples. Open Wed-Sun 10-18 (13-14). Leninskaya 20. Tel: 254-11.

Muzei Boyevoi Slavi (Military Glory Museum)   Go through the green gates to this small 2 floor museum. For such a built-up military peninsula, the museum has surprisingly little. The first floor is mostly dedicated to the failed Anglo-French invasion of 1854, while the second floor concentrates on Kamchatka's contribution to Soviet victory during World War II. Outside is a monument to the L-16 submarine that was sunk off San Francisco with a total loss of crew, including an American. To this day, the Russians are not sure if the sub was sunk by the Japanese or accidentally by the Americans. Open daily from 10-17 (14-15). Radiosvyazi 69. Tel: 250-94.

Kamchatski Theater of Drama and Comedy Ticket booth works from 10-19. Shows start at 7:00 on weekdays and at 6:00

on weekends.   Children's matinees at noon.   Leninskaya 75.
Information 231-18.

Puppet Theater (*Teatr Kukol*) Ticket booth on
Komsomolskaya Ploschad.   Maksutova 42.   Tel: 278-69.

Philharmonic Lenin 69 (but the ticket booth is across from
the post office), also houses the Evangelist Church.

Children's Theater (*Teatr Yunovo Zritelya*) Zvyozdnaya 26.
Tel: 756-93.

Marine Life Museum (TINRO) One room dedicated to
local fish and sea life.   Open Mon-Fri from 9-18 (12-12:30).
Naberezhnaya 18 . Tel: 219-35.

Museum of Geology Open Mon-Thu from 8-16 (12-13),
Fri 8-12. Beringa 117. Tel: 398-67.

Movie Theater Kamchatka Leninskaya 64. Tel: 226-53.

PLACES OF WORSHIP

Orthodox Church Constructed in 1992, this is the first
Orthodox Church in the city, led by Father Yaroslav.   Golden
cupolas catch the sun.   Inside, the iconostasis is still being
painted.   Take bus Nos. 22, 1, or 3 to TsUM or Rossiskaya
Kniga, then ask. Panfilova 30.

New Apostle Church 64 Leninskaya (in movie theater
Kamchatka). Services are held on Sundays at 11:00 a.m.

Organization of Religious Muslims Okeansky 62.

MARKETS

The main **food and clothing** market is at the junction of
Tushkanova and 50 Let Oktyabrya.   Open every day 9-17.
Another market stretches near Komsomolskaya Ploschad, behind
74 Leningradskaya.   This market has the usual shoes, leather
jackets, etc. but good caviar and crab can also be found.

On Sunday mornings, **coin, medal and stamp collectors**
gather at the Regional Library on Karl Marx 33/1 to sell and
trade.

SKIING

Ski season starts around the end of November and
continues through April, and sometimes through May.

Krasnaya Sopka (Red Hill) A thousand-meter slope with a great view of the city and bay, served by a T-bar lift. Lift tickets can be purchased individually, or in a book of 10 (*aboniment*). Western ski equipment is available for rental by the hour. Both rentals and tickets are obtained at the little house perched on the hill above the lift. Some snacks and drinks are also available (don't expect a Swiss Ski Chalet!) There is also a ski school—watch out for kids cutting in the lift line! The place is run by Vladimir Sinyetov and Anatoly Lyschnikov, both expert skiers. Vladimir skied on the Soviet National Team for 10 years and Anatoly trained Soviet skiers for the World Cup. The only problem with Krasnaya Sopka is getting there. Take bus #1, 2 or 3 to Krasnaya Sopka stop. Then start walking uphill. Just up from the bus stop there are steps, after that the "trail" is less clear—over a trash heap, avoiding the barking dog, and along a cliff. Just keep going up and to your left and eventually you will see the little rental house. Open Wed-Sun from 10-18.

Moroznaya Originally used as training ground for Soviet Olympic skiers, if you can get there it is well worth it. Located outside the town of Yelizovo, the easiest way to get there is by car. In Yelizovo, drive down Zaboika street to V. Kruchiny and keep going until you pass the sign in the shape of two large skis with the Olympic rings on them. Alternatively, stop anyone in town and ask them; everyone knows where Moroznaya is. Two T-bars will take you to the top of a mountain with a breathtaking view of Avacha volcano. The slope from the first lift is intermediate, the higher slope steeper and more advanced. Western ski equipment is available for rental by the hour (you'll need to leave your passport or some other ID). Lift tickets are available from the *kassa*, each ticket is good for one lift. The skiing is great, the view is just amazing. There is also a small buffet where you can warm up with some tea or small sandwiches. Ski equipment rentals from 9-12, 15-17 Tue-Fri and from 9-18 on Sat, Sun. Call ahead to see how the snow conditions are. Tel: (in Yelizovo) 612-08, 326-86.

Edelweiss Two slopes, but no equipment rental. Take bus No. 9 or 18 from Komsomolskaya Ploschad to Devyataya Shkola stop. You can see the hill from the bus stop—walk past *dachas* and a junkyard to the lift. Strelkovaya 13. Open Tue-Sun 10-18. Tel: 248-56.

Dinamo Lizhnaya Baza Downhill ski rental available. In Kirpichiki (a suburb of Petropavlovsk). Take bus No. 16 to last stop, or Nos. 17 or 18 to "torgovi center." You will see the slope. Tel: 700-06.

Lesnaya Lizhnaya Baza For cross-country skiing, rentals available. There is a very small (two rooms) "hotel" and they are working on opening a *stolovaya*, if you want to stay for a while. Take bus No. 25 to last stop, then about a 15-minute walk. They can also meet you at the airport with advance warning. Severo-Vostochnoye Shosse 50. Tel: 927-69.

Dolina Uyuta Ski School Near Yelizovo, this school is also for cross-country, rentals available. Tel: (Yelizovo) 637-45.

HOT SPRINGS

A trip to the hot springs is an essential part of any trip to Kamchatka. If you know any local people, they will probably recommend their favorite resorts or spas, as there are quite a few to choose from. Most are along the road from Yelizovo, which runs adjacent to the Paratunka River, about an hour from Petropavlovsk. Many can be reached by bus No. 210 from the Petropavlovsk Avtovokzal (bus station), or most easily by car.

Keep in mind when calling that the code for Yelizovo is 8-231 from Petropavlovsk, 41551 from outside Kamchatka.

Blue Lagoon (*Golubaya Laguna*) A new spot, this spa has a large pool, a bar and restaurant, and a hotel is under construction. Open 10-2 am, closed Tue. Tel: (Yeliz.) 583-96.

Paratunka Basein A large turquoise building surrounds two large outdoor pools, changing rooms, showers and a small cafe. If you're really enthusiastic you can rent rooms and stay overnight (book in advance). Take bus No. 210 from Petropavlovsk to the last stop. Modest entrance fee. Open 24

"Taking the waters" at the Paratunka hot springs

hours a day from Tue-Sun. Tel: (Yelizovo) 931-42.

Solnichnaya Divided into two parts. To enter the left side one must have a special permission from OVIR (evidently secret hot springs and curative methods). On the right side is the normal hot spring pool. Although those who wish to can stay overnight in their 2-3 person rooms, additional "special" services (cafe, restaurant) are not offered. Tel: (Yelizovo) 932-90.

EVENTS

In late March, Kamchatka organizes the international "Beringie" **dogsled races**. Ask your hotel or local tourist agency for exact dates and information.

The last Sunday in July is the **Dyen Morskovo Flota** (Navy Day). During the "old days," this was cause for large parades, speeches, and communist demonstrations. Nowadays, the navy ships just stand in the harbor, decked out in holiday flags.

October 17 is the **city's birthday (*Dyen Goroda)*** in Petropavlovsk. Depending on the year (and the city budget), various activities are organized throughout the city.

TRANSPORTATION

Taxi stand at Komsomolskaya Square, in front of Krugozor store. To order a taxi, call 235-86 (from Komsomolskaya Square), or 313-31 (central dispatcher).

The **airport** is about 1 hour away from Petropavlovsk, near the town of Yelizovo. So far there are no international flights, although it is rumored that there will be international flights by spring '95 (potential destinations are still secret). The International Hall is a separate building way off to the right of the main building. It has comfortable couches and polite service, but they charge a huge fee, and you have to go fight your way through the crowds at the regular building anyway. This situation might improve when they build a new baggage inspection section by the International Hall, but at the present time it is not worth paying the fee (unless your flight is delayed). To get there, take either bus No. 100 (Express Petropavlovsk to Airport), No. 103 (Petropavlovsk to Yelizovo and Airport), or No. 102 (local and slow). Information (in Yelizovo): 615-42. International Hall: 997-50.

City Aeroflot Office and Aerovokzal   Located near the Hotel Petropavlovsk, this office is convenient in that you can register for some flights here and the office has buses that will run you right up to your plane.   Confirm in advance if this service is available, and keep in mind that you are supposed to be at the airport two hours in advance of your flight.   Bus No. 3 goes from the center of town to the Aerovokzal.   Prospect Karla Marksa 31.   Hours from 9-19 Mon-Fri, 9-18 Sat.   Tel: 561-19, 567-19.

KamchatAvia   For flights within Kamchatka.   Leninskaya 52.   Tel: 283-13.

Krechet Airlines   Helicopter service to Valley of Geysers. Charter services.   Tel: (Yelizovo) 645-55.

Bus Station (Avtovokzal)   Buses go to Milkovo, Yelizovo and other towns around the peninsula.   Located at the "Desyaty kilometer" stop (10 Km) on the road out of the city.   To get there take bus No. 1 or 22 to last stop.   Ticket booth works from 14-19.   Tel: 577-14.

Morskoi Vokzal (Sea Terminal), due to open soon to international cruises.   On the second floor is the restaurant "Okean."   Tel: 248-90.

AROUND KAMCHATKA

Khalaktyrskii Plyazh (beach)   About 20 km from town, the Khalaktyrskii Plyazh is a popular place to swim.   Wild roses and irises grow on a striking beach of black sand.   July-September is the best time of year to go.   Take a bus to Khalaktyrskii village, then walk for 2 1/2 miles to the beach, or just ask a taxi to take you there.

To really experience the beauty and spirit of Kamchatka one has to leave Petropavlovsk and travel.   There are many *zakazniks* and *zapovedniks* (nature preserves), where untouched nature can still be experienced.   The choices are many.   Near Petropavlovsk is the ***Zakaznik Tri Vulcana***, which encompasses the Avachinski and Koryakski volcanoes.   There is a *tourbaza* in the saddle between the two volcanoes, and the protected Siberian bighorn sheep is found in the area.

About a four hour ride from Petropavlovsk is **Mutnovski Volcano.**   Take a bus to the geothermal station and follow the trail (about 5 km) to the foothills. From here you will walk through a mini Valley of the Geysers to the actual crater.

To the south is **Kurilskoe Lake**, a 50,000 year old caldera known as the "Pearl of Kamchatka" with its wealth of salmon and surrounding wildlife. During spawning season (July, August) bears can be seen in great numbers fishing for the salmon breeding in the lake. The lake is connected to the Okhotsk Sea by the Ozernaya River. Near the coast is the town of Ozernovski, with the first and only geothermal power station in Russia.

To the north lies **Milkovo**, a small town of approximately 15,000 inhabitants, that nevertheless has its own ethnographic museum with great examples of 17th century wooden buildings and an art gallery. More importantly, Milkovo is a great base from which to explore the surrounding countryside. Near Milkovo at the bus stop "41st kilometer" are thermal springs to bathe in. The **Kamchatka River** flows from the middle of the peninsula, between the Sredny (Middle) and Vostochny (Eastern) mountain ranges for 700 km. to the Bering Sea. Fishing for silver salmon and rainbow trout is popular, and bears, moose, and Canadian beaver can often be sighted. The river flows through Milkovo, which is a good place to start exploration. Milkovo can be reached by bus from Petropavlovsk in 5-6 hours, or by plane in less than an hour.

If you're looking for rafting, then check out the **Zhupanova** and **Bystraya Rivers**. Many Kamchatka rivers are named Bystraya (fast), but the best one for rafting is the one nearest Petropavlovsk.

The small town of **Esso** (pop. less than 3,000) in the (northern) Bystraya river valley is known for its beautiful surroundings and its thermal springs. Nearby is the Ichinski volcano, the only active one in the Sredny mountain range. Esso can be reached by plane or bus from Petropavlovsk or Milkovo.

In the town of **Ossoro**, located in the Koryakski Autonomous District, both the sedentary and the nomad groups of Koryaks can be found, and on nearby Karaginski Island are breeding grounds for seals and sea-lions.

One of the most famous places on Kamchatka is the *Kronotski Zapovednik,* which includes the **Valley of Geysers,** the second largest concentration of geysers on earth after Yellowstone. No roads go to the Valley of Geysers, and the only approach is by helicopter. The 200 km helicopter trip from Yelizovo is fascinating in itself, as it flies over the Koryakski and Zhupanovski volcanoes.

In the valley, wooden walkways with carved details have been placed to protect the fragile environment from the groups of tourists who come to visit the valley. Hundreds of plants here are listed in the *Krasnaya Kniga* (Red Book), the Russian endangered species list.

Of all the geysers, *Velican* (Giant) is the largest, sending steaming water up to 100 feet into the air every 2-6 hours. There are other geysers such as *Fontan* (Fountain) and *Dvoynoi* (Double), and the geyser *Schel* (Crack) puts on a show every 36 minutes. You may even approach the "Gates of Hell" (*Vorota Ada*), a double-vented crater.

Other remarkable sights in the Kronotski Nature Reserve are the 80 meter waterfall on the Shumnaya River, which flows from Central Lake in the Uzon Caldera, a triple waterfall, and "mud pots,"—pools of boiling mud. Of the 25 volcanoes in the preserve, 12 are active.

Cliffs overlooking the Kronotski Gulf are home to bird colonies, and during salmon spawning season it is easy to see some of the 500 bears which make their home in the preserve.

Although only one company (*Sogzhoi*) has the rights to fly into the Valley of the Geysers, there are many local companies which arrange trips. Arranging trips to remote areas is very difficult on your own. You might consider joining a group eco-tour if you wish to see the backcountry. If you attempt such travel individually, remember that fog and low clouds are frequent on Kamchatka, hindering helicopter travel. Structure your plans with room for delays.

KOMMANDORSKI ISLANDS

The **Kommandorski Islands** lie to the east of the peninsula. This small group of islands was "discovered" by Bering in 1741 when his ship, the St. Peter, was trying to find its way back to Kamchatka after exploring the coast of Alaska. Bering landed and wintered on the largest island, hoping to recuperate and set off again in the spring. However, it was not to be and Bering, along with many of his crew, succumbed to scurvy and died on this distant island which now bears his name.

When first discovered, the islands were uninhabited by man, populated only by native foxes, sea lions, sea otters, the flightless cormorant, and even the sea cow. Nowadays the foxes and sea lions are still around, but the flightless cormorant and sea cow have become extinct. In the late 1800's the animal population was increased by a reindeer herd imported by the Polish naturalist Dybovski. The main village, Nikolskoe, was founded in 1826 when the Russian-American company worked the islands, hunting whales, seals and sea otters. Competing companies also hunted the waters, and such was the demand for otter skins that each company would kill as many as possible, regardless of age or sex, in order to fill their holds as quickly as possible and sell their harvest. The result was obvious: the sea cows were hunted out of existence and the seal and otter populations dropped drastically. In 1871 exclusive rights to the islands for 20 years were granted to the American company Hutchinson, Cool and Co., an act which stabilized the hunting and allowed the herds to grow back to normal levels. Aleut families were shipped over to help with the work and nowadays there is an Aleutian National Cultural Center and a local lore museum, among other historical monuments. The Bering, Toporkov and Arii Kamen islands serve as nesting grounds for a variety of birds including fulmars, gulls, and puffins. The islands themselves are devoid of trees, but are covered with tall grasses, marshes and tundra in the north and mountains in the south. Lake Sarannoye, on Bering Island, is the largest lake on the islands, and is the main spawning ground for the local salmon. In the south of this island there are remarkable rock formations, including Steller's Arch. In April-May of each year one can see a great number of seals returning to the islands after wintering in Japan.

Tour agencies on the islands include:

Aglakh Yubileinaya 9, Nikolskoe, 684500. Tel: 453 or 400 (or see *Sogzhoi*, below).

Vitus Sovetskaya 11, Nikolskoe, 683500. Tel: 449 or 447.

Kamchatka Tour Agencies

For off-the-beaten-track adventures to any of the above-mentioned places, the following local travel agencies can help organize trips including hiking up volcanoes, river fishing, ski trips, bike trips, and more.

Sogzhoi **Joint Stock Company** One of the largest tour agencies in Kamchatka, Sogzhoi owns Krechet Airlines, which provides helicopter service to the Valley of Geysers and other regions around Kamchatka. They are also the head office for the Aglakh agency on the Kommandorski Islands. Main office located in Yelizovo, Sopochnaya 13. Tel: in Petropavlovsk 546-50, in Yelizovo 621-00 or 614-93 (tel./fax).

Puffins on Toporkov Island

Zateryanni Mir, "Lost World" or, as they translate it, "Derelict World." Hunting, hiking, fishing. Abelya St. 4-61, Petropavlovsk. Tel: 438-20.

Kamchib Russian/Italian joint venture, Norgali Tour Agency 16 Dalnaya St., Petropavlovsk. Tel: 745-77, tel./fax: 749-88.

KamchatTourist Toporkovo 10 (Geyser Hotel), Petropavlovsk. Tel: 563-71, 563-77.

Polyus Bokhnyaka 1. Contact Oleg Yurevich at 651-20.

Kamchatskie Priklyucheniya **(Kamchatka Adventures)** Specializes in alpine tourism and mountain climbing tours. Prospekt Karla Marksa 35. Contact the director, Alexander Mikhailovitch, at 527-10 or 517-21.

American Travel Agents:

East-West Discovery (specializes in travel to RFE) PO Box 69P, Volcano, Hawaii 96785. Tel: 1-800-985-8552.

Kamchatka Fishing Adventures Self-explanatory. 2825 90th St. SE, Everett, WA 98208. Tel: (206) 337-0326.

REI Adventures All levels of outdoor adventures, including volcano climbing expeditions, river rafting, hiking, bicycling, ski touring, etc. PO Box 1938, Sumner, WA 98390-0800. Tel: 1-800-622-2236.

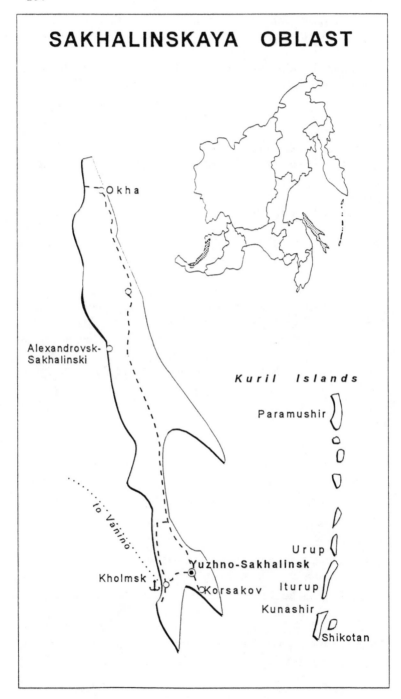

SAKHALINSKAYA OBLAST

Okha

Alexandrovsk-
Sakhalinski

Kuril Islands

Paramushir

ío Vañinò

Urup

Kholmsk

Yuzhno-Sakhalinsk

Korsakov

Iturup

Kunashir

Shikotan

CHAPTER 10

SAKHALINSKAYA OBLAST

Although Sakhalin Island is often described as "that big island above Japan" or "the island from which KAL 007 was shot down in 1985," Sakhalin might just go down in history as one of the economic miracles of Russia by the year 2000. Strategically situated near Japan, Korea and China and not far from Alaska, Sakhalin has already begun to attract enterprising business people.

Timber, fishing and oil are Sakhalin's biggest commodities, but the potential for production and service industries is very high. "Tourism" in its most natural form is available for next to nothing in Sakhalin's great outdoors. In winter locals enjoy downhill and cross-country skiing and ice fishing. In fall there is hunting, berry picking, and the great Russian "*shashlik*" barbeque. Sakhalin's biggest natural resource is its people, many of whom are only first and second generation Sakhaliners.

The best introduction to Sakhalin is to read Chekhov's account of early travels there, The Island of Sakhalin, or for a modern analysis, John Stephan's Sakhalin. John Stephan is the foremost authority on the region and author of a more recent publication, The Russian Far East: A History.

HISTORY

The "discovery" and exploration of Sakhalin and the Kuriles is probably best documented from the 17th to the 19th centuries. Captain Gennady Nevelskoy is one of the first and most famous Sakhalin explorers. His Amuro-Sakhalinskaya expedition of 1850-1855 marked the beginning of the systematic development and settlement of Sakhalin by Russia.   Muravyovski Post, founded in 1853 by Nevelskoy, was the first military base to be founded on Sakhalin.   This small military post was the only Russian presence on the island until 1875.   In this year the Japanese "traded" rights to southern Sakhalin for Russia's half of the Kuril Island chain.   Having gained complete possession of the island, the government, anxious to develop the area and relieve Siberia of some of its mass of criminal exiles, declared Sakhalin a penal colony for political prisoners and criminals. These prisoners were either sent to Sakhalin by ship from Odessa or by land, across the breadth of Russia.   For over thirty years Sakhalin was to remain one of the most feared and terrible places in all of Russia.   In 1890 the great Russia writer Anton Chekhov visited Sakhalin and wrote about the island.   Calling it a "hell," he said that "if only those who wanted to lived here, Sakhalin would be deserted..."   Using prison labor, the coal, oil, lumber and fishing industries were started and these raw materials shipped to Russia proper.

The Russo-Japanese War of 1904-1905, although centered around China, touched the soil and history of Sakhalin as well. Japan, having captured Port Arthur, decided to occupy Sakhalin. On June 24, 1905 the Japanese landed near Korsakov Port.   The Russian defenders, made up mostly of poorly armed untrained prisoners and their guards, were quickly reduced to carrying out guerrilla warfare.   One month later, on July 24,   the Japanese landed a 2nd force on the northern half of the island.   The Russians were forced to surrender, and under the Treaty of Portsmouth, all of Southern Sakhalin up to the 50th parallel was ceded to Japan, but North Sakhalin was to remain Russian. South Sakhalin (Karafuto) would remain Japanese and Yuzhno-Sakhalinsk (Toyohara) would be its capital until the end of World War II, when they were recaptured by the Soviet Union.

After World War II most of the Japanese population was repatriated.   The Korean population, most of whom had been "recruited" by the Japanese, was not repatriated and Korean Sakhaliners currently make up roughly 12% of the population.

The 50's were a time of expansion and development for the Soviet Union as a whole.   The CPSU (Communist Party) encouraged migration to diversify the economy of the region, a process which has continued throughout the reform process of the 80's and 90's and has greatly contributed to Sakhalin's diversity.   Although Sakhalin's independence from Moscow and continental Russia has not been officially manifested, given that it truly is an island, Sakhalin will always possess its own, unique nature.

Gennady Ivanovich Nevelskoy

Despite losing his wife and daughter to the rigors of the eastern climate, Gennady Nevelskoy was a fearless naval officer dedicated to the exploration and settlement of the Russian Far East.

Born in 1814, Gennady Nevelskoy came from a family with a long naval tradition. His father, uncle and cousins all served in the Tsarist navy with distinction and Gennady was to prove no exception. At the age of 15 he was already serving in a naval corps that prepared those who wanted to enter the naval academy. From 1836-1846 he served in the Baltic Fleet, making expeditions to the Northern and Mediterranean seas, yet he was drawn to the Pacific Ocean. Two of the unresolved debates of the day were whether Sakhalin was an island or a peninsula, and how to find the mouth of the Amur River and if it was navigable by ocean-going ships.

In 1847, Nevelskoy turned down a more promising assignment on a frigate to serve on the transport "Baikal," headed for Kamchatka. It was from here that he wanted to base his explorations to search for the mouth of the Amur and prove that Sakhalin was not a peninsula, but an island. To do this, however, he needed signed orders from the governor of Eastern Siberia, Nikolai Muravyov, and authorization from the Tsar. When Nevelskoy arrived at Kamchatka, he found Muravyov willing to write the necessary orders, but they would be invalid without the Tsar's authorization. Time passed and there was no word from the Tsar. Finally, Nevelskoy decided that on his next trip of delivering supplies to Kamchatka he would investigate Sakhalin "on the way," without official authorization. In this he was taking an enormous risk. If anything unfortunate happened, Nevelskoy's career would be ruined and he might possibly be imprisoned. Insubordination was not taken lightly in those days.

Fortunately, Nevelskoy's beliefs were well founded. He mapped and proved Sakhalin to be an island, found the mouth of the Amur, and found it to be navigable for large ships. These discoveries completely changed contemporary thinking of the area and reversed a 1/2 century belief about Sakhalin.

> *Returning to St. Petersburg, Nevelskoy was promoted and was assigned to Muravyov to carry out "specially important assignments." During the following 5 years, Nevelskoy continued to explore the coastline. He founded several settlements, including Petrovskoe, the first on the mouth of the Amur, and Nikolaevsk, which was the region's preeminent port until 1891. These settlements helped secure Russia's claim to the Amur region, and in 1854 Nevelskoy was promoted to Rear Admiral for his services. Hoping to continue his successes, Nevelskoy was bitterly shocked the following year when told that he was being retired to the reserves. For the next 20 years, he worked in a Naval Technical Committee in St. Petersburg. In 1876, he died at the age of 62.*

SAKHALIN REGION TODAY

Sakhalin today is quite different from the penal colony it once represented. In fact, it is unique within Russia. In 1990 the island's "closed" status was not only removed, but a new "Free Economic Zone" status was proposed to expedite social and economic development of the region. This stimulated international business interest in the region but the anticipated tax and customs incentives have yet to be fully applied.

With the exception of the oil industry, most of the industrial branches of Sakhalin are located in the southern half of the island. Some of the old Japanese factories are still in use. The northern portion of the island is less densely populated, but boasts a considerable concentration of highly-educated technical specialists to support the once-flourishing oil and gas industry.

THE KURILES

Stretching 1200 km from the southern tip of Kamchatka to the northern edge of Japan, the Kuril Islands are a place of great natural beauty and political confrontation. Divided into three administrative sections (Northern, Central and Southern), the islands have changed hands several times over the past 300 years but have been under Russian control since they were "liberated" in the last few days of World War II. Today the "Kuril question" is a major point of contention in Russo-Japanese relations and despite high level discussions on the matter, does not look to be resolved in the near future.

Fishing is the major industry in this "disputed territory." Altogether there are 56 islands, although only the five largest have permanent inhabitants: Iturup, Kunashir and Shikotan of the southern islands and Paramushir and Shumshu of the northern islands. While the population grows their own private supply of vegetables, the bulk of their supplies come from Sakhalin and are as good as cut off in winter. The three major towns are Severo (northern)-Kurilsk, Kurilsk, and Yuzhno (southern)-Kurilsk. The first has an established air route with Petropavlovsk-Kamchatski and the latter two receive flights from Yuzhno-Sakhalinsk.

Geologically, the islands are home to some 160 volcanoes, which make for great scenery. Kunashir Island is particularly striking with its fantastic rock formations at Cape Stolbchatiy, hot waterfalls of the Doctorski River, and imposing view of Tyatya-yama, "the Father of Volcanoes," which last erupted in 1973. Lake Ponto (the "boiling" lake) is also something which should not be missed. Due to their location, the Kuriles have damp and foggy weather almost year round, which might be depressing for humans, but is perfect for the various puffins, gulls and cormorants that inhabit the isles.

SAKHALIN INDIGENOUS PEOPLE

There are about 3,100 Sakhalin natives (the island's total population is approximately 700,000). This includes five distinct native groups, the largest of which is the Nivkhy (2,270) and the smallest of which is the Orokhi or "Ul'ta" (130). There are also Orochi, Nanaitsi, and Evenki. The Ainu, once indigenous to southern Sakhalin, were expatriated to Hokkaido after 1945. Native groups currently claim five separate settlements in the northern half of the island. Principal activities of the aboriginal population include fishing, seal-hunting, reindeer breeding and production of handicrafts. There is a native-run company called "Aborigen Sakhalin," based in the city of Poronaisk, which produces handicrafts. The island boasts several different native folk-lore ensembles, the most famous of which is "Pila Ken" based in the northern city of Okha. This group has performed in Japan, the US and Canada. The Nivkhi produce a newspaper and radio program in their own language which is also taught in a handful of schools and kindergartens in the north of the island.

For more information, Nadezhda Aleksandrovna Laigun, head of the Department of Peoples of the North at the Sakhalin Regional Administration, is a good reference. Tel: 3-41-55.

Memorial wall and dramatic sculpture "Eternal Glory to the Fallen Heroes" at the end of Kommunisticheski Prospekt.

YUZHNO-SAKHALINSK

Yuzhno-Sakhalinsk is the largest city in the region, with a population of over 160,000. It is also the center of government, industry, commerce, transport, education and culture. As the region's capital, the Regional Administration is located in Yuzhno, headed by the governor and several vice-governors.

Besides burgeoning joint-venture activity in communications, transport, energy, timber and fishing, there remain former state enterprises going it alone: confectionery and macaroni; brewing and distilling of beer and vodka respectively; construction; and paper.

Yuzhno-Sakhalinsk is the center of island air and ground transport, boasting an "international airport" (charters only) as well as extensive railway and bus systems.

As for education, the Yuzhno-Sakhalinsk Pedagogical Institute (Teacher's Training College) is the largest institute of higher learning on the island. Although the Institute is designed to prepare future teachers, new departments are preparing specialists in economics/management and important business languages such as English, Japanese and Korean. Junior Achievement's "Applied Economics" program is offered in several schools in Yuzhno-Sakhalinsk.

The Department of Culture is located in the city, through which one can find out about various cultural events taking place in Yuzhno and throughout the island. There are native and Russian traditional song and dance ensembles, a symphonic society, theatrical performances (by such diverse authors as Sam Shepard and Anton Chekhov), puppet theater, children's talent shows, regional and city festivals. The head of the Department of Culture is Alexander Georgievich Karlov. His deputy, Marina Germanovna Darovskaya, speaks English and is a wonderful source of information. Tel: 3-20-01.

WALKING AROUND TOWN

The best way to start a tour of Yuzhno-Sakhalinsk is to get to the top of *Gorni Vozdukh* (**Mountain Air**) ski "resort." The trail starts from Ulitsa Gorkovo (Gorkovo Street) which crosses the end of Kommunisticheski Prospekt. The walk to the overlook takes about half an hour. From the overlook, which is

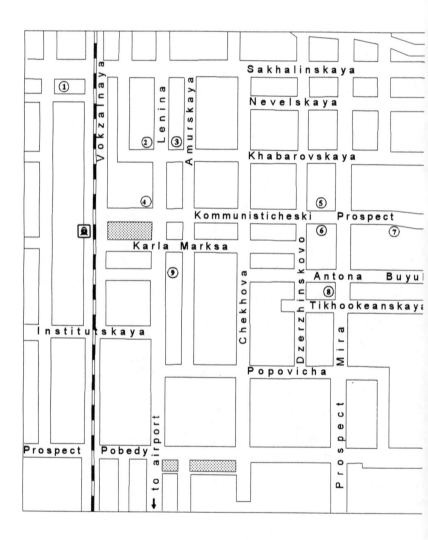

N

① Market
② Aeroflot office
③ Art Museum
④ Post office/telephone
⑤ SakhinCenter
⑥ Chekhov Theatre
⑦ Krai Museum
⑧ Dom Torgovli
⑨ Sapporo Hotel
Train / Bus Station

located at the bottom of a ski jump, you can enjoy a panoramic view of Sakhalin's capital city. The ski jump itself is not recommended, although the three ski runs are in use from December to April and the lift often works. Cross-country and alpine skiing equipment is available both at the mountain and down Gorkovo Street at the *Ploschad Pobedy* (Victory Square) ski base.

About half way down from the overlook on the right are two hotels, both having been called "the Gorka" and therefore creating some confusion. The first Gorka building, on your right, is smaller and is the newer of the two. The second, on your left, was built for Khruschev's one-day visit to Sakhalin and has a lot of character. A large dining room boasts a large rounded window with a truly picturesque view of the city through mountain pines. This is a nice place to have special dinners for large groups. Ask to walk out on the large balcony on the second floor -- you can imagine Khruschev getting up in the morning and surveying the land, cup of *chai* in hand...

Take a right coming down off of Gorni Vozdukh and turn left onto Kommunisticheski Prospekt. On the right hand side you will see some of the older Russian-style architecture for "single family homes." One building is a kindergarten, the rest are still being used as residences for high-ranking military officials.

Along the right side of Kommunisticheski Prospekt is the **Regional Park**, built by the Japanese industrial giant Fujiwara Ginjiro, and said to have been modelled after Chicago's Hyde Park. There is a lake in the center and many pretty trails for walking and jogging. There is a small city **zoo** which features a bear saved from hunters. There are tennis courts, a lake, a children's "auto park" (tricycles only please) and an operating children's locomotive. In the very back of the park is the Santa Hotel, where the service is international and the prices are out of this world. It's worth a look.

Continuing down Kommunisticheski Prospekt, on your left between Komsomolskaya and Mira you will find the **Kraevecheski Museum**. Opened in 1896 in Alexandrovsk, the museum's inventory of regional flora, fauna and ethnographic items is now housed in one of the few remaining Japanese structures on the island, in Yuzhno-Sakhalinsk.

Approaching the corner of Mira and Kommunisticheski you will see the press center on your right (local papers such as

"*Sovietski Sakhalin*" are located there) and on your left the Oriental Faculty of the Sakhalin State Pedagogical Institute (Teacher's Training Institute). If you have any pedagogical inclinations, you should contact them and offer to teach an English class to underclassmen. It's often difficult to decide who gets more out of the experience. Contact: Valentina Vasilievna. Tel: 3-51-29.

Continuing down Kommunisticheski, on your right you will see the **SakhinCenter** (Sakhalin Business Center) where many Russian and international representative offices are housed. On your left is the **Chekhov International Center**, the regional theater. Behind it is **Dom Torgovli** (House of Trade), the local department store which has the cheapest souvenirs in town. Next door to the Chekhov, still on your left, is Sakhalin's White House, the building of the **Regional Administration**, the head of whom is Sakhalin's governor.

Further down, on the intersection of Lenina and Kommunisticheski, is the Mayor's building which overlooks Lenin's statue, the generally acknowledged center of town.

You can end your tour here, or take a right on Lenina St. and head down toward Sakhalinskaya Street. On the first cross street, Khabarovskaya, you will find the **Regional Art Museum** (*Khudozhestvenni Muzei*). It is of a "neo-Greek" architectural style. Behind it is the **Regional Library.** Ask the director of the

Kraevecheski Museum

Foreign Literature section about the bi-monthly English Club. The club invites all English speakers and students of English to meet and chat over tea. Newcomers add the kind of variety that have kept the club going since 1991. Continuing down Lenina, take a left on Sakhalinskaya St. and you will find what was once referred to as the "Road of Life." This market is really more like a swap meet. Anything from car parts to puppies can be found here.

PRACTICAL INFORMATION

Unlike much of the rest of the former Soviet Union, Sakhalin has not, as of this writing, changed any of its Party street names. Lenin and Communist streets are still the main streets in town.

Moscow time +8 hours.

Code for calling Yuzhno-Sakhalinsk from outside Sakhalin: **42422** (for numbers with 5 digits) or **4242 (**for numbers with 6 digits).

Information when calling from inside Yuzhno: **09.**

Information from outside Sakhalin: **42422-5-61-21.**

Address Bureau Tel: 3-80-86.

To find out codes of other cities: **2-63-36.**

Main Post Office Located at Lenin Square, on the right as you face the square. Open 8:30-20:30 (14-15) Mon-Sun. There is also a **peregovorni punkt** around the corner (on Lenina) where you can order calls round the clock. There are *avtomati*, which you can dial yourself. Buy *zhetons* (tokens) from the cashier inside (one *zheton* lasts about 30 seconds). A list of cities which can be called hangs beside each phone (the row of phones to the right of the stairs can reach different cities than the row to the left). Check the list of codes hanging there—for some reason one row of phones needs different codes for large cities. When the phones actually work, this is a great system. Lay in a supply of *zhetons,* as they can also be used at the airport *peregovorni punkt*, where the cashier for buying *zhetons* is usually closed.

Sakhalin Telecom Service Centers International fax and phone are available for walk-in use. Located at the Lada, Nataliya, and Sapporo Hotels.

SakhsotsBank Change money before noon! Kommunisticheski Prospekt 47. Tel: 2-20-44.

IntoBank Chekova 130. Tel: 29-14-37.

Incombank Kommunisticheski Prospekt 32. Tel: 2-29-38.

HOTELS

Santa Resort Absolutely the most expensive place in town. You decide if the new modular construction, well-trained staff, sauna/jacuzzi rooms, bar, tennis courts, Japanese/European style restaurants, business facilities, etc. are worth the $242-$421 charge per night. Very expensive. Venskaya 3. Tel: 5-91-74, 5-92-10, Satellite Tel: (+7-509-85) 65550, Fax: 65555.

Gorka I This very small hotel (only three rooms) tries hard to please its customers. There is a private sauna, and laundry services are available. Satellite telephone and fax available. Very expensive. Kommunisticheski Prospekt 1B. Local Tel: 3-55-45. Satellite Tel: (+7-504-41) 62400. Satellite Fax: 62004.

Gorka II ("Zagorodnaya") Actually larger, older and more famous than Gorka I, and located right next door—taxi drivers and guests alike are liable to be confused. Has 5 rooms, and a good restaurant, ideal for holding stately dinners. Very expensive. Kruschev stayed here. Great view of the city. Local Tel: 3-89-30.

Eurasia Hotel Located next to the railway station, you might expect a seedier place, but this Russian-Japanese joint venture has pleasant rooms and a good restaurant, with helpful service. Also has a sauna. Vokzalnaya 54. Moderate. Local Tel: 27-44-66, 27-48-29. Satellite Fax: (+7-504-41) 62003.

Sakhalin Sapporo Average hotel offers satellite phone, fax, and car rental services. The hotel has a night club and a gift shop, but the rooms are on the small side. Restaurant is unremarkable. Moderate, breakfast included. Lenina 181. Tel: 3-66-29, 3-89-32. Satellite Tel: (+7-504-41) 62005 or 62550, Fax: 62001.

Nataliya Hailed as the perfect combination between Sapporo prices and Santa service. Too new to tell, however the price is reasonable. Also has a cafe which serves reasonably priced meals. Cafe open 8-20. Moderate. Antona Buyukli 38 (corner of Chekhova and Buyukli, one block from Hotel Viola). Tel: 3-66-83. Satellite Tel: (+7-504-41) 62700.

Bed and Breakfast This concept has not really caught on yet in Sakhalin, however there is a new group called "Address" which offers what appears to be this service. They have also offered airport pick up and drop off, local transport, translation and "connections" in the community. They are working with the Sakhalin International Center for Entrepreneurial Development, a non-profit effort by Loyola-Marymount University, to stimulate entrepreneurial activity on Sakhalin Island. Moderate. For advance bookings write to: "Address" c/o Entrepreneurial Center, 70 Pobedy, Yuzhno-Sakhalinsk, 693000. Or call local tel: 3-21-88. International Tel: (+7-504-41) 62226. Fax: 62227.

Hotel Maneron This blue hotel just off the square from the railroad station is centrally located and one of the few places with a friendly reception desk. Be forewarned that if you want a toilet, shower, or phone in your room, you must order a "lux" (suite). All ordinary single and double rooms have only a sink in the room, with other facilities down the hall. Some seedy characters lurk about, but the strict hall *dezhurnayas* keep an eye on things. The buffet/bar, supposedly open from 8-24 (closed 12:30-13), is unreliable, but you can usually buy soft drinks from the *dezhurnayas*. Cheap prices for singles, moderate prices for suites. Kommunisticheski Prospekt 86. Tel: 2-34-53.

Viola This hotel used to be apartments, so all the rooms are suites. They often have trouble with their heating system in winter, so ask for an extra blanket. All calls must be made through the desk clerk—no direct-dial phones. However, one expatriate company has established long-term residence here. Convenient location in a residential neighborhood, near center of town. The buffet on the top floor serves decent, if unexciting, meals. Chekhova 43. Tel: 3-32-99.

Some cars simply park for the winter in Yuzhno-Sakhalinsk

Concordia Rooms are simple, without telephones, but the hotel has its own hot water heaters. Inexpensive, breakfast included. Kruykova 35. Tel: 3-22-93.

Hotel Lada (formerly the "Vostok") Komsomolskaya 154. Local Tel: 3-31-45, 3-18-45, fax: 3-18-98. Satellite Tel: (+7-504-41) 62500.

Tourist A modest hotel, located within easy walking distance of the Slavianka cafe! Inexpensive. Sakhalinskaya 2. Tel: 3-33-92.

RESTAURANTS AND CAFES

M i M (Master and Margarita) Cheerful colored lights in the windows and quaint lanterns over the door make this worthwhile restaurant easy to find. Originally planned as a cafe/piano bar where "intellectuals" could gather, MiM (as it is affectionately called) has lately fallen on hard times. As the waitress explains it: nowadays intellectuals don't have the money to go to restaurants. The piano player may be gone, but MiM is still a pleasant place for lunch or dinner. The pop music is kept to a reasonable level so that conversations are possible, and best of all, the food is good and the waitresses are polite and friendly! Ulitsa Lenina 171. Open 9-11, 12-16, 18-23. Tel: 2-21-91.

Midzuumi Restaurant/Bar Nina For the passing "Geijin" the Japanese cuisine here represents a refreshing change of pace from the usual fare. Unfortunately, the Japanese chef has gone, to the possible detriment of consistency. After dinner, downstairs your group can take over a small table at the Nina bar, drink beer and partake of a little karaoke. Check the prices before you sit down—sometimes there is a cover charge, sometimes you pay per song, and sometimes you pay for both. If the bill seems inordinately high, argue. Keep in mind, however, that prices here are rivalled only by the Santa Resort. Restaurant stops cooking by 10 pm, closes at midnight. Nina has been known to stay open until 3 am, but has also closed early for no apparent reason. Lenina 182A. Tel: 2-63-92, 2-38-28.

Saigon Don't be fooled by the name, you won't find any Vietnamese food here, but you will find some tasty dishes. The name of the restaurant comes from the interior decor, which is bamboo, wood, and beaded curtains. The menu provides a large selection of seafood, as well as soups, salads and desserts. Try the chicken in garlic sauce. It's a toss up whether you'll get the friendly or the rude waitress, but service is usually quick in either case. Weekend evenings there is a live (loud) band. There are two small private dining areas. Best to make a reservation in advance, or they might not let you in, no matter how empty they are. Karla Marksa 27. Open Mon and Wed-Fri 12-24 (17-19), Tue 12-17, Sat, Sun 14-24. Tel: 2-40-23.

Binom If the large neon sign has lured you in, you may be surprised to find that the sign itself is probably larger than the interior of the restaurant. However, good food can be found in this small cafe-type hideaway. Brick walls, a bar with stools, and smoke in the air all add to the atmosphere. "Binom" apparently means something relating to the sea in Japanese (the waitresses could be no more specific than that), so there is seafood on the menu, but nothing Japanese. Seafood is also appropriate for this restaurant, as it is attached to the Hotel Rybak, which means "fisherman," on left side of Lenin Square. Open 12-23 (16-18).

Seoul Decent European and Korean cuisine. The restaurant is one of the newest in town, the atmosphere is Western, and the band, which cranks up after 7pm, is the best in town (with the most moderate volume). Unfortunately, one pays heavily for the upscale atmosphere. After the Santa and Mizuumi, Seoul is the most expensive place in town. Prospekt Mira 245. Open until 1 am every day except Monday. Tel: 5-13-42.

Slavianka (a.k.a. *Ruskaya Kukhnya* or Russian Cuisine) "Homey" atmosphere and traditional Russian cuisine. Prices are reasonable and service is usually very good. The cafe is too small for a band but the taped music can become oppressive. Best to reserve a place in advance and/or go early. Open every day until 9 pm except Sunday. After 8 pm they stop accepting customers. Sakhalinskaya 45. Tel: 3-56-67.

Cafe Rus Across the street from the Saigon in the Social Welfare building there is a well-hidden cafe. You have to walk through corridors of pensioners waiting to collect their monthly incomes, and down a flight of stairs before you reach your goal, but it will be well worth your time. The name of the cafe has about as much to do with the food as at the Saigon. Although called "Rus," this cafe is run by Koreans, with the result that many spicy Korean dishes are to be had. Anything with *ostri* in the title is spicy. The best thing about this place is the speedy service. When you come in, you will already find on your table a typed list of the day's menu, as well as some blank slips of paper and a pencil stub. Figure out what you want, write it down, and hand it to the waitress as she races by. She will shortly bring your dishes, and will toss a small cash register receipt at you. This is your bill. Unfortunately, the cafe is only open weekdays during business hours, but if you are looking for a quick bite, this is the place for you. Reasonable prices. Karla Marksa 24. Open weekdays 10-17.

Sapporo (in Hotel Sakhalin Sapporo) Food consistently decent and a table is almost always available. It's a good place to meet other business people, as most will be staying in the hotel. Moderate prices. Tel: 3-27-90.

Furosato Atmosphere is decent, with band and dance floor. The restaurant opened only in 1993. Seems to attract a disproportionately large crowd of young people in leather jackets. Prospekt Mira 420. Tel: 5-56-69.

Kurosivo Nice atmosphere. Korean and seafood. Prices medium to high. No band, but they tend to play tapes of MTV. Closes at 23:00. Tikhiokeanskaya 40A (hidden in apartment buildings across from Dom Torgovli). Tel: 3-35-04.

Chinson (*Vostochnaya Kukhnya* or **Oriental Cuisine**) Good, quick Korean food. Try one of everything. Vokzalnaya 13. Open till 23:00 Mon-Fri. Closes at 17:00 on Sat, closed Sun. Tel: 2-23-42.

Blue Bird Cafe (*Sinyaya Ptichka*) Only a few tables, so it's wise to reserve in advance. Open only Mon-Fri 12:30-15, unless reserved for parties of 7 or more. Dinners must be reserved in advance. Purkayeva 39. Tel: 5-66-79.

Lada (formerly *Druzhba* Restaurant in Hotel Lada) Fewer foreign travelers to be found here. It's a good idea to call ahead. Tel: 3-16-39.

Pearl Japanese restaurant in Santa Hotel. Tel: 5-92-65.

Rubin (Ruby) European restaurant in Santa Hotel. Tel: 5-92-65.

SHOPPING

Raicentr (name bears a double meaning, either Regional Center or Paradise Center). Owned by Alexander Borodin and his wife Natasha, this is an interesting family business combining arts, crafts, antiques and a commitment to collecting and displaying Russian culture, past and present. Located in the central hall on the 4th floor of the SakhinCenter,   internal telephone: 218.

Germes   A very well-stocked shop for souvenir buying. Hidden on Pogranichnaya St. No. 14. Tel: 3-35-29.

The **Art Museum** on Lenin St. features a souvenir shop, an interesting place to look at semi-precious stones. Lenina 137. Open from 10-18 (14-15), closed Sun, Mon.   Tel: 2-29-25 or 2-27-69.

Dom Torgovli   The cheapest place to buy souvenirs, although the quality might be inconsistent.   On Prospekt Mira behind the Chekhov Center. Tel: 3-26-42.

Tovari Dlya Detyei   By name, a store for children, but actually a regular department store.   Music tapes, household items, souvenirs. Ulitsa Lenina 123. Open Mon-Fri 10-19 (14-15), Sat 10-17.

Rubin (Ruby)   Private jewelry store.   Lenina 218.   Open Mon-Fri 10-19 (14-15), Sat 10-18. Tel: 2-63-57.

Zhemchuzhina (Pearl)   Government jewelry store.   Open Mon-Fri 10-19:30 (14-15), Sat 11-19:30.   Lenina 218.   Tel: 2-27-88.

MARKET

The market is located at Sakhalinskaya 85/A, but all along the street to the market there are various merchants.   There is also a market of Chinese goods across the street (and slightly before) the food market.

MUSEUMS

Kraevecheski Museum (Natural History, Political History, and Native Culture)   This small museum is a delight, truly with something for everyone.   Housed in one of the only remaining buildings built by the Japanese, it is nestled in a garden with a fountain, Japanese lion statues, and military hardware.   Inside there are dioramas with stuffed seals, bears and other animals indigenous to the island; information about the volcanoes still active in the Kuril Islands; archaeological remnants of early native cultures and the Russian and Dutch "discoverers" of Sakhalin; artifacts and reconstructions of native dwellings and lifestyles; and recollections of the conditions under Stalin and communism.   A small gift shop is chock full of jewelry, paintings, native birch-bark boxes and baskets, and all sorts of Russian crafts. A guidebook is available in both English and Russian, and you can even arrange for a tour with an English-speaking guide. Nominal entrance fee. Kommunisticheski Prospekt 29. Open Tue 11-17, Wed-Sun 11-18, closed Mon. Tel: 3-49-11.

Museum of Art *(Khudozhestvenni Muzei)* This small museum has changing exhibits, ranging from Russian icons and religious articles, to Japanese household shrines and wedding outfits. The ground floor is one large room, the upper floor consists of small rooms which must be entered from the interior balcony. These rooms are kept locked, opened for each individual guest as they progress from one to the other. Small gift shop on the premises. 137 Lenina. Open 10-18, closed Mon. Tel: 2-36-43.

Regional Library Has a foreign literature section. Khabarovskaya 78. Tel: 2-30-28.

ENTERTAINMENT

For night-time fun, those who can afford it book a table in a restaurant with a band and eat, drink and dance until about 1 a.m. Karaoke is also popular. Unfortunately, in the New Russia those who can afford it might not be those you ought to be partying with. Use common sense when "stepping out." Most people will opt to spend time at friends' houses in the evening and have no qualms about cranking the stereo, moving the dinner table and dancing in the living room.

Chekhov Theater Kommunisticheski Pr. 35. Tel: 3-42-13.

Philharmonic Sakhalinskaya 25. Tel: 3-74-15.

Puppet Theater Karla Marksa 24. Tel: 3-14-98.

Movie Theater Komsomolets Sakhalinskaya 52. Tel: 2-33-44, 2-63-29 (recording).

Movie Theater Oktyabr Kommunisticheski Prospekt 45. Tel: 3-66-12 (recording).

Lada Casino In Hotel Lada. Komsomolskaya 154. Tel: 3-29-58.

Royal Night Club In Sapporo Hotel. Tel: 3-19-02.

Nina Night Bar (See Midzuumi under food).

Department of Culture Can give tips on special events in Yuzhno. Dzerzhinskovo 23. Tel: 3-20-01.

Tourbaza Gorni Vozdukh Hotel Tel: 3-54-88, 3-47-16.

Lizhnaya Baza Locomotiv   Has both cross-country and downhill skis for rent. Take bus up Kommunisticheski Prospekt to the stop "city park" (*gorodskoi park*), walk to the boat rental (*lodochnaya stantsia*)   and ask for the Lizhnaya Baza.   Tel: 5-91-13.

Lizhnaya Baza Spartak   Cross-country skiing at *Ploschad Pobedy* (Victory Square). Tel: 3-51-32.

BANYAS

The following is a list of public *banyas* in Yuzhno. However, their condition is indicative of the condition of many public buildings these days.   The best *banyas* are those constructed for the exclusive use of a particular organization. For those you'll need connections, but it would be a worthwhile experience.

Korral   Formerly one of the better in the city.   Best to make reservations, especially if it's a bad water day in the city. Prospekt Mira 66. Open 15-23. Tel: 3-76-34.

Public Banya No. 1 Sakhalinskaya 69. Tel: 2-29-61.

Public Banya No. 2 Pobedy 84. Tel: 3-41-16.

PLACES OF WORSHIP

Korean Church   Christian services held Sundays at 10:00 am in the cinema Komsomolets. Lenina 78. Tel: 2-28-70.

TRANSPORTATION

Airport   Only about 20 minutes from downtown Yuzhno. Bus No. 108 leaves from in front of the train station, and runs frequently throughout the day.   The International Hall at the airport is to the left, a pleasant small room with a small, expensive bar.   It is a good idea to confirm your flight in advance, especially in spring, when sudden storms close the airport with alarming frequency.   Domestic Hall Tel: 3-52-30, 9-53-90. International Hall Tel: 5-54-46.

SakhAviaTrans   For internal flights up-island, twice/week flights to Hakodate, Japan, and once/week flights to Seoul, Korea.   Round-trip tickets to Hakodate bought in Yuzhno are currently half the cost of those bought in Hakodate.   Tel: 5-19-58.

City Aeroflot Agency One of the few Aeroflot offices that is actually helpful and where the clerk will smile at you, at least at the international desk. However, that doesn't make them any quicker than usual, so expect a wait. Lenina 198 (corner of Lenina and Khabarovskaya). Open from 9:30-19 (14-15). Tel: 3-32-55, 3-56-88.

Train Station/Bus Station Located in the center of town behind Lenin Square, which is located at the intersection of Kommunisticheski Prospekt and, you guessed it, Lenin Street. Long distance buses can be found in front of the train station. Information booths for both services are inside the train station or call 2-23-30 for bus information. It is best to ask the schedule for the train you want at the information booth, rather than checking yourself at the "self-serve" info schedules, since those lists tend to be misleading.

There are two train lines: one which goes halfway up the west side of the island, and another which goes up the east side to Nogliki. If you are going as far as Okha, you might prefer to take a plane or helicopter from Yuzhno, weather permitting, than an overnight train and bus. Train info: 2-71-13.

Taxis can often be found waiting outside the train station. You can order a cab at: 2-33-92 (passengers) or 3-46-77 (for cargo). For passenger service, generally you can expect a cab from 5-30 minutes after placing an order.

AROUND YUZHNO-SAKHALINSK

Since Yuzhno-Sakhalinsk is the capital of Sakhalinskaya Oblast, the city itself has adapted rapidly to its new international status with improved hotels, new restaurants, etc. Elsewhere on Sakhalin, while some cities are developing their industries and associated business-related services, many of the smaller cities are still essentially one-horse towns (although they don't think of themselves that way, of course!), with one hotel, usually imaginatively named after the town itself, a restaurant in the hotel, a local museum, and little else of interest to outsiders. However, this often also means that they are quite close to nature and it is easy to find great hiking routes through scenic mountains or pretty beaches and interesting coastlines. Mushroom and berry-picking in season are extremely popular among the locals, as is ice fishing.

It is also possible to go hunting, scuba diving, bird watching, skiing and more. Your best bet for organizing a special adventure trip is through InTRek-Sakhalin Agency, which acts as a clearinghouse for various smaller tour agencies. They offer tours ranging from volcano climbing in the Kuriles to archaeological excavations, to crab-catching, to simple tours around Yuzhno. For trips to the Kuriles you will need a special pass or permission (*propusk*), so be sure to make arrangements at least two weeks in advance. The same is true for hunting trips where you keep a trophy, such as a bear skull or ram horns. The staff at InTRek speak English and are helpful and polite.

InTRek-Sakhalin Chekhov International Center of Culture, Arts and Tourism. 35 Kommunisticheski Prospekt, Yuzhno-Sakhalinsk 693000. Local Tel: 3-48-89, 3-52-08. Satellite Fax: (+7-504-41) 62257.

Another local tour agency is:

Sakhalin Big Game for hunting and fishing excursions. Komsomolskaya 165. Tel: 2-81-61, 2-81-73, 2-81-75.

Just outside the city near the airport (ask your driver to show you) is a place where **water runs uphill**. Cars put in neutral will roll uphill as well. Due to a nearby magnetic lode stone or an optical illusion, it has to be seen to be believed.

KHOLMSK

Founded in 1870, **Kholmsk** is so named because it is built on a hill (*kholma*). It is the second largest city in the region (pop 51,000), and home of the Sakhalin Shipping Company (the main sponsor of the island's professional soccer team). Two and a half hours from Yuzhno-Sakhalinsk by car, the drive is a picturesque one. The mountain road (winding and in poor condition) passes through tunnels and the Kamyshoviy mountain range, forested hills and valleys, crosses ravines, and passes waterfalls for a scenic journey. If you weren't planning to go to Kholmsk but want to see the countryside of Sakhalin, it's worth a day trip.

PRACTICAL INFORMATION

Code for calling Kholmsk from outside Sakhalin: **42433**.

Code for calling Kholmsk from Yuzhno: **233.**
Post Office Ploschad Lenina 5. Tel: 4-79-47.

HOTELS

Hotel Kholmsk Inexpensive. Sovietskaya 60. Tel: 2-22-48.
Hotel Meridian Cheap. Sovietskaya 136/B. Tel: 3-28-55.
Hotel Chaika Pobedy 4. Tel: 4-51-77.

FOOD

Kusiro Opened before the Mizuumi in Yuzhno-Sakhalin, with a similar style. Japanese cuisine at Japanese prices. Upper floor serves European cuisine and features a band. Lower floor features a sushi bar. Sovietskaya 46. Tel: 2-44-87. 2-47-37 (sushi bar).
Azalea (Korean) Sovietskaya 103. Tel: 3-35-69.
Kholmsk Sovietskaya 60. Tel: 2-47-17.
Neptune Pobedy 18. Tel: 2-28-52.
Parus Sovietskaya 39 (Morskoi Vokzal). Tel: 2-29-37.
Pivbar (Beer Bar) Kapitanskaya 4. Tel: 2-20-06.
Volna (Wave) Kapitanskaya 4/A. Tel: 2-25-73.
Market on Lesozavodskaya.

MUSEUMS

Marine Fauna Museum (Vitas Marine Ecological Center) This museum research center also conducts small group marine tours (diving, bird watching on nearby islands, scientific studies). For a one to three week complete tour in a particular area of interest, you should make arrangements in advance through the InTRek agency in Yuzhno. If you already happen to be in Kholmsk, drop by the museum to see what is going on. Sovietskaya 23. Tel: 2-25-14, 2-28-31.

ENTERTAINMENT

At the top of the mountain overlooking the port, there is a **monument** to the Russian paratroopers who assaulted the Japanese forces here in the last days of World War II.

The **soccer team "Sakhalin"** is based at Molodyozhnaya St. To find out when they are playing call 2-29-33.

Intertourism association Sovietskaya 60. Tel: 2-26-97.

TRANSPORTATION

Kholmsk is 6 hours from Yuzhno by train (while the track is under repair), 2 hours by bus. It is 9 hours by ferry from Port Vanino, in Khabarovski Krai. This ferry mostly takes containerized cargo, but will take passengers as well. An interesting note is that because the Japanese built the railroad on Sakhalin, all inbound rail wagons must have their wheels changed to a different gauge than the rest of Russia. During navigation season (late May to Oct.), there is a ferry which runs about twice/month from Japan to Kholmsk (and/or Korsakov), and on to the Kuriles. Despite the fact that there is an Aeroflot office here, the closest airport is in Yuzhno.

Excursion Bureau Sovietskaya 75. Tel: 2-33-62, 2-30-63.

Aeroflot (Information) Zheleznodorozhnaya 93. Tel: 2-29-00.

Aeroflot Ticket Office at Morskoi Vokzal. Tel: 2-35-55.

Severny **Train Station (North)** Lesozavodskaya. Tel: 9-73-00 (info), 9-73-05 (tix).

Yuzhni **Train Station (South)** Sovietskaya. 9-72-07 (info), 9-97-52 (tickets).

Bus Station (*Avtovokzal*) Sovietskaya. Tel: 3-01-20.

Maritime Terminal *(Morskoi Vokzal)* Sovietskaya 39. Tel: 9-63-54.

Ferry Crossing Tel: 2-35-00.

KORSAKOV

The outpost of Muravyovski was founded in 1853 and named after the then governor of Eastern Siberia. When Mr. Korsakov became governor, the town name was changed as well. The third largest town in the region (population of 45,000), Korsakov is the center of the fishing industry and although run down, is still Sakhalin's largest sea-port. On the hill overlooking the town is a monument to the victorious Japanese troops in the Russo-Japanese War of 1905. During World War II, it was here in the environs of Korsakov that American POWs were held by the Japanese.

PRACTICAL INFORMATION

Code for calling Korsakov from outside Sakhalin: **42435**.
Code for calling Korsakov from Yuzhno: **235**.
Hotel Korsakov Gvardeiskaya 1. Tel: 2-49-00.
Restaurant Korsakov Gvardeiskaya 1.
Restaurant Vostok Oktyabrskaya 7. Tel: 2-57-22.
Bus Station Vokzalnaya 31. Buses to Yuzhno take approximately 45 minutes. Tel: 2-47-70.
Train Station Vokzalnaya 31. Tel: 9-27-30.
Maritime Terminal (*Morskoi Vokzal*) Per. Reidovy 2. Tel: 2-23-52.
Ferry About twice per month in the summer and fall there is a ferry from Wakkanei, Japan to Korsakov or Kholmsk.
Yacht Club Owners of locally owned sail boats are usually friendly and might offer to take you around for a day trip. Tel: 2-55-68.
"Experiment" A particularly active theater group featuring new interpretation theater. The Director, Lilia Shurigina, can be reached through the Korsakov Department of Culture at tel: 2-34-97.

OKHA

Founded in 1892, **Okha** (pop 36,000) in the north is the center of the oil and gas industry for the island and, as the city's energy is supplied by gas as opposed to coal in the southern cities, the air is purported to the cleanest and the snow the whitest on the island.

Code for calling Okha from outside Sakhalin: **424037** for numbers with 4 digits. Numbers with 6 digits must be ordered through the operator.
Code for calling Okha from Yuzhno: **2370**.
Tourism Bureau Lenina 35. Tel: 22-11.
Hotel Yaponskaya 13 rooms. Moderate prices. Lenina 40/1. Tel: 58-97.

Hotel Dom Rabotnikov Akobanka　Only 12 rooms.　You can also hire a car or mini-van through the hotel, by the hour or for the day.　Advance reservations suggested.　Airport pick-up available.　Inexpensive.　Sovietskaya 24.　Tel: 984-527.

Hotel Tsentralnaya　Cheap.　Komsomolskaya 25.　Tel: 35-51.

Art Cafe　Lenina 2.　Tel: 49-10.

Podarki (gifts)　Sovietskaya 23.　Tel: 27-92.

Kraevecheski Museum　Closed Mondays.　Sovietskaya 1. Tel: 984-357.

Airport Information　Tel: 47-35, 921-85 (ticket desk). Flights take about an hour and a half to Yuzhno-Sakhalinsk.

Aeroflot City Office　Dzerzhinskovo 42.　Tel: 47-35 (info), 48-24 (tickets).

Train Station Information　Tel: 97-06.

Bus Station　Dzerzhinskovo.　Tel: 22-67.

ALEXANDROVSK-SAKHALINSKI

In the center of the island on the west coast, Alexandrovsk-Sakhalinski can be reached by a beautiful hour and a half drive through the mountains from **Tymovsk**, (on the train line from Yuzhno-Sakhalinsk), and is one of the oldest cities in the region, founded in 1869.　Formerly the capital of Russian Sakhalin when the Russians only owned the northern half, the town had the dubious honor of being the first place exiles were sent when the island was declared a penal colony.　Chekhov stayed here during his visit to Sakhalin, which he called a "hell," but in the spirit of "all publicity is good publicity," the city has a Chekhov Museum to commemorate his visit (tel: 21-91).　Of note are the three huge rocks that stand in the bay, known as the Three Brothers.

Chapter 11

PRACTICAL INFORMATION

The Black Market
Technically, it is still illegal to change money on the street. Scams abound, so even though you will see people with dollar and yen signs pinned to their jackets, the abundance of banks and small exchange offices makes it unnecessary to take the risk of being robbed or cheated.

Cash, Credit Cards, Traveler's Cheques
A few hotels accustomed to dealing with foreigners accept credit cards, but often only one brand (usually Visa OR American Express). Some will not accept them on weekends, when the banks are closed! Traveler's cheques are almost unheard of and you will have great difficulty getting them exchanged. In short, Russia is a cash society.

Currency
The ruble is constantly losing value against the dollar due to high inflation, therefore we have not listed any ruble prices. Rubles currently come in coins of 1, 5, 10, 20, 50, and 100 rubles, and bills of 100, 200, 500, 1,000, 5,000, 10,000, and 50,000. Every few years the government changes the currency, and invalidates the old rubles. A word to the wise; although interesting to look at, Soviet money (i.e. anything with a picture of Lenin or a hammer and sickle), as well as Russian rubles from before 1993, are no longer valid and are good only as souvenirs.

Soviet rubles are no longer valid

Only rubles issued since 1993 are accepted as currency

Drinking Water

Although in most cities the drinking water is fine, the pipes are often quite old and the water is tinged with iron. There are also occasional "scares" about the drinking water. To be on the safe side, always drink bottled or boiled water.

Electricity

In Russia the voltage is 220, so make sure any electric device you bring over, such as a computer, hair dryer or electric razor, has the appropriate transformer.

Foreign Consulates

The following is a list of the countries with consulates in the Russian Far East. Most have embassies in Moscow. For more detailed information about office hours and services, check under Practical Information in the city where the consulate is located.

Australian Consulate General Uborevicha 17, Vladivostok. Tel: 22-86-28, fax: 22-87-78.

Chinese Consulate General Lenin Stadium, Khabarovsk. Tel: 34-85-37, fax: 34-85-37.

Indian Consulate General Aleutskaya 14, Vladivostok. Tel: 22-81-10, fax: 22-86-66.

Japanese Consulate General Mordovtseva 12, Vladivostok. Tel: 26-75-02, fax: 26-75-41.

Japanese Consulate General Komsomolskaya 79, Khabarovsk. Tel: 33-26-23, fax: 33-28-30.

Mongolian Consulate General Yerbanova 12 (2nd floor, Hotel Baikal), Ulan-Ude.

North Korean Consulate General Vladivostokskaya 14, Nakhodka. Tel: 55-53-10.

South Korean Consulate General Aleutskaya 45/A, Vladivostok. Tel: 22-77-29, fax: 22-94-71.

Philippine Consulate General Aleutskaya 14, Vladivostok. Tel: 22-13-51.

United States Consulate General Mordovtseva 12, Vladivostok. Tel: 26-84-58, fax: 26-84-45.

Vietnamese Consulate General Sportivnaya 41, Nakhodka. Tel: 2-76-46.

Holidays in Russia

Russians love their holidays and although some of the names have changed since the fall of Communism, there are still plenty of opportunities in the year to get together and celebrate. The proper way to congratulate someone on a holiday is to say "*s prazdnikom.*" Below is a list of the more important Russian holidays:

January 1 New Year's The biggest holiday of the year, New Year's combines Christmas and New Year's into one holiday. *Ded Moroz* (Grandfather Frost) and his daughter *Snegurichka* (the snow maiden) give children presents and help decorate the *Yolka* (Christmas tree). Russians usually spend New Year's Eve at home or at a friend's home with a huge spread of food and alcohol to celebrate till the wee hours of the morning. Toasts to friendship, women and the new year are obligatory. *S novym godom!* (Happy New Year!)

January 7 Christmas Russians didn't celebrate Christmas under Communism, as it was considered a religious holiday. Nowadays it is celebrated in January, due to the difference between the Julian and Gregorian calendars (Russia switched after the Revolution).   December 25 is considered to be the "Catholic" Christmas, and is not celebrated.

January 13 Old New Year's In case you forgot to toast to something on January 1, you have another chance.   Because New Year's is so popular a holiday, instead of celebrating by one calendar or the other (like Christmas), Russians celebrate it twice.

February 23 Defender of the Motherland Day As military service is obligatory, this holiday is considered to be the male's equivalent of March 8.   Previously called Soviet Army Day, men are given books and alcohol.

March 8 International Women's Day Women's Day is a big holiday where women throughout the country are congratulated and given flowers, candies and champagne at work, at home and even by passers by! On March 8, even the meanest Intourist or Aeroflot woman might turn nice and smile. *S prazdnikom!*

April 22 Lenin's Birthday A holiday that is no longer as popular as it used to be.   Nowadays, Lenin's birthday is sometimes celebrated by a *subbotnik* where workers volunteer to work on a day off to clean up their buildings, do repair work and so on.

Paskha   (Easter) The specific date changes according to the church calendar, but usually occurs in April or the beginning of May. Lots of *blini* (blintzes) are cooked and eggs are dyed red to celebrate Easter.

One week after Easter (end of April or beginning of May) Memorial Day Day on which Russians go to the cemetery to remember those who have passed

Proud Navy veterans on Victory Day

away.   Russian cemeteries have benches near the graves so families and friends can sit, talk and eat near their loved ones.

May 1-2 Labor Day May 1 used to be a huge holiday in the days of the Soviet Union, with large political demonstrations, marches, speeches and pictures of Lenin and Marx on every corner. Lately, Labor Day is a mere shadow of its former self and usually entails a demonstration by the remaining die-hard communists, calling for the overthrow of the "fascist democrats."

May 9 Victory Day The memory of the Soviet Victory in World War II, or the Great Patriotic War as it is called in Russian, is revered and May 9 is still one of the biggest holidays in every city. Veterans turn out bedecked with medals won in campaigns against Germany and Japan and there is usually a military parade. Speeches are made by various civilian and military leaders to peace and remembrance and a wreath is laid at an eternal flame. The year 1995 will mark the fiftieth anniversary of victory and grandiose celebrations are planned throughout the country. After the ceremonies the veterans gather together to remember fallen friends and times gone by and it is not unusual for an impromptu dance to begin to the sounds of "Kalinka." Victory day is not to be missed.

May 28 Border Guard Day Depending on where you are in the Far East, this holiday might pass unnoticed. Those who completed their service in the border guards gather together and remember the good times they had while in uniform. This is usually accompanied by lots of drinking and the groups tend to get rowdy at the end of the day, so be careful.

The square by the C-56 submarine in Vladivostok is a popular place for military parades

June 12   Independence Day   The first free election of a president of Russia (Boris Yeltsin) took place on this day in 1990, and it is celebrated as symbolic of "independence" from the Soviet Union.

Navy Day   Last Sunday in July   In military port cities such as Vladivostok, Navy Day is still a big holiday.   All the naval ships anchor out in the bay and pass by in review.   There are fireworks, a mock assault and displays of martial arts by the local marine battalion, and Neptune himself arrives to wish everyone a happy holiday!

September 1   Knowledge Day   On the first day of school, students all come to class with flowers and small gifts for their teachers.   As a rule, on the first day students do not study, but go on field trips or engage in some other fun educational activity.

November 7 Revolution Day   Another big Soviet holiday formerly celebrated by massive military parades in Moscow's Red Square with troops, tanks and missiles. Smaller towns emulated with what military hardware they had and everybody praised the revolution and the coming

Russian Cemetery

of Soviet Power in Russia.   Today, this holiday is no longer officially recognized and Revolution Day has been replaced with its democratic equivalent: Constitution Day.

December 12   Constitution Day   This holiday changes its date every time a new constituion is adopted. The most recent constitution was voted in in 1993.

Russian Embassies and Consulates in the United States

Russian Embassy   1825 Phelps Place NW, Washington, DC 20008. Tel: 202-939-8907.

Russian Consulate   9 E. 91 St., New York, NY, 10128. Tel: 212-348-0926.

Russian Consulate   2001 6th Ave., suite 2323, Westin Building, Seattle, WA 98121. Tel: 206-728-1910.

Russian Consulate   2790 Green St., San Francisco, CA 94123. Tel: 415-202-9800.

Safety

Russia, once so proud of its low crime statistics, has experienced an increase in crime in the past few years. Use common sense and the caution you would use in any big city when traveling. A few tips: if you travel by overnight train, put your valuables in the under-the-seat compartments and flip up the special metal lock which keeps the door from being opened wider than a crack. Women should be especially cautious at night—use public transportation when possible, but if you take a taxi, don't get in if there is more than one person already in the car. A small spray-can of pepper gas is a good idea. If you carry your passport with you, keep another picture ID in your suitcase. If your passport is lost or stolen, having a copy or another ID will speed the process of getting a new one at the U.S. Consulate.

Swimming

Before you can swim in a swimming pool, you will probably need a *"spravka"*, that is, a note from a doctor stating that you are in good health and free of skin lesions and AIDS. If you have a note from a U.S. doctor, that may or may not be accepted. A local doctor can give you a *spravka* after a cursory examination, and many pools ultimately make their own decision on how strictly to enforce this rule.

Telephone codes

The general procedure for direct dialing long-distance calls is to dial 8, wait for the new tone, then dial the city code and number. There should be a total of 10 digits, including the code and number. If the total number of digits does not add up to 10, add a two or a zero between code and number.

In some cases, when dialing <u>within</u> a Krai or Oblast, the city code is different than if you are dialing from outside the Krai. If you have trouble getting through to a number, dial 07 for the long-distance operator.

City Codes

Anadyr	41361
Birobidzhan	42162
Blagoveschensk	41622
Chita	30222
Khabarovsk	4212
Kholmsk	42433
Komsomolsk-na-Amurye	42172
Korsakov	42435
Magadan	41322
Moscow	095
Nakhodka	42366
Okha	42437
Petropavlovsk-Kamchatski	41522
St. Petersburg	812
Ulan-Ude	30122
Vladivostok	4232
Yakutsk	41122
Yelizovo	41551
Yuzhno-Sakhalinsk	42422

Tipping

Tipping is a relatively new phenomenon in Russia, however, it has caught on quickly. In some restaurants there is a "service charge" added to the bill, which, more likely than not, is for the restaurant and not the waiter. Rounding your bill up a couple of thousand rubles, IF service was particularly good, is probably sufficient in most small restaurants. In the fancier places a couple of dollars would be preferred.

For taxis, you should agree on a price before getting in, and no tip is necessary.

There are no porters at any airports except Moscow, where you must agree on a price before hand or be prepared for highway robbery.

Theater Season

Theater season runs from mid-October to the end of May.

Russian

Russian is a tricky language and due to certain grammar rules dealing mostly with stress, some letters may not be pronounced exactly the way they are written. We have tried to include a "tourist vocabulary" of useful phrases below. Many Russians speak some English and all will be pleased with even your most rudimentary attempts to speak their language.

(A note: we have tried to make it easier for non-Russian speakers to get along by writing words as they are pronounced, rather than using the standard transliteration. Therefore, for example, ulitsa Gorkovo, as it is pronounced, rather than Gorkogo, as it is spelled.)

The Russian Alphabet

А	a	Р	er (air)
Б	beh	С	es
В	veh	Т	teh
Г	geh	У	u (oo)
Д	deh	Ф	ef
Е	ye	Х	ha
Ё	yo	Ц	tseh
Ж	zh	Ч	ch
З	zeh	Ш	sh
И	i (ee)	Щ	shch
Й	i	Ы	y
К	ka	Э	eh
Л	el	Ю	yoo
М	em	Я	ya
Н	en	Ь	- (soft sign)
О	o	Ъ	- (hard sign)
П	peh		

Signs in Russian

RUSSIAN	ENGLISH
Внимание!	Attention!
Вход/Выход	Entrance/Exit
Этаж	Floor
Лифт (не работает)	Elevator (Doesn't work)
Открыто/Закрыто	Open/Closed
Санитарный день	Cleaning Day
Обед	Lunch
Ремонт	Repairs
Учет	Inventory day
Кассир/Касса	Cashier
Бесплатно	Free
Справочное бюро	Information desk
К себе/ от себя	Pull/Push
Гардероб	Cloakroom
Место для курения	Smoking allowed
Не курить	Smoking forbidden
Ресторан	Restaurant
Пропуск	Pass
Туалет (мужской, женский)	Bathroom (men's, women's)
Вокзал, Аэропорт	Train Station, Airport
Поезд	Train
Станция	Station
Ежедневный поезд	Commuter train
Расписание	Schedule
Рейс №	Flight #
Отправление	Departures
Прибытие	Arrivals
Платформа	Platform
Билет	Ticket
Таможня	Customs
Обменный пункт	Currence exchange
Камера хранения	Baggage check
Полиция, Милиция	Police
Госавтоинспекция (ГАИ)	Traffic Police

Useful Phrases

English	Pronunciation	Russian
Good day, (evening)	Dobry dyen (vyecher)	Добрый день (вечер)
Goodbye	Do svidanya	До свидания
My name is . . .	Menya zovut. . .	Меня зовут
I don't speak Russian.	Ya ni gavoryu po russki.	Я не говорю по-русски
Do you speak English?	Vwi govorite po angliski?	Вы говорите по-английски?
I, You, we, they	Ya, vwi, mwi, ani	Я, Вы, Мы, Они
Where, what	Gdye, shto	Где, что
Why, how	Pachemu, kak	Почему, как
No, yes	nyet, da	Нет, да
Thank you	Spasibo	Спасибо,
Please	Pozhalsto	Пожалуйста
I want	Ya hachu	Я хочу
That, this	Ehto	Это
How much does it cost?	Skolko stoit?	Сколько стоит?
Good, bad	Harasho, ploha,	Хорошо, плохо
Expensive, cheap	Doroga, dyosheva,	Дорого, дешево
Great	Otlichno	Отлично
Street	Ulitsa	Улица
Hotel	Gostinitsa	Гостиница,
Restaurant	Restoran	Ресторан
Store	Magazin	Магазин
I don't know	Ya ni znayu	Я не знаю
It is (im)possible	Ehto (ne) vazmozhno	Это (не) возможно
It is all right	Fsyo f paryadke	Все в порядке
I am a foreigner (masc.-fem.)	Ya inostran-etz, -ka	Я иностранец (ka)
I am an American (masc-fem.)	Ya amerikan-etz, -ka	Я американец (ka)
I don't understand	Ya ni panimayu	Я не понимаю
a little	Nyemnoga	Немного
Say it again, please	Paftorite, pazhalsta	Повторите, пожалуйста
Could you write that down?	Vwi bwi ne mogli ehto napisat?	Вы бы не могли это написать
What is written here?	Shto zdyes napisano?	Что здесь написано?

Can I have the menu?	Mozhno pasmotryet menyu?	Можно посмотреть меню?
Is smoking allowed?	Zdyes mozhno kurit?	Здесь можно курить?
What is the next stop (tram or bus)	Kakaya slyedushaya astanofka?	Какая следующая остановка?
Street	Ulitza	Улица
Square	Ploshad	Площадь
Boulevard	Bulvar	Бульвар
Prospect, Avenue	Praspyekt	Проспект
How do I get to... (by foot)	Kak mnye daiti do ..	Как мне дойдти до...
How do I get to... (by car)	Kak mnye doyekhat do ...	Как мне доехать до...
Bus	Aftobus	Автобус
Tram	Tramvai	Трамвай
Stop!	Stoi!	Стой!
Hospital	Bolnitsa	Больница

In a Restaurant

RUSSIAN	PRONUNCIATION	ENGLISH
Закуски	**Zakuski**	**Appetizers**
Салат мясной	Salat myasnoi	Meat/potatoes in mayonnaise
Салат из свежих овощей	Salat iz svyezhikh ovoschei	Fresh veg. salad (usually tomato and cucumber)
Под майонезом	pod mayonaisom	in mayonnaise
Столичный салат	Stolichni salat	potato/peas/egg/meat/ pickles/onion
Ассорти (мясное,рыбное)	Assorti (myasnoe, rybnoe)	Cold cuts, seafood selection
Икра (черная, красная)	Ikra (Chornaya, Krasnaya)	Caviar (Black, Red)
Бутерброд	Buterbrod	Open faced sandwich
Заливное	Zalivnoe	Aspic (meat or fish)
Холодец	Holodetz	Aspic (meat "parts")
Суп	**Soup**	**Soup**
Борщ	Borsch	Borscht

Бульон	Bulyon	Bouillon
с фрикадельками	s fricadelkami	with meatballs
Уха	Uha	Fish soup
Харчо	Kharcho	Tomato/rice/garlic soup
Пельмени	Pelmeni	Pelmeni (meat ravioli in broth)
Щи	Schi	Cabbage soup
Солянка	Solyanka	Pickle soup
Лапша	Lapsha	Noodle soup

Второе или горячее	**Vtoroe or Goryacheye**	**Second or Hot dish**
Шницель	Shnitzel	Veal schnitzel
Голубцы	Golubtzi	Stuffed cabbage leaves
Шашлык	Shashlik	Shish-kebab
Бифстроганоф	Bifstrogonof	Beef Stroganov
Цыплёнок по-киевски	Tsyiplyonok po-Kievski	Chicken Kiev
Котлета	Kahtleta	Beef cutlet
Варенники	Vareniki	boiled dumplings (usually potato or cabbage filling)
Свинина	Svinina	Pork
Курица	Kuritza	Chicken
Говядина	Govyadina	Beef
Мясо кабана	Myasa kabana	Boar
Гребешки	Grebeshki	Scallops
Кальмар	Kalmar	Squid
Креветки	Krevetki	Shrimp
Лосось	Losos	Salmon
Горбуша	Gorbusha	also salmon
Гарнир	Garnir	"garnish," veggies which come with a meat dish, usually potatoes and peas

Овощи	**Ovoschi**	**Vegetables**
Картофель	Kartofel, kartoshka	Potatoes
Картофель-фри	Kartofel fri	French Fries
Картофельное пюре	Kartofelnoe pyure	Mashed potatoes

Рис	Ris	Rice
Капуста	Kapusta	Cabbage
Помидоры	Pomidori	Tomatos
Грибы	Gribi	Mushrooms
Огурцы	Agurtzi	Cucumbers
Папоротник	Paparotnik	Ferns
Морковь	Markov	Carrots
Баклажаны	Baklazhany	Eggplant
Свекла	Svekla	Beets
Зелёный горошек	Zelyoni goroshek	Peas
Лук	Luk	Onion
Перец	Perets	Pepper (red or green)

Сладкое	**Sladkoe**	**Dessert**
Торт	Tort	Cake
Блины	Blini	Blintzes
Желе	Zhelye	Jello
Мороженое	Morozhenoe	Ice cream
Фрукты	Frukty	Fruit
Компот	Kompot	Fruit compote
Яблоки	Yabloki	Apples
Апельсины	Apelsini	Oranges
Груши	Grushi	Pears
Бананы	Banani	Bananas
Виноград	Vinograd	Grapes
Арбузы	Arbuzi	Watermelon
Ягоды	Yagodi	Berries

Завтрак	**Zavtrak**	**Breakfast**
Глазунья	Glazunya	Sunny-side up eggs
Каша	Kasha	Kasha (usually any grain - rice, buckwheat, macaroni, boiled in milk)
кефир	kefir	kefir (yogurt drink)

Дополнительно	**Dopolnitelno**	**Miscellaneous**
Блины	Blini	Blintzes
со сметаной	so smetanoi	with sour cream
с мёдом	s myodom	with honey

с вареньем,	s varenyem,	with jam
с джемом	s jemom	
Хлеб	Khleb	Bread
Булочка	Bulochka	Roll
с маслом	s maslom	with butter

Напитки	**Napitki**	**Drinks**
Чай, кофе	Chai, Koffi	Tea, Coffee
Молоко	Molako	Milk
Сок	Sok	Juice
Напиток	Napitok	Fruit drink
Лимонад	Limonad	Carbonated drink
Минеральная вода	Mineralnaya voda	Mineral water
Коктейль (молочный, фруктовый)	Kokteil (malochni, fruktovi)	"shakes," usually milk or ice cream mixed with juice

Спиртное	**Spirtnoe**	**Spirits**
Коньяк	Konyak	Cognac
Водка	Vodka	Vodka
Шампанское	Shampanskoe	Champagne
Ликёр	Likyur	Liqueur
Пиво	Pivo	Beer
Вино (красное, белое)	Vino (krasnoe, byeloe)	Wine (red, white)

Temperature Conversion

C	F	C	F	C	F
40	104	5	41	-30	-22
35	95	0	32	-35	-31
30	86	-5	23	-40	-40
25	77	-10	14	-45	-49
20	68	-15	5	-50	-58
15	59	-20	-4	-55	-67
10	50	-25	-13	-60	-76

Bibliography

Abramovitch, Raphael R. *The Soviet Revolution, 1917-1939.* International Universities Press Inc. 1962.

Bobrick, Benson. *East of the Sun, The Epic Conquest and Tragic History of Siberia.* Poseidon Press, 1992

Dobrobolskoi, Makarova. *1825: Zagovor.* Progress Publishers, 1990.

Kennan, George. *Exile by Administrative Process.* University of Chicago Press, 1958 abridged from the first edition, 1891.

Kim, N.V., editor. *Istoriya Buryatiya V Voprosakh I Otvetakh, volumes 1-3.* Ministerstvo narodnovo Obrazovaniya Buryatskoi SSR. 1991.

Kirby, E. Stuart. *The Soviet Far East.* Macmillan Publishers. 1971.

Lengyel, Emil. *Siberia.* Gardencity Publishing Co. 1943

Leon, Max. *A Frenchman Opens the Soviet Far East.* Foreign Language Publishing House. Moscow

Matveev, N.P. *Kratkii Istoricheskii Ocherk Vladivostoka.* Izdatelstvo Ussuri. 1990.

Mikhailov, Alexei and Yakovlev, Victor. *Yakutia, Sakha Sire.* Published with the cooperation of De Beers Centenary AG. 1992.

Mowat Farley. *The Siberians* Bantam Books, NY. 1982, Little, Brown & Co., Boston, MA. 1971.

Nemerov, Valery. *Chita: Istoriya, Pamyatnie Mesta, Sudba.* Chitinskoe Oblastnoe Knizhnoe Izdatelstvo. 1994.

Ryanskovo, F.N., editor. *Yevreiskaya Avtonomnaya Oblast.* Informatsionnno-Izdatelskii otdel Instituta kompleksnovo analiza regionalnykh problem DVO Rossiiskoi akademii nauk. 1992.

Sergeyev, Mark. *The Wonders and Problems of Lake Baikal.* Novosti Press Agency Publishing House. Moscow, 1989.

Sergeev, V.D. *Stranitsi Istorii Kamchatki.* Petropavlovsk-Kamchatskii Dalnevostochnoe Knizhnoe Izdatelstvo, 1992.

Unterberger, Betty Miller. *America's Siberian Expedition, 1918-1920.* Duke University Press, 1956.

Index

About the Authors

Erik Azulay

Born in Boston, Erik Azulay developed a passion for travel when his parents moved to Guadalajara, Mexico, where he graduated from high school. Since then Erik has lived in Spain, Indonesia and Mexico, and has traveled extensively throughout Europe and South East Asia.

Erik started his Russian career after receiving a degree in International Relations with a specialization in Soviet Studies from the University of Pennsylvania. Since graduation, he has spent the last 5 years living, working and traveling throughout the Former Soviet Union, the majority of that time in the Russian Far East.

Allegra Harris Azulay

Allegra Harris Azulay was born and raised in New York City, but began traveling at an early age with her mother, who wrote documentary films. This love of travel led her to work for 5 years on archaeological digs in Europe, before attending Georgetown University to study Russian. She has worked for various organizations in the Russian Far East, including the USIA Exhibit "Design USA," where she met her husband Erik. Allegra has spent the last 4 years alternating between New York and Vladivostok, working on various projects. Although she finds the Far East a fascinating place to travel, Allegra categorically refuses to use another Yakutian outhouse at -56C.

HIPPOCRENE BEGINNER'S SERIES

Do you know what it takes to make a phone call in Russia? Or how to get through customs in Japan? How about inviting a Czech friend to dinner while visiting Prague? This new language instruction series shows how to handle oneself in typical situations by introducing the business person or traveler not only to the vocabulary, grammar, and phrases of a new language, but also the history, customs and daily practices of a foreign country.

The Beginner's Series consists of basic language instruction, which includes vocabulary, grammar, and common phrases and review questions; along with cultural insights, interesting historical background, the country's basic facts, and hints about everyday living—driving, shopping, eating out, making phone calls, extending and accepting an invitation and much more.

Each guide is 250 pages, 5 1/2 x 8 1/2.

Beginner's Bulgarian
Vacation travelers and students will find this volume a useful tool to understanding Bulgaria's language and culture. Dialogues include vocabulary and grammar rules likely to confront readers, and background on Bulgarian history is provided.
0-7818-0300-4 • $9.95

Beginner's Czech
The city of Prague has become a major tour destination for Americans. Here is a guide to the complex language in an easy to learn format with a guide to phonetics. Also, important Czech history is outlined with cultural notes. This is another guide designed by Eurolingua.
0-7818-0231-8 • $9.95

Beginner's Esperanto
As a teacher of foreign languages for over 25 years, **Joseph Conroy** knows the need for people of different languages to communicate on a common ground. Though Esperanto has no parent country or land, it is developing an international society all its own. *Beginner's Esperanto* is an introduction to the basic grammar and vocabulary students will need to express their thoughts in the language.

At the end of each lesson, a set of readings gives the student further practice in Esperanto, a culture section presents information about the language and its speakers, a vocabulary lesson groups together all the words which occur in the text, and English translations for conversations allow students to check comprehension. As well, the author lists Esperanto contacts with various organizations throughout the world.
0-7818-0230-X • $14.95 (400 pages)

Beginner's Hungarian

For the businessperson traveling to Budapest, the traveler searching for the perfect spa, or the Hungarian-American searching to extend his or her roots, this guide by **Eurolingua** will aide anyone searching for the words to express basic needs.
0-7818-0209-1 • $7.95 paper

Beginner's Japanese

Author **Joanne Claypoole** runs a consulting business for Japanese people working in America. She has developed her Beginner's Guide for American businesspeople who work for or with Japanese companies in the U.S. or abroad.

Her book is designed to equip the learner with a solid foundation in Japanese conversation. Also included in the text are introductions to Hiragana, Katakana, and Kanji, the three Japanese writing systems.
0-7818-0234-2 • $11.95

Beginner's Polish

Published in conjunction with Eurolingua, *Beginner's Polish* is an ideal introduction to the Polish language and culture. Vocabulary and grammar instruction is combined with information on the history and politics of Poland.
0-7818-0299-7 • $9.95

Beginner's Romanian

This is a guide designed by **Eurolingua**, the company established in 1990 to meet the growing demand for Eastern European language and cultural instruction. The institute is developing books for business and leisure travelers to all Eastern European countries. This Romanian text is ideal for those seeking to communicate in this newly independent country.
0-7818-0208-3 • $7.95 paper

Beginner's Russian

Eurolingua authors **Nonna Karr** and **Ludmila Rodionova** introduce English speakers to the Cyrillic alphabet, and include enough language and grammar to get a traveler or businessperson anywhere in the new Russian Republic. This book is a perfect stepping-stone to more complex language learning.
0-7818-0232-6 • $9.95

SLAVIC AND BALTIC LANGUAGE DICTIONARIES FROM HIPPOCRENE

Bulgarian-English/English-Bulgarian Practical Dictionary
0331   ISBN 0-87052-145-4 $11.95 pb

Byelorussian-English/English-Byelorussian Concise Dictionary
1050   ISBN 0-87052-114-4 $9.95 pb

Czech-English/English-Czech Concise Dictionary
0276   ISBN 0-87052-981-1 $11.95 pb

Estonian-English/English-Estonian Concise Dictionary
1010   ISBN 0-87052-081-4 $11.95 pb

Latvian-English/English-Latvian Dictionary
0194   ISBN 0-7818-0059-5 $14.95 pb

Lithuanian-English/English-Lithuanian Concise Dictionary
0489   ISBN 0-7818-0151-6 $11.95 pb

Russian-English/English-Russian Standard Dictionary
0440   ISBN 0-7818-0280-6 $16.95 pb

English-Russian Standard Dictionary
1025   ISBN 0-87052-100-4 $11.95 pb

Russian-English/English-Russian Concise Dictionary
0262   ISBN 0-7818-0132-X $11.95 pb

Slovak-English/English-Slovak Concise Dictionary
1052   ISBN 0-87052-115-2 $9.95 pb

Ukrainian-English/English Ukrainian Practical Dictionary
1055   ISBN 0-87052-0306-3 $11.95 pb

Ukrainian-English Standard Dictionary
0006   ISBN 0-7818-0189-3 $14.95 pb

HIPPOCRENE LANGUAGE AND TRAVEL GUIDES

These guides provide an excellent introduction to a foreign country for the traveler who wants to meet and communicate with people as well as sightsee. Each book is also an ideal refresher course for anyone wishing to brush up on their language skills.

LANGUAGE AND TRAVEL GUIDE TO AUSTRALIA
250 pages • $14.95 • 0-7818-0166-4 (0086)

LANGUAGE AND TRAVEL GUIDE TO BRITAIN
336 pages, maps, photos, index
0-7818-0290-3 (119)

LANGUAGE AND TRAVEL GUIDE TO FRANCE
320 pages • $14.95 • 0-7818-0080-3 (0386)

LANGUAGE AND TRAVEL GUIDE TO INDONESIA
350 pages • $14.95 • 0-7818-0328-4 (0111)

LANGUAGE AND TRAVEL GUIDE TO MEXICO
224 pages • $14.95 • 0-87052-622-7 (503)

LANGUAGE AND TRAVEL GUIDE TO RUSSIA
293 pages • $14.95 • 0-7818-0047-1 (0321)

LANGUAGE AND TRAVEL GUIDE TO UKRAINE
266 pages • $14.95 • 0-7818-0135-4 (0057)

(Prices subject to change.)

TO PURCHASE HIPPOCRENE BOOKS contact your local bookstore or write to: HIPPOCRENE BOOKS, 171 Madison Avenue, New York, NY 10016. Please enclose check or money order, adding $4.00 shipping (UPS) for the first book and .50 for each additional book.

THE HIPPOCRENE MASTERING SERIES

MASTERING ARABIC
320 pages, 5 1/2 x 8 1/2
0-87052-922-6 $14.95pb
2 Cassettes
 0-87052-984-6 $12.95
Book and Cassettes Package
0-87052-140-3 $27.90

MASTERING FINNISH
278 pages, 5 1/2 x 8 1/2
0-7818-0233-4 $14.95pb
2 Cassettes
0-7818-0265-2 $12.95
Book and Cassettes Package
0-7818-0266-0 $27.90

MASTERING FRENCH
288 pages, 5 1/2 x 8 1/2
0-87052-055-5 $11.95pb
2 Cassettes
0-87052-060-1 $12.95
Book and Cassettes Package
0-87052-136-5 $24.90

MASTERING GERMAN
340 pages, 5 1/2 x 8 1/2
0-87052-056-3 $11.95pb
2 Cassettes
0-87052-061-X $12.95
Book and Cassettes Package
0-87052-137-3 $24.90

MASTERING ITALIAN
360 pages, 5 1/2 x 8 1/2
0-87052-057-1 $11.95pb
2 Cassettes
0-87052-066-0 $12.95
Book and Cassettes Package
0-87052-138-1 $24.90

MASTERING JAPANESE
368 pages, 5 1/2 x 8 1/2
0-87052-923-4 $14.95pb
2 Cassettes
0-87052-938-8 $12.95
Book and Cassettes Package
0-87052-141-1 $27.90

MASTERING POLISH
288 pages, 5 1/2 x 8 1/2
0-7818-0015-3 $14.95pb
2 Cassettes
0-7818-0016-3 $12.95
Book and Cassettes Package
0-7818-0017-X $27.90

MASTERING RUSSIAN
278 pages, 5 1/2 x 8 1/2
0-7818-0270-9 $14.95
2 Cassettes
0-7818-0270-9 $12.95
Book and Cassettes Package
0-7818-0272-5 $27.90

MASTERING SPANISH
338 pages, 5 1/2 x 8 1/2
0-87052-059-8 $11.95pb
2 Cassettes
0-87052-067-9 $12.95
Book and Cassettes Package
0-87052-139-X $24.90

MASTERING ADVANCED SPANISH
300 pages, 5 1/2 x 8 1/2
0-7818-0081-1   11.95pb
2 Cassettes
0-7818-0089-7 $12.95
Book and Cassettes Package
0-7818-0090-0 $24.90

HIPPOCRENE INTERNATIONAL COOKBOOK CLASSICS

All Along the Danube
by Marina Polvay

The Art of Brazilian Cookery
by Dolores Botafogo

The Art of Hungarian Cooking
by Paula P. Bennett and Velma R. Clark

The Art of Israeli Cooking
by Chef Aldo Nahoum

The Art of Syrian Cookery
by Helen Corey

The Art of Turkish Cooking
by Neşet Eren

The Best of Russian Cooking
by Alexandra Kropotkin

Eat Honey and Live Longer
by Maria Lo Pinto

The Joy of Chinese Cooking
by Doreen Yen Hung Feng

The Best of Ukrainian Cooking
by Bohdan Zahny

A Selection of

Hippocrene

PHRASEBOOKS AND GRAMMAR AIDS

Arabic Grammar of the Written Language
$19.95•0-87052-101-2•(397)
Elementary Modern Armenian Grammar
$8.95•0-87052-811-4•(172)
Czech Phrasebook
$11.95•0-87052-967-6•(599)
American Phrasebook for Poles
$8.95•0-87052-907-2•(135)
Polish Phrasebook and Dictionary
$9.95•0-7818-0134-6•(118)
Romanian Grammar
$6.95•0-87052-892-0•(232)
Russian Phrasebook and Dictionary
$9.95•0-7818-0190-7•(597)
Cassettes (separately)
$12.95•0-7818-0192-3•(432)
Spanish Grammar
$8.95•0-87052-893-9•(273)
Swahili Phrasebook.
$8.95•0-87052-970-6•(73)
Ukrainian Phrasebook and Dictionary
$12.95•0-7818-0191-5•(28)

(All prices subject to change.)

TO PURCHASE HIPPOCRENE BOOKS contact your local bookstore, or write to: HIPPOCRENE BOOKS, 171 Madison Avenue, New York, NY 10016. Please enclose check or money order, adding $4.00 shipping (UPS) for the first book and $.50 for each additional book.

Self-Taught Audio Language Courses

Hippocrene Books is pleased to recommend Audio-Forum self-taught language courses. They match up very closely with the languages offered in Hippocrene dictionaries and offer a flexible, economical and thorough program of language learning.

Audio-Forum audio-cassette/book courses, recorded by native speakers, offer the convenience of a private tutor, enabling the learner to progress at his or her own pace. They are also ideal for brushing up on language skills that may not have been used in years. In as little as 25 minutes a day — even while driving, exercising, or doing something else — it's possible to develop a spoken fluency.

All Audio-Forum courses are fully guaranteed and may be returned within 30 days for a full refund if you're not completely satisfied.

You may order directly from Audio-Forum by calling toll-free 1-800-243-1234.

For a complete course description and catalog of 264 courses in 91 languages, contact Audio-Forum, Dept. SE5, 96 Broad St., Guilford, CT 06437. Toll-free phone 1-800-243-1234. Fax 203-453-9774.